Stambeli

MUSIC, TRANCE, AND ALTERITY IN TUNISIA

Richard C. Jankowsky

The University of Chicago Press CHICAGO AND LONDON

Richard C. Jankowsky is assistant professor of music at Tufts University.

The University of Chicago Press, Chicago 60637
The University of Chicago Press, Ltd., London

Printed in the United States of America

19 18 17 16 15 14 13 12 11 10   1 2 3 4 5

ISBN-13: 978-0-226-39217-2 (cloth)
ISBN-13: 978-0-226-39219-6 (paper)
ISBN-10: 0-226-39217-1 (cloth)
ISBN-10: 0-226-39219-8 (paper)

Publication of this book has been aided by a grant from the AMS 75 PAYS Endowment Fund of the American Musicological Society.

Library of Congress Cataloging-in-Publication Data
Jankowsky, Richard C.
Stambeli : music, trance, and alterity in Tunisia / Richard C. Jankowsky.
p. cm. — (Chicago studies in ethnomusicology)
Includes bibliographical references and index.
ISBN-13: 978-0-226-39217-2 (cloth : alk. paper)
ISBN-10: 0-226-39217-1 (cloth : alk. paper)
ISBN-13: 978-0-226-39219-6 (pbk. : alk. paper)
ISBN-10: 0-226-39219-8 (pbk. : alk. paper) 1. Stambali (Rite) 2. Blacks—Tunisia—Rites and ceremonies. 3. Spirit possession—Tunisia. 4. Music—Tunisia—History and criticism. 5. Music—Tunisia—Religious aspects. I. Title. II. Series: Chicago studies in ethnomusicology.
ML3760.6.J255 2010
781.62'960611—dc22

2010004535

♾ The paper used in this publication meets the minimum requirements of the American National Standard for Information Sciences—Permanence of Paper for Printed Library Materials, ANSI Z39.48-1992.

Stambeli

MUSIC, TRANCE, AND ALTERITY IN TUNISIA

CHICAGO STUDIES IN ETHNOMUSICOLOGY

A series edited by Philip V. Bohlman, Bruno Nettl, and Ronald Radano

In memory of

Bābā Majīd (1922–2008)

and

Jeanne Jeffers Mrad (1938–2009)

CONTENTS

ILLUSTRATIONS

Figures

Tables

Musical Examples

ACKNOWLEDGMENTS

This book owes its existence to the Barnāwī/Mihoub family at Dār Bārnū. To Bābā Majīd (a.k.a. Muḥammad Mihoub), Baya, Belḥassen, Emna, Saʿida, and Sayda I express my deepest gratitude for welcoming me into the Dār Bārnū household and into the world of *sṭambēlī*. I also thank the network of Dār Bārnū *sṭambēlī* musicians for sharing so much of their time, music, and thoughts with me. Special thanks to Ṣālaḥ Warglī for inviting me to attend and record some of the ceremonies he led, and for allowing me to include some of those recordings on this book's accompanying compact disc. I also offer my sincerest thanks to the Mrad family for their support, hospitality, and friendship over the years. To you I also affectionately assign blame for fostering my initial interest and continual involvement in Tunisian cultural expression.

Mounir Hentati of the Centre des musiques arabes et méditerranéennes (CMAM) in Sidi Bou Said, Tunisia, helped me locate relevant articles and recordings and facilitated my first meeting with Bābā Majīd. Besma Sudani provided invaluable help in transcribing interviews and in solidifying my spoken Arabic. I also thank Vaffi Sheriff and Ismael Musah Montana for aiding my archival research in Tunis, and Matthieu Hagene for generously sharing his photographs and preparing the accompanying Web site. Adam Jerbi provided unfailing friendship and practical support during each of several fieldwork trips. Thanks also go to the staff at the Centre d'études maghrébines à Tunis (CEMAT), in particular, Riadh Saadawi, for their invaluable assistance and support.

Martin Stokes and Philip Bohlman encouraged and inspired me throughout the many stages of this project, and Robert Kendrick's insightful questions helped me to refine some of the arguments presented in these pages. I benefited greatly from formal and informal discussions with colleagues over the two years I spent on the faculty of the School of Oriental and African

Studies at the University of London; I especially thank Owen Wright for his helpful comments on a very early draft of portions of the book. I am deeply grateful to my colleagues in the Department of Music at Tufts University for their encouraging and accommodating support of this project. Amahl Bishara, Kenneth Garden, Sarah Pinto, and Mary Talusan Lacanlale offered invaluable writing-up camaraderie as well as useful suggestions that rendered chapter 5 more cohesive. A special thanks goes to Timothy Rommen, who commented on several chapters and eagerly helped me conceptualize and sketch the visual representations of temporal transformations found in chapter 5.

I extend my deepest thanks to my mother Joan and brother Mike, who have provided unwavering encouragement and put up with my history of making numerous impromptu and sometimes open-ended trips to North Africa. A special thanks goes to my sister Debbie, who in her infinite love and generosity has often provided me a place of refuge, recovery, and renewal during my transitions between jobs and fieldwork trips. The greatest share of my gratitude goes to my wife Tola Donna Khin, whose untiring support, through long hours and even longer absences, has inspired me to put my all into this project while ensuring that I keep a healthy sense of perspective.

Funding for fieldwork in Tunisia was generously provided by the Fulbright Institute for International Education, the American Institute for Maghrib Studies, the Arts and Humanities Research Council, and the Faculty of the Arts and Humanities at the School of Oriental and African Studies. The book manuscript was finalized during a research leave generously awarded by Tufts University.

NOTE ON SPELLING AND TRANSLITERATION

I transliterate the Arabic terms in this book using a slightly modified version of the system employed by the International Journal of Middle East Studies. While my overriding concern is to remain faithful to the pronunciation of Tunisian spoken Arabic, I have also attempted to provide enough technical information to facilitate comprehension and comparison for those conversant in other Arabic dialects or Modern Standard Arabic. The most common resultant compromise is found in my treatment of the Arabic letter *alif*. While this letter is conventionally transliterated as *ā*, its pronunciation in Tunisian Arabic can be either *ā* (as in the English "bat") or what I represent as *ē* (as in "bet"), depending on its neighboring letters. Thus, my transliteration of the word *sṭambēlī*, for example, remains true to its local pronunciation, while the line over the *e* signals to readers of Arabic that the letter is an *alif* (rather than the short consonant *e*). (It is worth noting that the French literature transliterates the term as "stambali.") When preceding certain consonants, the *l* sound of the Arabic definite article *el-* or *il-* (or *al-* in standard Arabic) is replaced by the consonant it precedes. In such cases, I have privileged pronunciation over conventional transliteration; thus, I write Sīdī ʿAbd es-Salēm instead of Sīdī ʿAbd el-Salēm. The *sṭambēlī* lexicon is replete with Arabicized terms originating in several, sometimes unattributable, sub-Saharan languages. I apply the same transliteration system to these words as I have for Arabic terms, to best approximate local pronunciation.

Arabic words, such as *Ramadan* or *imam*, that are represented in English dictionaries appear here without diacritical marks. For the sake of readability and reference, the names of people and places that have conventional Europeanized forms maintain those forms rather than more technically accurate transliterations of the Arabic; so Tunisian President Habib Bourguiba rather than Ḥabīb Abū Ruqayba, or the city of Kairouan rather than Qayruwān. Because of the idiosyncrasies of plurals in Arabic, which can alter the appearance of a transliterated word significantly, I have opted to simplify matters by presenting plurals for often-used words by appending an unitalicized "s" to the end of the singular form, e.g., *nūba*s rather than *nuwab*.

Introduction

I could feel the heat of the flames approach and recede each time the dancer turned to his left and back, swinging burning stalks of hay (*ḥalfa*, or alfa grass) held in each hand. With every beat of the music, he twisted his white-cloaked, upright body from side to side, holding the flames to the skin of his outstretched arm (fig. 1 shows a similar trance). I was one of several musicians seated along the forward perimeter of the dance space singing and playing the heavy handheld iron clappers known by the onomatopoetic term *shqāshiq*. Our unrelenting rhythms followed the cyclic patterns of the *gumbrī*, the three-stringed, bass-register chordophone whose melodies "speak" to the spirits in order to coax them to descend into the bodies of dancing hosts. In this case, the *gumbrī* melody, played skillfully and authoritatively, yet seemingly effortlessly, by the octogenarian master musician Bābā Majīd, had lured the powerful Muslim saint Sīdī ʿAbd es-Salēm to possess a male Arab Tunisian *ʿarīfa* (healer; lit. "she who knows") and compel him to engage in self-mortification by dancing with fire. Despite the increasing number of burning embers flying at us as his movements matched our accelerating tempo, we closed in on the dancer, rising onto our knees in order to surround him with the loud, metallic pulses of our *shqāshiq*, producing overlapping sheets of sound that were now becoming increasingly multilayered as some of us introduced carefully chosen, syncopated rhythmic variations. His trance intensified with deeper, repeated forward bends at the waist accompanied by increasingly persistent applications of fire to flesh.

At this point, it is usually just a matter of time before the dancer passes out, indicating that the possessing entity has had its fill of dancing and has exited the host's body. Sīdī ʿAbd es-Salēm, however, does not always take leave of his host immediately after completing his dance. Sometimes he will drop the stalks of hay in order to hold his hands in front of him, palms up, to lead the gathering in the recitation of the *fātiḥa*, the opening verse of the

FIGURE 1. Trance dance, with fire, to Sīdī ʿAbd es-Salēm, 2009. (Photograph by Matthieu Hagene.)

Qur'ān. This time, however, he kept one burning stalk, holding it behind his back as he bowed in front of us, signaling for the music to stop. Sīdī ʿAbd es-Salēm was ready to speak. For the next ten minutes or so, he conferred individually with numerous members of the gathering who had rushed over to consult with the saint. He foretold futures, provided advice on personal matters, and informed individuals of the well-being of the souls of deceased friends or family members. After each consultation, he demonstrated his protective power by passing the flaming stalk under the bare arms of those seeking his knowledge and guidance, without eliciting any apparent damage or pain.

The consultations provided the musicians with a brief opportunity to rest, towel sweat off hands and faces, sip from small glasses of sweet, but now lukewarm, mint tea, or light cigarettes. Some left the ritual area to make cell phone calls or chat with friends among the hundred or so attendees gathered for the possession ceremony, which constituted a focal event of the annual three-day pilgrimage to the shrine of Sīdī Frej. The shrine is an unassuming, whitewashed edifice situated on a quiet side road in Sūkra (Fr. La Soukra), an agricultural region several miles northwest of Tunis. Like most North African Muslim saints, Sīdī Frej is venerated by many local residents, who may visit his shrine to make offerings and prayers in exchange for the saint's blessing, protection, or guidance. His importance, however, extends well beyond the neighborhood. Sīdī Frej was from the Bornu region of central Africa, where he was captured, forced to cross the Sahara Desert, and then sold into slavery in Tunis. His miraculous powers were recognized by other displaced sub-Saharans and Arab Tunisians alike. After his death centuries ago, he was incorporated into the pantheon of saints and spirits who heal through *sṭambēlī*, the trance and spirit possession music developed by slaves, their descendants, and others of sub-Saharan ancestry in Tunis. Now, in the middle of a hot July night in 2005, musicians, healers, adepts, and other members of the *sṭambēlī* network continued the tradition of annual pilgrimages to his shrine, a practice believed to have started more than two hundred years ago. As *sṭambēlī* ritual music, simply described as *dwā'*, a "cure," is largely concerned with healing people suffering from spirit affliction, the pilgrimage attracts many patients who are eager—or obliged—to enter trance in order to gain the blessing and protection of a saint or to placate their possessing spirit in order to defend against further spirit attacks for the rest of the year.

We were now deep into the second of three nights of spirit possession rituals. The musical routes we were taking through the *sṭambēlī* pantheon had already brought us to Sīdī Frej, who had induced trance in several dancers. The subsequent appearance of Sīdī ʿAbd es-Salēm usually meant that the performance for the "Whites" was nearly over and the next section of the ritual, for the "Blacks," would soon commence. The Whites, the majority of whom are Muslim saints (*awliyā'*, or "close to God"; sing. *walī*), were historical figures recognized by Tunisians as possessing a rare and powerful blessing *(baraka)* from God, usually demonstrated through exceptional piety or miraculous acts. In contrast, the Blacks, otherwise known as "holy" spirits (*ṣālḥīn*), were never living beings and are understood as originating in sub-Saharan Africa. Typical *sṭambēlī* ceremonies, performed in a single evening to placate the spirit of a single, possessed client, generally follow a trajectory that attends mostly to the Whites before shifting attention to the Blacks. During the pilgrimage, this progression occurs gradually over three days. Most of the spirits would have to wait until tomorrow night to take hold of their hosts, after a day of offerings to them that would include a large street procession, rituals at a sacred water well, animal sacrifices, and the preparation of special victuals.

With facial muscles convulsing and one eye still rolled back, the *ʿarīfa* returned to the front of the dance space, which was our cue to start the music for Sīdī ʿAbd es-Salēm one last time before the possessing saint took leave of his host's body. Although physically exhausted, the *ʿarīfa* would be returning the next day for another taxing possession. If all the right offerings were made, and if we played our music skillfully to invoke members of other spirit families in a ritually appropriate order, several Royalty spirits would possess him successively to end the pilgrimage, which, by placating the members of the *sṭambēlī* pantheon, would defend *sṭambēlī* patients from further spirit attacks for the remainder of the year.

* * *

In *sṭambēlī*, music does more than facilitate trance by communicating with the spirit world. It also structures and organizes the entire ceremony, effectuating the ritual's dual role as a technical site of healing and an imaginal space of social, spiritual, and historical encounter. Music, in this context, is not epiphenomenal, or even merely expressive, but is rather pragmatic; it constitutes a bodily, sensory intervention through which realities are constructed, perceived, and transformed (Friedson 1996; Kapferer and Hobart 2005). This is not the case only for musician, spirit, and trancer; engulfed in the overwhelming sounds of *sṭambēlī*, all who attend the ceremony, while differently positioned in their ritual experience, are nevertheless all situated within the same matrix of aesthetically mediated perceptual possibilities.

The impact of *sṭambēlī* aesthetics is conditioned by their alterity. Musical instruments such as the *gumbrī* and *shqāshiq*, as well as the *sṭambēlī* musical aesthetic, with its cyclic form, pentatonic modes, and distinctive metallic timbre, are understood from within and without as *sūdānī* (sub-Saharan) and thus non-Tunisian. The lyrics, which are sung mostly in dialectical Arabic, are nevertheless considered *ʿajmī* (non-Arabic) due to the occasional appearance of words from sub-Saharan languages and the nasal, understated delivery of the lyrics, which, in contrast to the ideals of enunciation in Arabic music, is not explicitly concerned with the (human) listener's comprehension of the words. *Sṭambēlī* aesthetics are not common components of the Tunisian public sphere; they are not readily available, or even recognizable, to many Tunisians.[1] They are radically other.

Yet while *sṭambēlī* was developed by displaced sub-Saharans, and most *sṭambēlī* musicians are of sub-Saharan descent, many of *sṭambēlī*'s healers and clients are not. There is much evidence in the oral and written record to suggest that, even when a much larger sub-Saharan population existed in Tunis, at the height of the trans-Saharan slave trade, such interaction between sub-Saharans and Arab Tunisians in the context of *sṭambēlī* was the norm, not the exception. *Sṭambēlī*, then, is not usefully or accurately reducible to a practice only of and for the black community, especially in contemporary Tunis, where there is little sense of a "black community," let alone one that is unified through common participation in the *sṭambēlī* tradition. *Sṭambēlī* is more usefully and accurately understood as mediating the encounter between selves and others, creating a space for humans and spirits, as well as sub-Saharan and Arab Tunisians, to forge, reinforce, and reconfigure their relationships.

As each member of the extensive *sṭambēlī* pantheon is identified with and summoned by its own unique and individualized tune or *nūba* (lit. "[one's] turn"; pl. *nuwab* or, less commonly, *nūbēt*), *sṭambēlī* musicians must master an equally vast repertoire of music. Musicians' ritual knowledge and responsibilities, however, do not end there. Each member of the pantheon has its own preferences and idiosyncrasies and is situated within larger groups of saints or families of spirits, each with its own internal hierarchies as well as distinctive relationships with other groups and families. Failure to acknowledge and act according to the specific identities and social relations of each member of the pantheon, by applying certain musical techniques and making musical choices, could lead to a compromised and potentially ineffectual ceremony. Musicians, then, are immersed in the performative, corporeal immediacy of producing trance *and* have privileged access to the cumulative knowledge of the *sṭambēlī* pantheon that informs their ritual actions.

This book is an account of how *sṭambēlī* musicians actualize this ritual knowledge in performance, through musical aesthetics, ritual decisions, and embodied interactions with humans and spirits. I pay particular attention to how musicians simultaneously condition the experience of individual healing and evoke social histories predicated on displaced sub-Saharans' histories of slavery, subjugation, and shifting relations with the Tunisian state and society. Ritual healing, as Thomas J. Csordas (2002) notes, often resonates well beyond an individual's specific ailment. In the somatic movements of *sṭambēlī* rituals, musicians and trancers generate real change on, and through, the physical body; that is, they heal. Yet they also evoke, through embodiment and the senses, histories "from below" that remain unrecorded by conventional historiography; that is, they embody cultural history (Stoller 1997: 47).[2] In *sṭambēlī*, these healings and histories are utterly interdependent; one cannot be fully grasped without the other. The two are also inextricably linked to alterity: the story of *sṭambēlī* is a history *of* others and about healing *by* others, both visible and invisible. Its rituals of possession demand participants and observers to reimagine their worlds, worlds that are influenced by relationships with unseen characters and involve a largely suppressed history of trans-Saharan movements and the ensuing experiences of subjugation.

Within this space of ritual, shaped by legacies of otherness and saturated with the aesthetics of alterity, sub-Saharan and North Africas interact with each other in both human and spirit forms. This privileged space is defined more by inclusion than exclusion and enables the polyphony characteristic of spiritual traditions described by Michael Lambek (2006) as "both/and" (as opposed to the "either/or" ethos of institutionalized monotheistic religions). Such traditions, however, especially when they involve spirit possession, have long suffered from analyses that reduce ritual meaning to terms, logics, and rationales that are external to them, thus overlooking ritual's own theoretical potential (Kapferer 2005a: 39). When these traditions are products of subjugating processes of slavery or colonialism, scholars concerned with the relationship between ritual and a wider sociopolitical context may impose a politics of resistance or subversion on ritual at the expense of the participants' actual experience.

In this book I am more concerned with how the internal dynamics of ritual direct participants into meanings. These meanings, as I will discuss, do indeed connect to sociopolitical structures and relationships located outside ritual, but they are produced for and by participants in a ritual where the phenomenological sensations of ritual aesthetics and motion evoke and connect to those domains of nonritual knowledge and experience. In other words, I feel it is important to approach an understanding of *sṭambēlī*'s ethos and meanings from within, through extensive ritual coparticipation, and connecting with others by approaching *sṭambēlī* on its own terms.

Such an approach was only possible thanks to the generosity of Bābā Majīd and the nurturing encouragement of the Dār Bārnū household. After suffering a barrage of questions from me about ritual meanings, spirit pantheon membership, and the nature of trance, Bābā Majīd looked at me and, with the calm sagacity that one might expect from an active ritual elder, replied, "All the answers are in the music." With this statement, he had invited me onto the "path" (*thnīya*) of an apprentice *gumbrī* player and member of the Dār Bārnū household. Upon accepting, I no longer approached Bābā Majīd with prepared questions, but rather listened, observed, and learned. I immersed myself in the music, training on the *gumbrī*, at his pace and on his terms, almost daily throughout most of the year 2001 and the summer of 2002. After finishing my doctoral dissertation on *sṭambēlī*, I conducted six more months of fieldwork in 2005 and 2006 at Dār Bārnū. In addition to continuing my *gumbrī* apprenticeship, during these latter visits I also performed with Bābā Majīd's troupe as one of the *ṣunnā'*, the musicians who play the *shqāshiq* and sing responses.[3]

Did I find the answers to my questions "in the music," as Bābā Majīd had promised? Not at first. But that was because I had been asking the wrong questions, questions that were shaped by my own assumptions and preconceived notions about music, trance, and the spirit world. This book is a product of my efforts to ask questions that are relevant and important to *sṭambēlī* practitioners themselves, and, just as important, questions that address *sṭambēlī* on its own terms, as a healing practice in which music communicates with the unseen members of the *sṭambēlī* pantheon who have the power to intervene in people's lives in complex and meaningful ways. This is not to say that there is uniformity of opinion within the community regarding what is and is not "important," or that I avoided altogether certain topics of interest to me that may be peripheral or of little interest to others. Rather, I approach *sṭambēlī* as someone convinced of the value of its embodied and aesthetic epistemologies, and as someone willing to expand my "imaginative horizons" (Crapanzano 2004) by opening up to the sensory, corporeal, and shared experience of *sṭambēlī* ritual, with all the implications that involves.

Stambeli begins in chapter 1 with a consideration of three domains of encounter that frame my understanding and experience of *sṭambēlī*. The first is the encounter between displaced sub-Saharans, mostly slaves, who brought with them *sṭambēlī*'s material and spiritual precursors, and the urban, Arab-Islamic society of Tunisia that constituted their destination and became home to subsequent generations of slaves and their offspring. The second domain consists of the encounter between human and spirit worlds. I introduce the relationship between humans and spirits in the context of *sṭambēlī* and situate my approach in relation to academic trends in the study of music and spirit possession. The third domain of encounter concerns the relationship between ethnographer and the *sṭambēlī* practitioners of Dār Bārnū. A description of the ethnographic context leads to a consideration of the opportunities and limitations of a research methodology that emphasizes coparticipation (Fabian 1990) and an ethnography of the particular (Abu-Lughod 1991).

Sṭambēlī is a product of the extensive, yet relatively undocumented, trans-Saharan slave trade. Chapter 2 describes Tunisia's participation in this trade and discusses the appearance of a system of "communal houses," which included Dār Bārnū, established by the ever-increasing population of new and freed slaves, their descendants, and other sub-Saharans in Tunis. Inside these houses, displaced or diasporic sub-Saharans could find others who spoke their languages, shared their customs and beliefs, and could help ease their transition into their host society. The houses anchored the histories and identities of sub-Saharans in Tunis and provided the setting for *sṭambēlī*'s development, which I chronicle in terms of the ontological and aesthetic foundations of *sṭambēlī* and its emerging sociocultural significance in Tunisian society. A recounting of the legend of Bū Saʿdiyya, the mythic first musician of *sṭambēlī* and the historical guide for displaced sub-Saharans in Tunis, highlights the multiple meanings engendered by *sṭambēlī*'s histories of displacement and healing. Here I will suggest that the potent combination of *sṭambēlī*'s proximity to certain popular yet contested religious beliefs and practices and its distance from local aesthetics and ontologies contributed to its continual demand among certain sectors of Tunisian society. This success, paradoxically perhaps, secured simultaneously the integration and marginalization of *sṭambēlī* within Tunisian society.

By way of introducing the saints and spirits that populate the *sṭambēlī* pantheon, chapter 3 also provides an overview of the overarching musico-spiritual structure of the *sṭambēlī* event. I discuss the pantheon in relation to *sṭambēlī*'s histories and geographies of encounter, situating the range of meanings its constituent members evoke in the context of Tunisian history and society. Chapter 4 examines the aesthetic ideals cultivated by *sṭambēlī* musicians, most often described as *sūdānī* and *ʿajmī*, and examines how these sonic qualities are understood and produced through musical instrument morphology and performance technique. I delve deeper into *sṭambēlī* ritual musical aesthetics in chapter 5 through a detailed consideration of the *nūba*. Here I describe the production and manipulation of timbres, textures, and intensities necessary for ritual efficacy, paying particular attention to the central, if elusive, dynamics of rhythmic elasticity and sonic density.

The organization of *nūbas* into larger "chains" (*silsilēt*) structures all *sṭambēlī* ceremonies and, by extension, the entire *sṭambēlī* pantheon. Since the actual presence of a spirit or saint is *only* manifested publicly and witnessed through the musical performance of its *nūba*, aesthetics are pragmatic not only in terms of producing the conditions for the phenomenological experience of spirit possession, but also in bringing into being the numerous members of the *sṭambēlī* pantheon, along with their histories of movement and their capacities for hurting and healing, for contemplation and reflection. Chapter 6 presents this knowledge in action, in the context of a private healing ritual for one of Bābā Majīd's clients. Here I describe the *sṭambēlī* healing process, from affliction and diagnosis to divination and placation, and the central role of music in this process. A detailed examination of a client's possession ceremony reveals the underlying knowledge that informs the musicians' decisions and actions in order to produce a successful ceremony. This example also considers the importance of *sṭambēlī* aesthetics not only for the client, but also for the ritual experience of the multitude of others gathered for the ceremony. The "audience," I argue, is composed not of passive observers, but of active participants who experience the aesthetic and ontological conditions for the patient's transformation and bear witness to the histories evoked by the succession of saints and spirits who make that transformation possible.

Chapter 7 focuses on the pilgrimage to the shrine of Sīdī Frej, which brings together *sṭambēlī* initiates and numerous other pilgrims for three days each summer. Of all *sṭambēlī* rituals, the pilgrimage attracts the most people and invokes the greatest number of saints and spirits as it charts a geocultural history of encounter on many levels. The majority of noninitiates who encounter *sṭambēlī* do so in the context of the pilgrimage, which is a semipublic event and a defining feature of other traditions associated with the veneration of saints in Tunisia. While chapters 6 and 7 explore private and semipublic rituals, respectively, chapter 8 considers the role of public, nonritual contexts of *sṭambēlī* and its shifting and often contested position within the public sphere. Concert stage performances of *sṭambēlī* are infrequent but important in terms of new audiences and public attitudes toward *sṭambēlī*. Viewed from inside the history of Dār Bārnū, such performances are not usefully understood as inauthentic or "selling out," as *sṭambēlī* has a long history of performing on stage for influential others. While staged ceremonies are not new, they do reflect changing trends in patronage due to shifting relations with the state and society that must be understood in the context of *sṭambēlī*'s encounters with colonialism, nationalism, modern developmentalism, and globalization.

The conclusion presented in chapter 9 pulls together the main theoretical points I have been making on ritual dynamics and the transnational imagination in light of the ethnographic examples presented in chapters 6, 7, and 8. Here I also reflect on some of the salient transformations and continuities of *sṭambēlī* throughout its history to assess its current situation, especially as a younger generation of *sṭambēlī* musicians takes over the responsibility of maintaining and developing the tradition. The death of Bābā Majīd, the last of the Dār Bārnū elders, marks the end of a *sṭambēlī* leadership shaped by Dār Bārnū's prior role of sheltering slaves and other sub-Saharan Africans. Unlike Bābā Majīd, these younger musicians did not grow up surrounded by freed slaves, servants, and their descendants or others with memories of sub-Saharan Africa, and they never experienced *sṭambēlī* as a part of the activities of a functioning network of communal houses. But renewed demand for *sṭambēlī* in ritual and onstage suggests that, while the practice is in danger of losing some meanings as it transitions away from an era in which the communal houses were active, *sṭambēlī* is accumulating other meanings that involve the reinterpretation of "Africanness" and a reconsideration of the place of *sṭambēlī* in Tunisian society.

PART I

Histories and Geographies of Encounter

CHAPTER ONE

Encountering the Other People

ALTERITY, POSSESSION, ETHNOGRAPHY

Khemīsī Ḥdīd died the sixth day of Ramadan, in the year 2000. A black Algerian, Khemīsī had arrived at Dār Bārnū (the "Bornu House") in Tunis thirty-eight years earlier, and it remained his home until his death. Dār Bārnū was part of a network of houses established during the time of slavery, on the periphery of the Tunis medina, that served to help freed slaves and other displaced sub-Saharans find others from their places of origin to help them adjust to life in Tunisia. Dār Bārnū, as its name suggests, originally served as a shelter for those from the Bornu region of central Africa, near Lake Chad. After the last of his family in Algeria had died, Khemīsī came to Tunis to find an uncle on his mother's side of the family. The uncle, however, refused him. Soon thereafter, he met Bābā Majīd (whose surname is Barnāwī, meaning "of Bornu"), who brought him to Dār Bārnū. Although Khemīsī was not of Barnāwī descent, he, like many other marginalized or disenfranchised individuals in Tunis, was nonetheless welcomed into the Dār Bārnū household.

We are in the open-air courtyard of Dār Bārnū. Emna is wearing a green kashabiyya *(hooded cloak) and holding a green, wooden staff in her right hand. She is possessed by Sīdī ʿAbd el-Qādir, a Muslim saint known as "master of the spirits"* (sulṭān iṣ-ṣālḥīn)*. She is on her knees, head down, directly in front of the* gumbrī *being played by her father, Bābā Majīd. To either side of him sit two younger musicians, each of them playing two pairs of* shqāshiq, *which saturate the air with their cyclic rhythms and metallic overtones. Emna's feet begin to move to the beat, and she rises gradually, stamping the rod on the ground until finally throwing it down. It falls and hits her father, who does not seem disturbed. She is now on her feet. When the music stops, she stands in place, swaying back and forth. Her mother removes the* kashabiyya, *leaving Emna in her "Los Angeles, California" T-shirt. The musicians begin to play the* nūba *of*

Sīdī Frej, who, like Sīdī ʿAbd el-Qādir, is one of the "Shaikhs," the most powerful group of sṭambēlī saints. Emna's body rocks back and forth to the music in increasingly intensifying movements until she passes out, falling flat on her back. Her mother and a friend calmly step over to her, stroke her head, and call for the white cloth. Bābā Majīd shakes his head, indicating no, it is not yet time, and continues to play. . . .

The Barnāwīs loved Khemīsī dearly and considered his death to be a great tragedy. They described him to me as pious, quiet, gentle, and caring. When they spoke of him, tears would often well up in their eyes. They would also inevitably mention his great singing voice, which has become legendary in the *sṭambēlī* network of Tunis. A single homemade cassette recording of a *sṭambēlī* ceremony in 1991 ensured his voice would not soon be forgotten and was often played for me so I could hear his voice. "That's Khemīsī's style. There's nothing like that here any more, nothing," Bābā Majīd would say with a distant look in his eyes. "He never wanted anything from life," I was also told, "he never even wanted to marry. All he wanted to do was to pray and to sing." Khemīsī's death also left the ageing Bābā Majīd as the sole bearer of the Dār Bārnū *sṭambēlī* tradition. Without Khemīsī at his side, he would now have to rely on younger musicians, whose ritual knowledge he viewed as, at best, minimal, and whose interests, he worried, were privileging making money over the tradition of healing.

. . . Emna begins to writhe on the ground, trembling convulsively, inching forward until her head nearly hits the gumbrī. *As the music subsides, Bābā Majīd finally calls for the white cloth. Three women take the cloth and use it to cover her body, which is now sprawled on the ground. The music begins again. Each of the women takes a corner of the cloth and pulls it up and down in time with the music. After some time, the music ends and they clothe her in a black* kashabiyya. *Emna rises slowly as she becomes possessed by a spirit named Kūrī and dances on her knees, stomping her leg as she throws her arms into the air, one after the other, over and over. Then she passes out again, indicating that Kūrī has left her body. When she awakes, it appears that Sīdī ʿAbd el-Qādir has taken advantage of her vulnerable state and possessed her yet again. This time, however, he does not dance but rather foretells the future, in secret, to the women who are now gathering around her. Tears well up in the eyes of some of the women as they consult, in hushed voices, with Sīdī ʿAbd el-Qādir, who speaks to them about, among other things, the well-being of Khemīsī in the afterlife. . . .*

Upon hearing the news that Khemīsī had died, Emna had run from her room at Dār Bārnū to his to be by his side. She cried over his body and kissed his forehead. The following day, her legs became paralyzed. She remained immobile, in her room, for nearly three months. The Dār Bārnū healers determined that Kūrī, a powerful sub-Saharan spirit who had afflicted Emna in the past, had once again struck her. Spirits are often present at times of death, and coming into physical contact with the dead makes one especially vulnerable to a spirit attack.

. . . After the short break, the musicians resume playing. Emna's kashabiyya *is removed, and she soon becomes possessed by May Nasra, a young, male spirit belonging to a family known as the Bēyēt, or Royalty spirits. The women cover Emna in a pink and white* sunjuq *(large cloth banner), place a red tarboosh on her head, and slide a tray of toys and a* luḥa *(young student's personal chalkboard) in front of her. May Nasra complains that he does not like the tarboosh and wants a new one. A Tunisian medical doctor and friend of mine in attendance asks me whether Emna had gone through a traumatic experience related to school. I respond in the affirmative. After the request for a new tarboosh is fulfilled, May Nasra indicates that he is finally placated by throwing candy from the tray to everyone present. Emna passes out once more. The musicians lead the congregation in the* fātiḥa*, and Emna's mother and friends help her up and slowly usher her into the house. The sṭambēlī is over. Positive relations with the spirits have been reestablished. Emna is "all better (for) now."*

* * *

I begin by interweaving this ethnographic description of Emna's possession with an account of Khemīsī's death not only because they are intimately connected, but also because both vignettes mark moments of profound transition in the Dār Bārnū *sṭambēlī* tradition. The loss of Khemīsī highlighted a moment of historical rupture. Historically, Dār Bārnū's main function had been to address the experience of suffering for displaced sub-Saharans, which took many forms, including the violence of slavery, displacement, and loss, as well as the experience of prejudice and social marginalization. His death brought to a tragic end an era in which Dār Bārnū served as a refuge for enslaved and free black Africans.

The second transition, namely, Emna's transformation from afflicted to healed, highlighted a moment of historical continuity. Through music and trance, Emna's ceremony evoked Dār Bārnū's historical and spiritual legacies, while also underscoring *sṭambēlī*'s continued relevance in its role of alleviating the suffering of spirit affliction. For Emna, a bright, shy young woman who was her high school's valedictorian but stopped her university studies due to harassment by what her father calls *khumaynistes* (radical Muslim students; the term combines the name Khomeini—referring to the Iranian ayatollah—with an ascriptive French suffix commonly used in Tunisian

Arabic), the possession ritual was both taxing and cathartic. By allowing a succession of sub-Saharan spirits and North African and Middle Eastern Muslim saints to use her as a vessel for their enjoyment of music and dance, she reestablished positive relations with members of the *sṭambēlī* pantheon who, in their ritual appearance, not only heal but also collectively evoke the trans-Saharan movements and encounters of *sṭambēlī* itself.

The Other People: Sub-Saharans in Tunisian Society

"The other people" (*in-nās il-ūkhrīn*) refers collectively to the spirits in the *sṭambēlī* pantheon. This appellation confers on the spirits a humanlike quality and calls attention to the potential for social relationships both among spirits and between human and spirit. Their otherness is manifested not only in their invisibility and elusive metaphysical presence, but also in their historical and geocultural identities connecting them to distant places and times.

"The other people," however, may also be used to describe how *sṭambēlī* practitioners and other blacks in Tunisia have been perceived by mainstream Tunisian society. They have been othered in different ways throughout different periods of history, beginning with the earliest days of the trans-Saharan slave trade, at which time they were brought from sub-Saharan Africa into North Africa and sold as slaves. Their non-Muslim status—later conflated with their race—situated them within the category of *kuffār*, or unbelievers, making them candidates for slavery within the purview of Islam. Converting to Islam, or even being born Muslim, however, did not protect Tunisia's black population from the experience of prejudice. Noted historian L. Carl Brown observes that Husaynid Tunisia (ruled by an Ottoman dynasty from 1705 to 1881, and still present under French "indirect" rule from 1881 to 1957) was "far from color blind," and the "only Muslim element in the population subject to discrimination tending to keep them at the lower social and economic rungs of society were the Negroes" (Brown 1974: 185–186).

Tunisia's black population must be understood in its historical and geocultural heterogeneity. A general distinction is maintained between the *wārgliyya*, who are the blacks from the southern Tunisian oases and who are considered more or less indigenous, and the rest of the black population, which is understood as descendants of displaced sub-Saharans, the vast majority of whom were slaves (Zawadowski 1942). Within this latter group we must distinguish broadly between the overlapping populations of slaves that arrived in Tunis before the advent of the Husaynid Dynasty in 1705 and those that arrived in much larger numbers in the eighteenth and nineteenth centuries, bringing with them specific cultural practices and identities that led to a distinctive sub-Saharan slave culture within which *sṭambēlī* crystallized (Montana 2004b).[1]

Blacks in Tunisian society, whether or not they are associated with *sṭambēlī*, continue to experience racism. Conversations with members of the *sṭambēlī* community and close Arab Tunisian friends confirmed the existence of widespread prejudice limiting the social, marital, and employment options of dark-skinned Tunisians. This is reinforced in a variety of ways. The government still uses a stamp of a "Negro head" to denote the lowest grade of silver in its grading system of precious metals. The servitude of slavery remains linguistically inscribed on the black body in Tunisia, where the most common socially acceptable term for black people is *waṣfān* (servants), and where it is not uncommon to hear a speaker specify someone's race by designating that person *maḥrūq* (lit. "burnt," i.e., black) or *ḥurr* (lit. "free," i.e., Arab).

Overarching sociocultural politics of identity in the Maghrib are generally framed in religious (e.g., Muslim vs. Jewish) and/or ethnolinguistic (e.g., Arab vs. Berber) terms. While these identities are by no means static (indeed, they are often situational and overlapping), the sub-Saharan presence in Tunisia complicates such divisions in particular ways. Whereas Berbers and Jews have been considered, for all practical purposes, indigenous others to politically dominant Arabic-speaking Muslims, sub-Saharans have been understood to be geocultural outsiders. However, it has not always been possible to categorize them as non-Muslim and non-Arabic speakers, as most slaves were converted to Islam before or after their arrival in North Africa and learned to speak Arabic once there.[2] Like Arabic-speaking Jews and Muslim Berbers, sub-Saharans in Tunisia have continually negotiated nuances of sameness and difference vis-à-vis Arab Tunisian society. Shared or overlapping identities include common membership in the *umma* (community of Muslims), in an Arabic-speaking society, and in the Tunisian nation-state (constructing an image of national homogeneity has been a priority of both postindependence ruling regimes). Difference is manifested in their racially marked bodies, which evoke histories of servitude, prejudice, and ritual practices that are both contentious and in high demand by some Arab Tunisians.

Many Tunisians ascribe to black Africans a mysterious and powerful ability to manipulate the spirit world and to protect against misfortune.[3] Writing in 1914, A. J. N. Tremearne noted that "in certain cases the presence of a young negress is a necessity even to the Arab magician" (1914: 187). Traditionally, black female servants known as *dada* would look after the children of the house, accompanying boys to their circumcision in order to give them courage, and even breastfeed Arab Tunisian boys so that they would grow up, in Bābā Majīd's words, "strong and brave."[4] The presence of black women was desired in order to bring good fortune at weddings and at childbirth. When this was not possible, the mere image or likeness of a sub-Saharan would suffice. According to M. G. Zawadowski, in early twentieth-century Tunisia,

> the dark pigmentation of the Blacks also seems to constitute an effective "scarecrow" against the jnūn [spirits] in Maghribi popular magic. The presence of a Negro in a family meeting is regarded as bringing good luck, and, in the Tunisian Sahel, one invites a Negro to attend marriage ceremonies for the express purpose of "making the evil eye fly away" (*iteyyer el-ʿîn*), according to the picturesque Arabic expression. Their power to protect them from the jnūn is considered so strong that it is enough to make an image of a Negro out of cardboard, wood, bronze, or stone, and place it in a conspicuous place on a wall, for example, to obtain the same result. (1942: 151)

The perception of otherness is inseparable from a mysterious power to bring good luck or misfortune. As in many other sub-Saharan diasporic communities around the world, while this otherness limits social mobility, it also creates certain opportunities. Despite social and institutional prejudice toward black Africans in Tunisia (see Messaoud 1984), there also remains a common belief that sub-Saharans have particularly powerful efficacy in manipulating the world of spirits, a world that continues to hold sway (at least outside the public sphere) in Tunisian society. *Sṭambēlī* practitioners are considered specialists in dealing with some of these spirits.

Situating *Sṭambēlī*

Communities of displaced African slaves throughout the Islamic world developed ritual healing and devotional musics that refracted and transformed ritual traditions from their African places of origin and synthesized them with elements from their new societies. The trade in African slaves contributed to the spread of *zār* spirit possession practices throughout the Sudan, Somalia, and Ethiopia and into Egypt and the Persian Gulf (Natvig 1991). In Iran, African Baluchis are specialists in trance rituals such as *guāti-demāli* and *lewā*, as well as *zār*, each of which combines in some way local Sufi and African aesthetics and symbols (During 1997). Slaves and their descendants brought *ṭumbura* rituals from the Sudan to Saudi Arabia (Makris 2000),[5] while ritual practices involving elements of *bori* and other sub-Saharan possession rituals were known throughout the Ottoman Empire, including cities in modern-day Turkey (Hunwick 2004).

Sṭambēlī shares many aesthetic and spiritual features of Hausa, Songhay, and other sub-Saharan spirit possession traditions that factor in its ancestry, and it exhibits family resemblances to other healing practices based on music and trance rituals led by sub-Saharans in the Middle East. It is also a node in a larger constellation of related traditions across the Maghrib, where the interface of sub-Saharan possession rituals and the veneration of Muslim saints is evident in the *gnāwa* traditions of Morocco (Chlyeh 1999; Hell 1999), the *derdeba* (Dermenghem 1954) and Seven Springs of Algeria (Andrews 1903), and the *sambānī* of Libya (Tremearne 1914). While there are many similarities among these Maghribi traditions, each developed its own distinctive practices and meanings shaped by such factors as the numbers and geocultural origins of slaves and other displaced Africans, the organization and maintenance of ritual groups, the level of demand for their healing services by local clientele, and their relations with sociopolitical powers.

The term *sṭambēlī* is used to refer to the music, the trance ceremony, and the entire ritual healing tradition. The etymology of the term is unclear and contested, and the differing assumptions about its origins reveal the presence of competing sociohistorical narratives, as well as connections to powerful others, both human and spirit. Bābā Majīd asserts that *sṭambēlī* derives from *sambeli,* which he understands to be a sub-Saharan term for spirit possession activities involving music and dance.[6] Indeed, among the Songhay, *sambeli* refers to an illness or misfortune resulting from an attack of sorcery in which spirits are summoned, and in the Hausa language, *sambale* is "a dance of youth and maidens" (Stoller 1997: 12–13; Bargery 1934: 894). According to Bābā Majīd, *sambeli* is difficult for Tunisians to pronounce and therefore evolved into *sṭambēlī*, which is more intuitive for Tunisian Arabic speakers.[7] The transformation from *sambeli* into *sṭambēlī* was noted by 1920s Tunisian writer Ṣādiq Rizgī, who viewed this transition in nomenclature as evidence of *sṭambēlī*'s "pagan" origins (Rizgī 1989 [1968]: 156).

The more common perception from outside the *sṭambēlī* network, however, is that the term derives from *istanbūlī*, the Arabic for "from Istanbul." This interpretation speaks to *sṭambēlī*'s historical links to the Ottoman court and its rulers' home base of Istanbul. Indeed, *sṭambēlī* did have close ties to, and some patronage from, certain rulers when Tunisia was part of the Ottoman Empire. Yet again, no reason has been given for the potential change from *istanbūlī* to *sṭambēlī*. It seems likely that both the historical association of *sṭambēlī* with Istanbul and its connection to sub-Saharan spirit activities, as well as the pragmatics of pronunciation, may have contributed to the evolution of the term. *Sambeli,* according to numerous Arab Tunisians, is not an intuitive succession of sounds and is somewhat awkward to pronounce, while the practice of *sṭambēlī* did become associated with the late Husaynid regime, which not only tolerated *sṭambēlī*, but even hosted performances at the court during holidays.[8] The ambiguity of the etymology of the term *sṭambēlī* is, in fact, congruent with two recurring themes of this book, namely, that *sṭambēlī* elicits often competing reactions and interpretations that speak to Tunisian history and society, and that it is a complex, contested, and adaptable domain of cultural performance that draws on, but is not reducible to, any of its sub-Saharan, Islamic, Tunisian, or Ottoman referents.

Etymology aside, the main controversy surrounding *sṭambēlī* involves its place in Tunisian society. Two broad and interrelated ideological positions are often mobilized in statements critical of *sṭambēlī*. In the first, the moral-religious perspective, *sṭambēlī* and other possession rituals are deemed incompatible with Islam. Accusations of paganism, immorality, charlatanism, and even lesbianism have been leveled against *sṭambēlī* in diatribes penned by outraged observers such as al-Timbuktāwī in 1808, and scholars such as Ṣādiq Rizgī in the 1920s, and have proven influential among the Tunisian ruling and intellectual elite (see chap. 2). While such attitudes are axiomatic in urban Tunisia, especially among younger Tunisians and those from more privileged or educated backgrounds, they sometimes contradict practice. On numerous occasions, especially early on in my fieldwork, I encountered individuals who made the annual pilgrimage to Sīdī Frej yet would tell me that what I was seeing was "not Islam," or, more subtly, would use word choices (always French, at least at first) that distanced them from *sṭambēlī* participants, such as "they believed" that a saint was present.[9] In his study of trance in Tunisia, Ezeddine Dekhil also encountered a range of attitudes, including those of a female university student who attended ceremonies but, in a creative misreading of Marx, stated that she was "against" *sṭambēlī* because it is an "opiate of the masses" that is incompatible with Islam (Dekhil 1993: 271).

Such religious-based condescension finds an improbable bedfellow in a second attitude, namely, the high modernizing perspective, in which *sṭambēlī* and other rituals are seen as primitive, superstitious, and incompatible with the drive toward modern development.[10] This was dramatically demonstrated after Tunisian independence in 1956, when a new nationalist regime, zealously wedded to the ideologies of developmental modernism and secularism, targeted Tunisian blacks, along with Arab Tunisians, for their participation in the so-called cult of saints (Dermenghem 1954) based on supposedly backward, premodern beliefs and practices. Public performances of *sṭambēlī* were suppressed by the state, and an informal ban on the television and radio remained in place through the 1990s, after Ben ʿAlī took over the presidency with a bloodless coup d'état in 1987. During a short-lived resurgence in the public sphere in 1966, several newspaper articles asked whether *sṭambēlī* had the potential to become "modern" like American jazz, another "music of slaves" (see chap. 8).

Yet many Tunisians are intrigued by *sṭambēlī*, and more than a few I encountered over the years were surprised to find out that Tunisia has "something like" the Moroccan *gnāwa*, with which they are more familiar owing to the success of the *gnāwa* in the world music market. A handful of public *sṭambēlī* events over the past six years or so—one a concert featuring Khemīsī and Bābā Majīd, and the others involving *mūlid* (the Prophet's birthday) ceremonies at the shrine of Sīdī ʿAlī el-Asmar—gave *sṭambēlī* another small and short-lived presence in the public sphere. Such sporadic attention has contributed to *sṭambēlī*'s ambiguous location within Tunisian society, which, influenced by the ethos of the world music market, sees in *sṭambēlī* an exotic but internal other.[11] In this context, however, *sṭambēlī*'s continued presence may direct Tunisians toward a public rethinking of modern Tunisian identity and history, which asserts national homogeneity and suppresses the history of slavery.

Conceptualizing Possession Trance

Sṭambēlī healing is predicated on three fundamental assumptions. First, the individual body is permeable by unseen, outside forces. Second, humans and spirits cohabit the natural world and therefore the actions of one have the potential to influence the other. Third, music and dance are the active agents in reestablishing positive relations between human and spirit. These relationships are thoroughly embodied: affliction involves unforeseen and unwelcome violation of the host's body by the spirit, while the healing process invites possession by enticing the spirit to enter the host's body to dance, within the proper spatial and temporal context of ritual, until it is placated, thus bringing the spirit-host relationship into healthy balance. The palpable yet enigmatic connection between music and trance has fascinated generations of scholars, and as *sṭambēlī* ritual efficacy is predicated on this relationship, it warrants situating the present study within the landscape of various attempts to explain or render it comprehensible.

The relationship between music and possession trance has long exercised the anthropological and ethnomusicological imagination. The precise nature of this relationship, however, has proven elusive, resulting in an abundance of methodological and theoretical approaches. Like the study of spirit possession itself (Boddy 1994: 410), scholarship on spirit possession musics is characterized by a tension between rationalizing, scientistic, and universalizing tendencies on the one hand and more culturally contextualized, phenomenological approaches on the other. Despite their sometimes irreconcilable differences, many studies near both ends of this spectrum share an implicit assumption that possession trance poses some sort of "problem" to be solved.[12]

In the 1960s, anthropologists proposed several musically deterministic hypotheses on the relationship between music and trance. Based on their own field encounters, or those documented by others, anthropologists postulated that loud and repetitive drumming led to trance through sensory overload (Walker 1972) or disturbances of the inner ear (Jackson 1968; Needham 1967). Andrew Neher (1961) conducted laboratory experiments to demonstrate that repetitive rhythmic stimuli could affect brainwave pulsations, resulting in involuntary eye-blinking patterns and subjective reactions he found comparable to anthropological descriptions of possession trance (Neher 1962). Veit Erlmann (1982) tested—and ultimately refuted—Neher's claims in his study of the music of Hausa *bori* possession trance. Erlmann found that only 6.1 percent of the 179 tunes he recorded had tempos in the range Neher identified as necessary to produce such reactions. Gilbert Rouget provided the most comprehensive refutation of such scientistic claims, which elicited his now famous suggestion that, if they held true, then "half of Africa would be in a trance from the beginning of the year to the end" (Rouget 1986: 175).

In his magisterial and meticulous consideration of the diversity of possession musics throughout the world, Rouget called attention to the paradoxical relationship between music and trance: while ritualized trance by and large cannot occur without music, there are no formal qualities (rhythms, modes, tempos, frequency, instrumentation, etc.) of music that appear necessary for trance. The missing variable in previous approaches, for Rouget, was culture, which conditions the way that trancers are socialized into modes of connecting music and trance. Different cultures have different ways of understanding both trance and music, as well as the principles underlying the relations between the two. While he imposed a sweeping structuralist typology of trance types by fitting them into categories alien to their cultures, he did leave us with the invaluable insight that any relationship between music and trance is first and foremost culturally conditioned.

The "crisis of representation" (Clifford and Marcus 1986) in anthropology and the ensuing "crisis of experience" in ethnomusicology (Barz and Cooley 1997) resulted in several case studies employing more experimental and self-reflexive modes of analysis and writing. While experiential narrative strategies have been criticized for telling us more about the ethnographer than the people and practices under study, they do provide unusually deep access to the shifting subject positions, personal feelings, and music and trance experiences of ethnographers embarking on potentially life-transforming initiations into possession trance traditions such as Afro-Cuban *santería* (Hagedorn 2001), Brazilian *candomblé* (Wafer 1991), and Tumbuka *vimbuza* in Malawi (Friedson 1996).[13]

Steven Friedson's deeply phenomenological study of musical healing among the Tumbuka is based on his deep and intimate experience of spirit affliction, which required learning to "dance his disease." Convinced that the "radically different" Tumbuka experience of music, possession, and healing necessitated an equally radical ethnographic methodology, Friedson turned to the phenomenological theories of Martin Heidegger and Wilhelm Dilthey to provide his framework for interpretation. Focusing on his deeply personal experience of drumming and dancing, he conveys vividly and powerfully his experience of the perceptual ambiguity of the multistable 3:2 polymeter of Tumbuka drumming. Creatively and effectively likening the acoustic experience of this phenomenon to optical illusions (such as the Necker cube) that allow for multiple viewpoints and conceptions, he describes his experience of the music as collapsing the boundary between subject and object.[14] Music is described as a "technology" enabling "this loosening up of perceptual boundaries," which, he proposes, "seems to be a significant factor in the promotion of trance states" (1996: 143).[15] An important contribution here is Friedson's concern for musical affect, especially at it relates to the structural and sensory impact of timbre. The strengths and limitations of his study are simply those of phenomenology itself: perception, of course, is culturally mediated, and the 3:2 temporal relationship may or may not be as mind altering for Tumbuka as it was for Friedson. As he emphasizes from the outset, phenomenology "is fundamentally a self-interpreting activity" (1996: 7). Nevertheless, his study constitutes an important step forward by demonstrating the value of engaging with spirit practices and their practitioners on their own terms.

Representing a positivist swing toward the other end of the spectrum is Judith Becker, whose influential study *Deep Listeners: Music, Emotion, and Trancing* (2004) championed musical determinism and universalism in a search for a rational, scientific, and secular humanistic explanation of trance states associated with music. In contrast to Friedson's subject-based approach, Becker focused on the object, or other. After brilliantly contextualizing the continued Western aversion to trance, she argues that trancers and deep listeners necessarily experience a different type of self—a more emotional self—from that of their (mostly Western) counterparts who assume the Cartesian sense of a disengaged, controlled, and bounded self. Grounding her inquiry in recent neuroscientific research, she postulates that trance is brought about by musical rhythmic entrainment, a kind of structural coupling—the synchronization of multiple bodies and brains—that shifts the autonomic nervous system into "overdrive." She associates the profound emotional response to this process with "the production and release of certain hormones and monoamines" that lead trancers to "feel themselves to be in the presence of spirits" (2004: 148). She concludes that trancers are deeply emotional people who achieve deep satisfaction from the chemical floods engendered by trance. For Becker, the autonomous self is at the heart of all activity, and cultural practice merely masks the similarities, that is, the deep emotionality, of trancers universally.[16] But in the context of indigenous spirit possession practices, even if we found groundbreaking synapse firing or intensification of hypothalamic activity in trance-state brain mapping, this would probably be of little interest to participants, for whom the framework of spirit possession is crucial to finding meaning personally and situating the experience socially. Indeed, if pressed, people involved with possession practices might see this incredible activity as further proof that possession did in fact occur. Thus, we reach the epistemological ceiling of such an inquiry, and are left at a far remove from the reality of others' experiences. We might equally ask, to paraphrase Michael Lambek (1989: 48), whether the strange activities of joggers or poets might be explained away as neurochemical activity associated with emotion.

Both Friedson and Becker consciously employ innovative methodologies in their attempts to render trance comprehensible, and their works illustrate vividly the enduring tension between scientistic, universalizing tendencies and contextual, phenomenological approaches. My own approach to possession trance is what I have referred to, drawing on Michael Herzfeld, as a "militant middle ground" between such extremes (Herzfeld 1997; Jankowsky 2007). This should not be interpreted as a compromise between phenomenological and scientistic approaches to trance, largely because I do not identify trance as some sort of problem that needs to be solved. It is the space between universalizing tendencies and extreme reflexivity that I aim to navigate. This is not "neutral" territory, for it is not the negation of the other two, but is rather a purposeful, if elusive, space of in-betweenness.[17] The middle ground I tread is populated by ritual musicians, who inhabit the in-between space mediating between human and spirit worlds. I focus on this space because I am less interested in explaining trance than in understanding how the conditions for trance are produced and the kinds of meanings it is capable of generating in the specific context of Tunisian *sṭambēlī*.

I am therefore encouraged by deep ethnographic studies that eschew both extreme reflexivity and universalizing tendencies in order to consider spirit possession practices on their own terms. For Paul Berliner (1993), the serious study of *mbira* music was inseparable from the instrument's connection to ancestor spirits and the context of *bira* possession ceremonies. By acknowledging the importance of spirit activities among the Shona, he was able to delve into the complex role of *mbira* music in communicating with the spirits (who are "shrewd judges" of talent, thereby upholding musical values), enabling communal participation in ritual, and inviting Shona to reflect deeply on history and apply its lessons to present-day social conflicts. Ron Emoff's (Emoff 2003) study of possession music in Madagascar mobilized the indigenous concept of *maresaka*—an aesthetic of reconfiguring various sonic, visual, and historical textures—to access the subtle ways in which *tromba* spirits and their music combine fragments into meaningful wholes by reordering and recollecting the past in order to empower the present. John Blacking engaged in a similar search for meaning—rather than explanation—among the Venda, from whom he learned that music, when performed well, in the proper context, and for the right person, enables a dancer to "come face to face with her/his other self, the real self of the ancestor spirit" (1985: 67). Blacking's study is also notable for explicitly raising the question of the relationship between music and spirit possession. Like Erlmann and Rouget, he found no convincing evidence for any kind of causal link, and concluded with the provocative proposal "that what at first seems to be a dramatic example of the power of music, namely, possession by spirits during musical performance, had little to do with musical influences and that its explanation may have to be sought elsewhere" (1985: 69).

The scholarly fixation on the mechanisms of trance has diverted attention away from other important aspects of possession musics, such as how they signify meaningfully in their cultural contexts. Paul Stoller (1989) understands the music of spirit possession rituals among the Songhay of Niger as enabling the "fusion" of past and present, as well as social and spirit, worlds. For the Songhay, the "cries" of the *godji* fiddle evoke Songhay ancestors and bring them into contact with humans in the here and now. In a similar vein, I understand possession rituals to be imaginal sites, where social issues connecting the past with the present are brought to the fore through corporeal, sensory experience. I also consider the aesthetic experience—especially the distinctive aesthetics of *sṭambēlī* and their significations within Tunisian society—as central to experiencing the nonverbalized information that rituals are designed to convey.

Ritual Reconsidered

Much of this book is concerned with *sṭambēlī* ritual performance and thus comes with the risk of accusations of "reducing" possession to ritualized practice (Masquelier 2001: 26).[18] I rather view my approach as doing the opposite, that is, amplifying or expanding possession outward from within ritual. By delving deeply into the ritual experience and its aesthetic sensorium, by taking at face value the healing that occurs and the spiritual and supernatural beings who manifest themselves in ritual, I attempt to convey how a perspective from within ritual is one that spills out into the realm of the sociopolitical landscape but does so in a way that reveals the relationships and historical referents that are salient for members of the *sṭambēlī* network. In doing so, I hope to contribute to recent discussions of ritual healing that suggest ritual possesses its own theoretical possibilities, and that it is from within that its meanings resonate beyond it.

Ever since Arthur Kleinman's (1980) landmark study of healing in cultural contexts, a vast ethnographic literature has affirmed that the cultural impact of ritual healing extends far beyond an individual's affliction. The explicit objective of *sṭambēlī* is to alleviate specific types of individual suffering resulting from spirit affliction. Individual suffering, however, "must be understood in the context of both larger political realities and local moral worlds" (Csordas 2002: 161), which in the *sṭambēlī* context involves histories of trans-Saharan movements and ensuing social, religious, and racial encounters. I am convinced that *sṭambēlī* ritual performance has the power to evoke these multiple worlds simultaneously, to put them into play with each other, and to make them manifest for individual and collective reflection. It does so by creating what Don Handelman calls a "temporary microworld," which is "predicated on the potential for change . . . [and] answers to its own horizons of cultural possibility" (cited in Herzfeld 2001: 262). A crucial aspect of this microworld of ritual is its temporal dimension, which involves a "radical slowing down . . . of the tempo of ordinary life, its speed, continuous shifts in standpoint, changes in perspective and structures of context—the chaos of lived existence" (Kapferer 2005a: 48). It is here, at the interstices of spatial and temporal transformation, that ritual aesthetics redirect participants into new horizons of meaning and possibility. There has been an increasing recognition of the phenomenological and symbolic power of the music that is central to healing rituals in creating such transformations (Becker 2004; Crapanzano 1973; Emoff 2003; Friedson 1996; Gouk 2000; Kapferer 1991; Roseman 1991; Stoller 1989, 1996). Broadly speaking, in the context of ritual, "musical performance binds the participants to the associative webs they construct, encompassing them within a meaningful—yet ineffable—world" (Reily 2002: 14). More specifically, according to Rachel Harris and Barley Norton, ritual music has the power to

1. structure ritual time—to create a "virtual" time which creates a sense of shared experience and to collapse the temporal boundaries between past, present and future;
2. structure ritual space—to acoustically mark out the space in which rituals

are carried out and in religious rituals to collapse the boundaries between "human" and "spiritual" worlds;

3. articulate and/or transform ethnic and gender identities and differences, and social values and hierarchies;
4. express and/or evoke emotion;

and, particularly in rituals involving spirit possession, to:

5. promote healing;
6. invite and, in some cases, ward off spirits;
7. identify spirits and "socialize" possession (Harris and Norton 2002: 2).

These are important observations. In *sṭambēlī*, as in the rituals described in the ethnomusicological literature considered by Harris and Norton, music is not mere accompaniment to ritual activities, nor is it simply a vehicle for delivering the words of ostensibly more important sacred texts. It is not merely an expressive act, but also a pragmatic force that is constitutive of experience (Kapferer 2005b). In other words, rather than seeing music as merely a part of ritual, it may be useful to understand ritual more as a *context for music to act and to reveal its powers of intervention and transformation*. Such a shift in perspective allows us to move beyond analysis of ritual structure and elucidation of ritual process (although both remain important analytical undertakings) in order to explore "ritual dynamics," which are the compositional elements of rite that establish the perceptual ground for the construction of meaning (Kapferer 2005a).

The concept of "ritual dynamics," as proposed by Bruce Kapferer (2005a), should not be confused with ritual process, although the two are mutually implicated. Victor Turner's (1969) shift of focus from the stasis of ritual symbols to the kinetics of ritual action, as is well known, constituted a paradigm shift in ritual studies that remains an invaluable contribution to our understanding of ritual. Kapferer's notion of ritual dynamics builds on the spirit of Turner's prioritizing of the ritual process, especially moments of heightened transformation (such as the "betwixt and between" of liminality), but avoids the potential pitfalls of emphasizing the structuring (usually tripartite) grammar of ritual, which runs the risk of reducing ritual to a linear, teleological process that is then analyzed in terms of its symbolic and predictable outcome. Ritual dynamics emphasize not this larger structuring, but rather the inner forces and processes—the compositional elements—that shape perception, transform experience, and generate meaning. Kapferer, who is indebted to Susanne Langer's use of the term "dynamics" as opposed to "process" to accentuate these forces, also argues that through their capacity to construct "complexity through relative economy or simplicity," aesthetic processes communicate "simultaneously the immediately concrete and abstract" (Kapferer 2005a: 39). Reacting against analyses that interpret ritual as a suspension of reality, Kapferer draws on Gilles Deleuze and Félix Guattari's concept of the "virtual" to convey this sense of ritual as both "really real" and as a self-contained imaginal space. This virtuality is distinct from that of technologically produced virtual reality in that the latter is a simulacrum, concerned with reproducing real realities or an alternate reality, while the former is "a fully lived existential reality" (Kapferer 2005a: 47). Ritual virtuality, nevertheless, is distinct from everyday reality or "actuality," which is chaotic in that it is always emergent, continually constructed by individuals whose actions and attitudes are variously forming, shifting, and intersecting in relation to the flow and immanence of everyday situations. For Kapferer, the salient feature of this virtuality is not that it suspends reality, but that it slows down the tempo of everyday life and holds at bay the chaotic and fractured nature of quotidian experience. In other words, rather than being other than real, the virtuality of ritual "constitutes a descent into processes of the really real" which would otherwise be "impossible to address in the tempo and dynamics of ordinary lived processes as these are lived at the surface" (Kapferer 2005a: 48). Ritual, then, is at once a concentration of force and a protraction of focus, simultaneously producing experiential density *and* expansion. In this book I argue that, in *sṭambēlī*, these processes constitute, and are constituted by, the aesthetics of musical production.

Fieldwork Context and the Ethnographic Experience

Tunisia is often characterized in the popular and scholarly imaginations as a crossroads of European, Middle Eastern, and to a lesser extent, African worlds. With over 95 percent of its population Sunni Muslim and Arabic speaking, it has been described as remarkably homogenous, though not without a certain historical cosmopolitanism resulting from its encounters with, and absorption of, foreign cultural elements. The northernmost country on the African continent, Tunisia is nestled between Algeria to the west and Libya to the east. It is roughly the same size as Florida, but with over seven hundred miles of Mediterranean coastline, and a mere eighty miles from Sicily, it has been coveted for its strategic location by a succession of occupying regional forces including the Phoenicians, Romans, Vandals, Byzantines, Arabs, Ottoman Turks, and French. Tunisia also received significant numbers of immigrants traveling under more dire conditions, most notably Jews and Muslims fleeing the Christian Reconquista in Andalusia and innumerable forcibly displaced sub-Saharan slaves. While each left cultural imprints of varying degrees, the most indelible and pervasive legacy was left by the Arabs, whose language, religion, and culture remain central to the innermost identity of Tunisians nearly fourteen centuries after the arrival of the first Arab invaders (Perkins 2004: 5; Abun-Nasr 1987: 26). While indigenous Berber populations factor into most Tunisians' ancestry, Berber cultural identity is rarely expressed outside a handful of small villages on the edge of the Sahara Desert.[19] The spread of Islam, Arab culture, and twentieth-century nationalist policies of Arabization successfully established Arabic as the country's lingua franca, leaving only an estimated fifty thousand speakers of the Berber dialect Shilha in Tunisia at the end of the twentieth century. These dwindling numbers, the absence of monolingual Berber speakers, a lack of Berberophone mass media, and increased intermarriage all suggest that Berber language and culture in Tunisia are already in the final stages of becoming obsolete (Battenburg 1999).[20]

Berber dynasties reigned in Tunisia from the eleventh to the early sixteenth centuries, ending Arab rule first initiated by Arab military chiefs from Egypt, zealous to spread Islam as well as gain prestige and the spoils of conquest, who invaded Tunisia in 670 CE and established the city of Kairouan as their base (Abun-Nasr 1987: 28–29). The main threat to the success of the Arab invasion was resistance from Berber tribes united into confederacies, the most famous of which fought and won several battles in Tunisia under the leadership of the legendary queen al-Kahina before it was defeated and she was killed (Abun-Nasr 1987: 31).

In 1574 Tunisia came under the control of the expanding Ottoman Empire. Too distant to be ruled effectively from Istanbul, the garrison state developed relative autonomy under a succession of leaders culled from a local but nonnative ruling class that perpetuated the Ottoman tradition of marking a clear distinction between rulers and ruled (Brown 1974: 29). Central power relied on the military force of the army, whose members, like the ruling class, were also drawn from a corps of foreigners or outsiders. Maritime piracy constituted Tunisia's major economic activity during this time, as North African Muslims were systematically excluded from legitimate trade by Europe's monopoly on trans-Mediterranean commerce (Perkins 1986: 58). Reliance on corsair activity gradually gave way to legal international trade in the late seventeenth century as European naval threats persuaded Tunisia to accept commercial treaties that furthered European dominance of trans-Mediterranean trade (Perkins 1986: 59).

Tunisia's integration into the wider Mediterranean market increased during the ensuing Husaynid Dynasty, established in 1705 by Ḥusayn ibn ʿAlī, who inaugurated an era of diminishing Ottoman control while acknowledging allegiance to Istanbul, which maintained the local regime's Ottoman legitimacy. The Husaynids cultivated diplomatic and commercial links with Europe, which enabled Tunisians to benefit from European demand for goods such as olive oil, wheat, and animal hides but also made the Tunisian economy vulnerable to disruptive events on the Continent. When faced with diminished demand for its goods abroad or poor harvests at home, the Tunisian state and independent merchants received substantial loans from Europe. Increasing foreign indebtedness and the French occupation of Algeria in 1830 created a climate of uncertainty to which Tunisia responded with mostly European-inspired reforms. Reformist leaders such as Aḥmad Bey (r. 1837–1855), whose ad hoc development strategies met with mixed results, nevertheless helped instill an attitude toward reform that viewed modernization as compatible with local cultural practices and religious beliefs. He developed a military-industrial complex that included factories, mills, and foundries dedicated to producing goods to support a standing army drawn for the first time from the local citizenry. While this proved too expensive to become self-sustaining (and led to more international debt and unpopular local taxation), the army's broad-based conscription contributed to the development of a national consciousness (Perkins 1986: 71).

A tradition of top-down reform became entrenched in Tunisia in the mid-nineteenth century as the state designed and imposed social, political, and constitutional reforms. Ironically, the state was also borrowing heavily from the West in order to protect itself from the West (Largueche 2003: 330). Both of these situations only bolstered the colonial theory of "the advanced state" governing and reforming a "backward society" (Largueche 2003: 330). State-level pressure to "modernize" Tunisia from abroad also increased as Great Britain and France persuaded Tunisia to make judicial and constitutional reforms to create social and economic stability and to protect foreign nationals. These reforms, made to benefit foreigners and their investments, failed to restructure Tunisian society (Perkins 1986: 83). But increasing debt, especially after the spending increase needed to quell the tax-related 1864 rebellion, increased Tunisia's dependence on the French, who marched into the country in 1881 and took it over with very little armed resistance. Two years later France declared Tunisia a "protectorate" and guaranteed its international debt in exchange for control over the bey's administrative, judicial, and fiscal decisions (Perkins 1986: 86).

In addition to reforms in land distribution and taxation that benefited colons while impoverishing many Tunisians, the French developed nationwide transportation, communication, and education infrastructures designed with the needs of colons in mind. It was not until World War I introduced tens of thousands of Tunisians to French citizens sympathetic to the plight of the Tunisians, and showed them that even the mighty French military could suffer heavy losses, that widespread organized resistance to colonization developed in Tunisia (Perkins 1986: 97). Resistance crystallized around the Neo-Dustūr (New Constitution) party, founded in the 1930s by Western-educated Tunisians initially dedicated to creating a modern nation-state that combined European political ideals while maintaining pride in Tunisia's Arab-Islamic heritage. Led by Sorbonne-trained lawyer Habib Bourguiba, the Neo-Dustūr took advantage of Morocco's successful calls for independence during the full-scale anti-French rebellion in neighboring Algeria (the cornerstone of French North Africa, with the status not of a colony but of a French political subdivision) to demand its own independence, which it was granted in 1956. Bourguiba became the Republic of Tunisia's first president after winning national elections a year later, at which time the last of the Husaynid rulers, Amīn Bey, was deposed.

As part of a larger strategy to integrate Tunisia into the world economy, Bourguiba's newly independent regime embarked on an aggressive agenda of Western-inspired social reforms. The Personal Status Code of 1956 radically improved the rights of women through enfranchisement, education, and equality in divorce and inheritance. The code also required a woman's consent to marry and set minimum ages for marriage. Bourguiba also carried out public campaigns encouraging family planning—including contraception and abortion rights—and discouraging the wearing of the veil.

The Personal Status Code, which challenged traditional interpretations of Islamic law, was part of a broader, systematic offensive by Bourguiba against the influence of Islam in Tunisian society. Islamic courts were abolished in favor of secular judiciaries, and *ḥabūs* properties (religious endowments) were taken over by the state. But there were limits to such sweeping reforms. Irritated by the decline in economic productivity as Tunisians observed their religious obligation to fast during the daylight hours of the holy month of Ramadan, Bourguiba publicly ignored the fast by ingesting food at midday on television. Although he couched his defiance in religious terms, encouraging the nation to join him in his "jihad against underdevelopment" (since those engaged in jihad are absolved of the obligation to fast), his campaign against fasting failed (Perkins 2004: 119). Opposition to this demand was insurmountable, even among relatively nonobservant Tunisian Muslims. The fasting tradition, which is accompanied by all sorts of festivities and social activities, was simply too deeply entrenched in Tunisian culture. Although this reform failed, most others, such as the Personal Status Code, were successful and enduring, if not always immediately and universally accepted. Bourguiba was careful to position himself not as anti-Islamic, but as an Islamic reformer. The success of his religious reforms resulted in part from the discrediting of the Tunisian religious establishment from its collusion with the French and its failure to guide the country out of colonization. In fact, it was not the country's religious clerics but the Tunisian nationalists who were the most outspoken defenders of Tunisian Islam during the colonial era (Perkins 1986: 118).

Bourguiba was a shrewd and pragmatic politician who preferred agile maneuvers and accommodation to outright confrontation, a style of governance he himself coined "Bourguibism." He supported negotiating with Israel while also providing refuge to the PLO after it was expelled from Lebanon. He championed women's rights but had little regard for human rights and freedom of speech. He promised democratic reform but built a single-party political system and accepted the official status of president for life. Historian Kenneth Perkins notes that, in all but title, Bourguiba had become the bey, "exercising his authority, working and residing in his palaces, and reveling in the pageantry and rituals once reserved for the Husainid rulers" (2004: 208).

In the 1980s, Bourguiba's declining health, which compromised his mental faculties, transformed national politics into a "collective wager" on his mortality (Alexander 1997: 36). His rule ended on November 7, 1987, after a bloodless—and constitutional, as Bourguiba would be declared senile—coup d'état led by his former interior minister, Zīn al-ʿAbidīn Ben ʿAlī, a military officer who had built the state's security apparatus and directed Bourguiba's increasingly militant crackdown on Islamist opposition. While Bourguiba was revered as the father of modern Tunisia, there was a sense of relief that he was ushered away with little trauma, and there was renewed hope that the paralyzed political system could be rejuvenated. Ben ʿAlī immediately memorialized his own accession, which he simply, if portentously, dubbed "The Change" (*al-taghrīr*), by establishing the seventh of November as the new holiday of national pride. He removed all public reminders of Bourguiba, whose name and image were eliminated from coins, banknotes, and postage stamps; many streets and squares named after Bourguiba were renamed November the Seventh.

Despite instituting multiparty politics, promising to improve human rights, and broadening freedom of speech, Ben ʿAlī has imprisoned political opponents, human rights activists, and journalists critical of his policies; foreign press reports on Tunisia are often blocked from dissemination. Human Rights Watch asserts that the Ben ʿAlī regime uses the threat of Islamic terrorism as a pretext for suppressing any form of peaceful dissent, and Reporters without Borders cites Ben ʿAlī's "obsessive control over the news" (Reporters without Borders 2008) and describes his regime's Internet censorship and surveillance policies as "among the most repressive in the world" (Reporters without Borders 2007). Suppression of free speech, imprisonment of opponents, and a steadily improving economy (with prodding from the International Monetary Fund and World Bank, he has embraced globalization and privatization) have largely neutralized any viable opposition to the president, who ran unopposed in 1989 and 1994, received 99.44 percent of the votes in 1999, and, after a referendum extending the number of terms a president may hold office, was reelected in 2004 with 94.49 percent of the votes. He was elected to a fifth term by a similar margin again in 2009.

Islam in Tunisia

Since independence, there has been a continual tension between religion and the secularizing policies of the country's leadership. Although the Tunisian constitution declares Islam the country's official religion, both Bourguiba and Ben ʿAlī have fought painstakingly, and often violently, to prevent Islam from infiltrating the political system. Islamic parties are banned, imams are selected and employed by the state, and nonelderly Muslims who attend mosque services too regularly are regarded with suspicion. Yet many Islamic practices and beliefs are so entrenched in Tunisian culture that overt anti-Islam measures, as Bourguiba found out during his Ramadan fiasco, can be counterproductive. As Mark Tessler (1978: 361) argues, religion in Tunisia has been gradually redefined over the past fifty years. While religious observance may have declined, Islam has remained important, arguably for its sociological rather than its theological impact. The government has therefore begun to encourage moderate and nonpolitical Islamic voices. In 2005, Ben ʿAlī's son-in-law established the country's first religious radio station for precisely this purpose, and the government has begun to sponsor Sufi music festivals to showcase a more "tolerant" form of Islam.

Sufi orders in Tunisia have enjoyed a tenuous and shifting relationship with the state that has ranged from patronage and encouragement to systematic repression. In Husaynid Tunisia, Sufi orders were a part of everyday life for the rulers and ruled alike, and most beys belonged to a religious brotherhood and thus maintained the importance and legitimacy of the orders. Aḥmad Bey was a devoted member of the Shādhiliyya brotherhood and would visit the tomb of its founder, Sīdī Belḥassen (Sīdī Abū al-Ḥassan ʿAlī esh-Shādhilī) before and after major journeys, including his monumental state visit to Paris (Brown 1974: 176). The beys respected the tradition of Sufi sanctuaries as asylums for fugitives, and many beys built or renovated shrines for saints they venerated (Brown 1974: 176). The Husaynids were not necessarily altruistic in their encouragement of Sufism, as it was also a means for integrating, and thus regulating, those members of society that were not part of other major institutions (Montana 2004b).

The Sufi orders (*ṭuruq*; sing. *ṭarīqa*, lit. "way" or "path") active in twentieth-century Tunisia included the Qādiriyya, ʿĪsāwiyya, Shādhiliyya, Madaniyya, Raḥmāniya, ʿArūsiyya, Sulāmiyya, Ṭaybiyya, Tijāniyya, ʿAmariyya, and ʿAzūziyya (Rizgī 1989 [1968]). It was still common to hear the saying "He without a [Sufi] path is on the path of the devil" in the early twentieth century (Rizgī 1989 [1968]: 101). While the ancestry of most Tunisian Sufi orders can be traced to the twelfth-century mystic Abū Midyān, the *ṭarīqa*s often differ greatly in their rituals, teachings, beliefs, and membership. Some, such as the Sulāmiyya, have histories characterized by conservative teachings, close relationship to the state, and elite membership. Others, such as the ʿĪsāwiyya, have been politically and religiously suspect to many for their sometimes violent trance ceremonies and more "popular" membership, although their stage performances, part of the widespread folklorization of religious ritual in Tunisia, are increasingly perceived as good for tourism.

But not all Tunisian saints and their teachings became the focus of highly formalized religious associations such as a Sufi order. In fact, one of the defining features of North African Islam is the widespread veneration of saints who are not founders of Sufi orders. Instead, the veneration of saints takes the form of a variety of practices and beliefs surrounding sacred sites associated with sacred personages—living or, more commonly, deceased—believed to be capable of intervening in the lives of humans. These sanctuaries, called *zwāyā* (sing. *zāwiya*), may be as simple as a pyramid of stones or as grandiose as a lavish complex of buildings adjoining a mosque but are most commonly modest, single-story, whitewashed edifices with domed roofs. In any case, the site either houses the tomb or was a significant place in the life of a saint, or *walī*, whose spiritual presence resides or can be summoned there. More than with their teachings, saints are associated with the performance of miracles or other acts that demonstrated that God had chosen to bestow upon them his *baraka*. This blessing is understood as transferable from a saint to supplicants. Michael Gilsenan notes that it is their "capacity for significant action" in a person's life that is central, not their status as spiritual teachers (1973: 45). Their following is often limited to a neighborhood, village, or region, although several are recognized across Tunisia and its neighbors. Offerings ranging from individual prayers over the saint's tomb or the lighting of a candle purchased from the caretaker of the *zāwiya* to trance rituals and group pilgrimages, are made in order receive the saint's blessing and protection, and as an advance on the saint's intercession on behalf of the supplicant. As in Morocco, the relationship between supplicant and saint involves the same dynamic of exchange and expected reciprocity that characterizes traditional Maghribi social relations (Crapanzano 1980).

Situating Dār Bārnū

Dār Bārnū is situated in the neighborhood of Tunis known as Bēb Sīdī ʿAbd es-Salēm (lit. "gate of Saint ʿAbd es-Salēm"), in reference to the gate that was historically one of the entrances to the city through its walled fortifications and named after the area's most significant landmark, the shrine of Sīdī ʿAbd es-Salēm. It is a low-income, working-class area, what the French would call a *quartier populaire*. At independence in 1956, it had the second-highest population density of all of Tunis's neighborhoods (Sebag 1998: 532–533). It is located at the farthest periphery of the medina, or old city, of Tunis. The development of the medina, like that of other Islamic urban areas, followed a pattern of spatial hierarchization. At the center of the medina is the Zitouna Mosque, first built when Tunis was founded in 698 CE. The city fanned out from this center, with the most prestigious and pleasant markets—of perfumers, booksellers, and jewelers—situated closest to the mosque. The least pleasant markets—the loud or malodorous markets of such tradespeople as greengrocers, wool dyers, and coppersmiths—were located farthest from the center (Brown 1974: 125, 188).[21] Residential patterns ran a parallel course, with the old Tunisian elites living closest to the heart (*qelb*) of the medina, and migrants and ethnic or religious others inhabiting the margins.

Before colonization by France, geographic origins and religious background played a major role in determining the city's residential patterns. The Husaynid regime's administrative policies reified such categories by appointing an overseer (*gaʿīd*) for each of the city's largest or most significant minorities: the blacks, Jews, Europeans, and rural immigrants. With the intensification of urban migration in the twentieth century, socioeconomic factors began to overtake these distinctions. Like many other Maghribi cities, the medina housed a *hara*, or Jewish quarter, and a *quartier franc* for a sizable European population. Outside the medina, but still within the city walls, were the *barrānī* (lit. "stranger" or "foreigner") neighborhoods, mostly populated by rural, mainly Bedouin, Tunisian immigrants (Signoles et al. 1980). At the farthest periphery of the city, just at the city walls, were ghettos (what the French called *gourbivilles*), densely populated by the poorest and (literally) most marginalized outsider groups. Bēb Sīdī ʿAbd es-Salēm is the northernmost of these neighborhoods.

This section of the ancient wall now abuts a four-lane highway. The cars that zoom by rarely stop here, their drivers paying little heed to a district that has little to offer them. After a short walk from a nearby tram or bus stop and a bit of traffic dodging to cross the highway, one enters the neighborhood by walking down the steep slope through the wide gap in the ancient walls. Immediately, the landscape changes drastically. There is no automobile traffic, save for the occasional delivery truck or daring taxi, for the streets are too narrow. At 6:00 a.m. each day, street vendors begin to set up their makeshift stalls. The majority have on display impressively large piles of used, and often broken, parts for radios and televisions. Others sell cheap socks, poor copies of designer T-shirts, plumbing supplies, or (to this Red Sox fan's chagrin) New York Yankees baseball caps. The loud, crackly speakers of the cassette kiosk typically blare *mizwid*, a bagpipe-based music associated with rural immigrants and denigrated by critics for glorifying immoral behavior; it constitutes the most popular indigenous music style. The only regular exception is Fridays, when this music is replaced by Qur'ānic recitation. The bustling "informal economy" of the neighborhood is not composed only of merchants.[22] Behind the closed doors of some homes, clairvoyants may be consulting with clients, or Islamic healers may be inscribing passages from the Qur'ān onto charms. Behind one traditional, light blue wooden double door, in an alley just off the main thoroughfare of the street market, a patient may be seeking diagnosis for suspected spirit affliction, or a spirit possession ceremony may already be well underway. This is the door of Dār Bārnū.

Upon entering, the visitor is situated in a small foyer that leads to an open-air courtyard. Despite the traditional architectural style, a number of features signal immediately that this is not a typical Tunisian home. Inside the entryway, one quickly comes face-to-face with a large carving of a goat's head protruding from the wall. On either side, several decorative swords of various sizes and shapes hang inside their sheaths. Small plaques of passages from the Qur'ān also hang conspicuously. In the midst of these objects hang a number of framed photographs of Bābā Majīd, Khemīsī, and other *sṭambēlī* musicians in performance. One photograph portrays Bābā Majīd, alone, playing the *gumbrī* on a concert stage in Germany. Another shows him performing at the American embassy with Charlie Byrd during the jazz guitarist's 1966 visit to Tunis.

The juxtaposition of sub-Saharan, local Tunisian, and pan-Islamic symbols intensifies further inside the house, where a room houses ritual paraphernalia such as cloaks, banners, spears, a variety of drums, and the mask and costume of Bū Saʿdiyya (*sṭambēlī*'s first musician; see chap. 2), in addition to a small area outfitted in honor of the powerful spirit Kūrī, who is also from Bornu. A bedroom doubling as a sitting room houses numerous *sṭambēlī* musical instruments, more swords and daggers, and family photographs. The ease with which these multiple referents were managed in the daily life at Dār Bārnū led me to question early on the appropriateness of artificially separating out what is "local" and what is "sub-Saharan," however they might be defined, in *sṭambēlī*. This is not a simple "here" vs. "there" equation; much of Bornu was Islamicized as early as the sixteenth century, and spirit possession ceremonies probably existed in the Maghrib even before the arrival of Islam. Bābā Majīd often brought up such points of contact and shared histories, pointing out, for example, that even "the name *barnū* comes from [the Arabic] *barr nūḥ* [land of Noah]: home of our Saint Noah."[23] Eventually I became convinced that after at least three hundred years of *sṭambēlī* development here, all of these referents are equally "at home" at Dār Bārnū and among members of the *sṭambēlī* network. This is not to suggest that they have lost their association with other places and times, but rather that being at home can be about recognizing connections and performing routes across geocultural, racial, and national boundaries.

Historically, these connections were experienced on a daily basis in numerous, palpable ways at Dār Bārnū. Kanuri, the language of Bornu, was widely spoken there, and many also spoke Hausa. Bābā Majīd described the ambiance as an "African market" and often spoke of the common mingling of people of various ethnolinguistic groups (on track 5 of the accompanying compact disc, he performs a medley of songs associated with Tuareg, Barnāwī, and Bambara communities). Today, the atmosphere is much more subdued, sub-Saharan languages are no longer spoken, and the buzz of the "African market" is all but gone. Nevertheless, the historical and geocultural connections to sub-Saharan Africa permeate life at Dār Bārnū. These connections are elicited in the present day, not only through the material culture present in the house, or through the occasional presence of potential patients seeking diagnosis for suspected spirit affliction, but also through the house's role as a site for *sṭambēlī* ritual performance, involving musical aesthetics, dances, spiritual and supernatural presences, ritual knowledge, histories, and ontologies carried and cultivated by displaced sub-Saharans and their descendants in Tunis.

While the actual composition of the household varied due to extended residencies by family and friends, as well as the regular comings and goings of musicians, diviners, and clients, the permanent residents during my research were Bābā Majīd, his wife Baya, their son Belḥassen, and their daughters Emna, Sayda, and Saʿida. Bābā Majīd was the *galadīma kbīr* (*galadīma* is Hausa for "chief" and *kbīr* is Arabic for "great" or "big"), or head, of Dār Bārnū. His surname, Barnāwī, immediately evokes the house and Bornu. He led the house's *sṭambēlī* troupe and was therefore also the *yinna*—a master of the *gumbrī* and of the ritual knowledge of music, spirits, diagnoses, and medicines the title *yinna* presupposes. He was born to what he described as a white Tunisian mother and a black father from Bornu. Longevity runs in the family: his mother reportedly lived to be 102 years of age, his father 110. During the time I knew him, Bābā Majīd always looked remarkably youthful and energetic for an octogenarian (fig. 2). His father was born in the Bornu region and was taken to Tunis, where he served the Husaynid court. He became the last appointed *gaʿīd* of the black community in Tunis, a position that gave that population a voice at the court. According to Bābā Majīd, his father always yearned to return to Bornu but never could. Bābā Majīd

FIGURE 2. Bābā Majīd Bārnāwī, 2001. (Photograph by Richard Jankowsky.)

himself never expressed any desire to see Bornu. Although his history is inextricably tied to sub-Saharan Africa, Bābā emphasized that, like *sṭambēlī* itself, he was born and raised here; despite his sub-Saharan ancestry, Tunisia was his only home.

While Bābā Majīd provided my training and guidance in the performative world of *sṭambēlī*, he was also an important historical source. In the *sṭambēlī* ceremonies he directed, his musical structuring of ritual through the invocation of identifiable spirits and saints presented suggestive fragments of *sṭambēlī* history. Understanding the parameters of those performed, embodied histories came from formal and informal discussions with Bābā Majīd and other *sṭambēlī* practitioners. The distinction between remembrance, which is social remembering, as takes place in ritual, and memory, which is an individual process, is relevant here. Bābā Majīd was a repository of history through his memories and the only *sṭambēlī* practitioner old enough to have experienced firsthand, or heard from others, historical events and stories from the time when Dār Bārnū was a highly active communal house. His informative, highly detailed, and often entertaining oral narratives about the history of Dār Bārnū—from his own experience and from histories passed down to him—provided compelling vignettes of Tunisian history through the cultural lens of the sub-Saharan minority in Tunis. While this history is virtually absent from Tunisian historiography, there are written documents that allude to *sṭambēlī* and the network of communal houses, often supporting Bābā Majīd's factual information but differing in their attitudes and conclusions. This highlights the subjectivity of historical narrative, whether oral or written; both are creative productions that are not—indeed, cannot be—objective accounts of "things the way they were," but are rather modes of making history. Recollections of the past must be read, or heard, in the context of the struggles and issues of the present, which in Bābā's case, so soon after the death of Khemīsī, certainly involved a sense of loss and a palpable nostalgia for the past. Indeed, on many occasions Bābā's historical narratives returned abruptly to the present, often to point out how *sṭambēlī*, whether it be the technique of the younger musicians or the place of *sṭambēlī* in Tunisian society, was no longer what it used to be. I interpret this nostalgia not as something that distorts history, but rather as something that sheds light on the meaning of history for individuals, especially as it relates to a discomfiting present.

Bābā Majīd's wife, Baya, runs the household efficiently and affectionately. *Sṭambēlī* activities constitute a large part of her household responsibilities. She has a deep knowledge of the *sṭambēlī* spirit pantheon and the various symptoms and ritual processes associated with its members. While Bābā Majīd was alive, Baya was the first point of contact for potential clients and was therefore often found fielding phone calls and administering initial consultations at the house. She also often made the scheduling and transportation arrangements for *sṭambēlī* ceremonies. Baya attended many of Bābā's ceremonies, where she assisted with ritual preparations and attended to clients and other dancers during and after trance. Traditionally, these activities were the responsibility of the *ʿarīfa*, a ritual healer with extensive trance experience and skills in divination. After the last of the trustworthy *ʿarīfa*s at Dār Bārnū had passed away, Bābā had trouble finding honest, knowledgeable, and dependable *ʿarīfa*s with whom to work. He had been disappointed, and even misled, by subsequent *ʿarīfa*s, one of whom began to offer Bābā's *sṭambēlī* services to clients not afflicted by spirits, such as students desperate to pass exams. Deeply dismayed by such charlatanism, Bābā and Baya began to share the majority of the duties traditionally assigned to the *ʿarīfa*s. And, while balancing all of this, Baya still made time to make virtually all of her food from scratch, including items such as *harīssa* (a spicy red pepper paste) and rosewater that many other Tunisian families can now buy ready made. She was much younger than Bābā and, like his mother, was not of African descent.

Belḥassen learned to play the *shqāshiq* by accompanying his father's troupe. Over time, he cultivated a reputation for being an honest and reliable musician who acquired extensive ritual knowledge from a venerable source. He became the lead *shqāshiq* player in the troupes led by his father's apprentices and is sometimes hired to accompany Tunisian popular musicians, such as Hedi Habbouba and Hedi Dounia, interested in adding *sṭambēlī* sounds to their live or recorded performances. After his father's death Belḥassen continued to play in the Dār Bārnū troupe, which he now coleads with Ṣālaḥ al-Wārglī, one of Bābā Majīd's apprentices, on *gumbrī*.

We met Emna, the eldest of their daughters, at the beginning of this chapter. Her affliction is serious, and although she is a smart young woman with a gentle demeanor, her affliction puts her in a disadvantageous position that affects her future. Her two sisters, with the very similar names Sayda and Saʿida (resulting in some early confusion on my part!), are not *maskūn* ("inhabited" by the spirits) like Emna, but regularly dance in ritual. While no single member of the family has memories of or any experience in sub-Saharan Africa, they all take part in acts of remembrance by using and cultivating the specialized knowledge transmitted to them from their elders, most of whom are now deceased.

* * *

As I was quickly integrated into the household's routines, I felt a remarkable sense of belonging that went far beyond that accorded a guest, even considering the renowned hospitality of which Tunisians are rightfully proud. I seemed to fill a role in the household that was uncontrived, even preexisting. Although the nature of interpersonal relationships ultimately dictated the extent of my presence at Dār Bārnū, the very possibility itself, I learned, was conditioned by the household's historical role of taking in the displaced, helping the needy, and cultivating ritual musicianship. No visitors to the house would bat an eyelash at a stranger who could pass for Algerian (according to local consensus, as the combination of my light skin and dark hair and eyes is prevalent in Algeria, owing to a long history of intermarriage with the French), spoke decent but by no means perfect Tunisian Arabic (adding fodder to the Algerian descent theory), and was learning the *sṭambēlī* repertoire from Bābā Majīd and accompanying him and his troupe to ceremonies. Before long, I found that Bābā had assigned me a new name (Neji), children and teenagers started referring to me as uncle (*ʿām*, a term they used for older *sṭambēlī* musicians), and Bābā and Baya started introducing me to others simply as "one of ours" (a phrase that also forestalls further inquiries about the person in question).

After Bābā's insistence that all of my answers were "in the music," and his suggestion that I should therefore embark on the path of apprenticeship, I spent almost every day at Dār Bārnū, accumulating hundreds of hours practicing the *gumbrī* and learning the repertoire of *nūba*s under his tutelage. I accompanied Bābā's troupe to *sṭambēlī* rituals held at private homes, *zāwiya*s, and back home at Dār Bārnū. I was present for many consultations with clients and, just as important, casual discussions about the clients, their afflictions, and their diagnoses. Such everyday discourse in the household was essential to understanding *sṭambēlī* holistically, not just as ritual, but also as a web of events, decisions, and processes that only eventually culminated in ritual. After several months, I also started performing with the *ṣunnāʿ* at rituals held at shrines and at Dār Bārnū, since skills in playing *shqāshiq*, singing, and elusive ritual knowledge had to be developed largely through embodied ritual interaction.

The unspoken and embodied register of my *sṭambēlī* education was perhaps the most important in understanding the subtleties, parameters, and varieties of *sṭambēlī* ritual experience. Since each of the members of the *sṭambēlī* pantheon has its own *nūba*, the more I learned of the musical repertoire, the more I was able to identify the presence (or absence) of particular saints and spirits in rituals that I attended and eventually performed in. Not only did this enable me to learn their particular dance movements, requisite animal sacrifices, and favored incenses and colors, but it also revealed the normative structuring of the ritual through music, the hierarchies within the pantheon, and the interdependence of musicians and spirits. I realized that the spirit world of *sṭambēlī* was, as promised, progressively revealing itself to me, and that, indeed, it was only "in the music" that the members of the *sṭambēlī* spirit pantheon, their rich history of trans-Saharan movements, and their continual relevance in modern Tunisia became manifested publicly.

It was through such an intensive and extensive fieldwork experience within a single household and its *sṭambēlī* troupe that I feel that I was able to gain meaningful access to the *sṭambēlī* ritual experience, an experience that signifies well beyond an individual's trance or ailment, broadening out—in often contested and complex ways—into wider Tunisian historical and sociocultural domains. A focus on specific individuals in a particular household, therefore, does not mean ignoring larger social forces. In fact, these larger forces and dynamics are really only comprehensible in terms of how they are experienced at the local level, with all of their complexities and contradictions intact. This is one of the strengths of the type of research experience that Lila Abu-Lughod calls an "ethnography of the particular" (1991). Such an approach provides a strategy for avoiding overgeneralization and rather emphasizing how a particular group of people understand their world and create meaning in and of it. Given the embodied nature of my ethnographic experience as well as the emotional ties that have been cultivated, for several years now I have not been able to separate clearly my "research activities" from my personal relationships with the members of the household. The result is a deep sense of belonging, one that is fraught with emotional responses when, for instance, I sympathize with the frustration of Belḥassen and other young *sṭambēlī* musicians with their limited social and economic opportunities, share joy at Sayda's engagement and subsequent marriage, share concern over Emna's affliction and future, and mourn the passing of Bābā Majīd.

Such a sense of belonging, however, comes with certain obligations and scholarly limitations. No longer was I aloof from the household's more problematic interactions or antagonistic relationships with others. These others include certain other troupes, clients, or healers, as well as Tunisians with disparaging attitudes about *sṭambēlī*.[24] It also means that my understanding of *sṭambēlī* is largely shaped by my experience inside the Dār Bārnū household. While the *sṭambēlī* that exists today in Tunis is largely a product of the Dār Bārnū tradition—the leaders of most other troupes were Bābā's apprentices and members of the household at one time or another—I do not wish to give the impression of *sṭambēlī* as a monolithic institution whose meanings are uniform across its membership. Although there is a great deal of overlap in performance practice, there are also salient differences among troupes in spirit pantheon membership, the relative importance of certain saints and spirits, and other interpretations and meanings from other perspectives to which I had less direct access. Similarly, I also try not to give an impression of Tunisian society as unified and undifferentiated in its views of *sṭambēlī*. I am helped in this endeavor by the fact that years before I encountered and researched *sṭambēlī*, I had spent considerable time living in Tunis and had cultivated enduring relationships with many Tunisians of varying backgrounds, whose personal and professional perspectives provided a useful backdrop against which to situate the experiences and attitudes of *sṭambēlī* practitioners vis-à-vis wider Tunisian society.

Ethnographic reporting on ritual knowledge carries with it a weight of responsibility that is only compounded by the politics of representing minorities in autocratic states. Decisions I have made regarding inclusion of statements and observations err on the side of caution, resulting, to the very best of my knowledge, only in the occasional exclusion of some voices. It is nevertheless imperative to emphasize from the outset that responsibility for statements in this book—including those attributed to others—is mine alone.

CHAPTER TWO

Displacement and Emplacement

THE TRANS-SAHARAN SLAVE TRADE AND THE EMERGENCE OF *SṬAMBĒLĪ*

Unlike the African diaspora in the Americas, the descendants of slaves and other sub-Saharans in Tunisia have not produced a group of outspoken scholars, novelists, and other public figures who have written "Africa" back into national cultural and historical narratives. As Edward A. Alpers (2000) has shown in the context of the Indian Ocean, other African diasporas, particularly those within the Islamic world, do not necessarily map cleanly or usefully onto intellectual paradigms resulting from the experience of slaves and their descendants in the Americas, where racism, the place of blacks in society, and the debates over those subjects took on particular forms. In the context of Husaynid Tunisia, the institution of slavery was shaped largely by the dynamics of Islamic culture and jurisprudence, as well as an Ottoman system of governance that relied heavily on populating many of its most influential positions with slaves. Husaynid palaces were full of non-Muslim European slaves called mamluks, who were provided with the most prestigious education, religious training culminating in conversion to Islam, and practical preparation for important administrative roles in the highest echelons of the government (Perkins 1986: 63; Valensi 1967). Black slaves in Tunisia participated in a wider array of social contexts, from the palaces and offices of the Ottoman rulers and the homes of wealthy elites to the difficult and dangerous mass labor of construction projects in the city and agricultural and irrigation work in rural areas and the southern oases.

Just as important as their interaction with numerous spheres of Tunisian society was the common membership of slaves and owners in the Islamic community of believers. While a slave's formal, if initially superficial, conversion to Islam typically took place on the slave caravan or soon upon arrival (Hunwick 2004), subsequent generations of offspring would grow up knowing only Islamic society. Trance ceremonies held by slaves at the shrines of Muslim saints, sacred and public spaces visited by Arab and black Tunisians alike, coincided with the first reports of their rituals at communal houses in the early 1700s. While *sṭambēlī*—like other Tunisian practices that invoke the spirit world or involve the veneration of saints—has been condemned by Islamist and secularist critics alike, within the *sṭambēlī* network there is no discourse of opposition between "Islamic" and "animist" belief systems such as Adeline Masquelier (2001) has reported among *bori* practitioners in Niger. *Sṭambēlī* practitioners and clients are Muslim (and in some cases, Jewish, though the number has decreased significantly since the mid-twentieth century), and many *sṭambēlī* elders pray often and visit the mosque weekly. In fact, to speak of *sṭambēlī* in terms of religion (*dīn*) would not only be inaccurate, but would also be considered offensive to participants, for whom *dīn* unequivocally denotes Islam. These factors, along with the common perception among Arab Tunisians that Africans have special powers to communicate with the spirit world, have all facilitated the integration of *sṭambēlī* into the fabric of Tunisian society.

Nevertheless, there has been little room for black Africans in dominant Tunisian historical narratives. In Tunisian society, as in the Arab world more generally, collective identities and social histories begin with the arrival of Islam and are situated within, and legitimated by, genealogical lineages that connect to important Islamic personages, even if they involve collective "lapses of memory" that erase autochthonous Berber and pre-Islamic heritages (Dakhlia 1993). As Jocelyn Dakhlia has shown in southern Tunisia, these identities are often defined in terms of what they are not: Islamic versus pagan, civilized versus barbarian, Arab versus non-Arab. While these dichotomies also represented the distinction between slaveholder and slave, in fact the majority of slaves were converted to Islam—however nominally—since potential buyers would have "grave reservations" about integrating a so-called pagan, by definition "unclean," into their households (Hunwick 2004: 149–150). Lack of conversion would have also prevented slaves from carrying out many of the duties expected of them, such as preparing meals, slaughtering animals, having sexual relations with their masters, or fighting in the army (Makris 1996: 162). Yet conversion to Islam, proficiency in Arabic, adherence to Arab customs—all of which became the norm for generations of children born of slaves in Tunisia—did not eradicate prejudice or pave the way for upward social mobility. In fact, conversion to Islam may have facilitated slaves' acceptance, in religious terms, of their subordinate status (Makris 1996: 162). Thus, even urban, Muslim, and Arabic-speaking descendants of Africans in the Arab world remained racially marked signifiers of sub-Saharan Africa, the dominant stereotype for the non-Islamic, noncivilized, and non-Arab, and by default excluded from "respectable" genealogies in Tunisian society. (Meillassoux 1991; Makris 1996; Dakhlia 1993).

With their own familial and community bonds destroyed by the experience of being uprooted and dispersed, however, displaced sub-Saharans in

Tunis addressed this geocultural distancing and "denial of coevalness" (Fabian 1983) by creating, developing, and ritually concretizing specific genealogies of belonging that not only provided them with new identities salient to their host environment, but also simultaneously connected them to their homelands in sub-Saharan Africa *and* to the very heart of Islam in Arabia. They accomplished this in part by creating a self-support network of communal houses, each associated with a specific geocultural site in sub-Saharan Africa and affiliated with patron spirits brought with them from their homelands, and simultaneously adopting Tunisian and other Muslim saints into their ritual pantheons. In later chapters I will show how, by appearing together within the same ritual space and responding to the same distinctive aesthetics of *sṭambēlī*, sub-Saharan spirits and Muslim saints performatively display the compatibility of these genealogies and suggest a common ground between sub-Saharan-ness and dominant Arab-Islamic notions of history and identity. In what follows here, I describe the historical conditions for *sṭambēlī*'s emergence in Tunis, highlighting the performance contexts such as the community's communal houses, saints' shrines, and the palace of Husaynid rulers. By bringing *sṭambēlī* into contact with different spheres of Tunisian society, each of these contexts became a site of social encounter characterized by the potential for both accommodation and resistance.

Bū Saʿdiyya: Guide and First Musician

Shaped by the experience of displacement, senses of history in *sṭambēlī* are inseparable from senses of place. The legendary figure of Bū Saʿdiyya—simultaneously the mythic first musician of *sṭambēlī* and the historical figure responsible for guiding displaced sub-Saharans to the appropriate communal house in Tunis—demonstrates this inseparability in profound ways. As it transitions from displacement to placelessness to emplacement, his is the most explicit narrative of the mythographies of movement cultivated by *sṭambēlī* at Dār Bārnū.

The legend of Bū Saʿdiyya is verbalized in a very brief fashion, one in which the details of the narrative are less important than its themes of displacement and alterity and its geocultural trajectory from sub-Saharan Africa to North Africa. Bū Saʿdiyya, according to legend, lived in sub-Saharan Africa and hunted to support his family. One day he returned home from hunting to find his only daughter, Saʿdiyya (Bū Saʿdiyya literally means "father of Saʿdiyya"), missing. During his search for her, he discovered that she had been captured by slave raiders from a Tunis-bound caravan. Desperate to find his daughter, Bū Saʿdiyya left his home to follow the same trans-Saharan caravan routes to Tunis. Upon his arrival, his clothing tattered and torn from his weeks crossing the desert, he would wander the streets, playing the *shqāshiq* and singing of his pain and sorrow, begging onlookers to help him find his daughter.

Bū Saʿdiyya never did find his daughter. But his persona did continue to play an important role in the *sṭambēlī* network of Tunis, where individuals would dress up in the mask and costume of Bū Saʿdiyya and wander the streets singing, dancing, and playing the *shqāshiq*, *ṭabla* (double-headed barrel drum), or *gūgāy* (one- or two-stringed fiddle). The costume is a dramatic sight (fig. 3). The mask, which covers the entire face and drapes over the shoulders, has cutouts for the eyes and mouth that are lined with cowry shells, whose bright whiteness contrasts starkly with the dark leather of the mask. Atop the mask is a conical headdress topped by a tuft of feathers and the head of a bird with a long beak. The headdress is elaborately and densely decorated with cowry shells, beads of many colors, small mirrors, and pendants. Over the body is draped a long, bright red vest decorated with cowries and dangling amulets. Across the waist is tied a kind of skirt fashioned from of dozens of animal tails and long strips of colorful cloth tied to a rope belt. Wandering through the streets, or performing at feasts or festivals, this "eccentric itinerant dancer," dressed like a "fetishist magician," according to A. J. N. Tremearne's 1914 observations, was the only Hausa contribution to festivals put on by Arab Tunisians, performing for the donations of spectators (Tremearne 1914: 241). He continues to entertain and frighten onlookers, especially children, who are fascinated by "the phantasmagorical character of this bizarre being, which they could not compare to any known creature" (Ben Abdallah 1988: 179–180).[1]

While good Bū Saʿdiyyas played up these expectations of the fearsomely exotic in their performances, they also masked a more serious social responsibility that is emphasized in the oral history at Dār Bārnū. From within the exiled sub-Saharan community, Bū Saʿdiyya was not exotic or frightening. In fact, it was precisely the otherness of his appearance and music making that attracted the attention of freed slaves and newly arrived sub-Saharan migrants, whom he would then lead to the communal houses associated with their places of origin. Bābā Majīd explained: "Who was it that would show [the Africans] the world here [in Tunis]? It was Bū Saʿdiyya. [When they arrived] he would tell them, 'You have people from your country over there [in that communal house], and you have yours over here [in this communal house]'" (personal communication, 2001).

According to Bābā Majīd, if language was a barrier, Bū Saʿdiyya could still identify the origins of newcomers, because geography was inscribed on their bodies through scarification, painted markings, and clothing: "[The Africans] were tattooed and painted in order to tell where they were from, and Bū Saʿdiyya knew all of their markings . . . he knew them all. Their tattoos were their ID cards" (personal communication, 2001).

FIGURE 3. Bū Saʿdiyya, accompanied by *ṭabla* and *shqāshiq*, 2009. (Photograph by Soumaya Hagene.)

Later, Bābā Majīd picked up his *gambara* to play the *nūba* of Bū Saʿdiyya (CD track 1). The rectangular-bodied, three-stringed *gambara* is the softer-sounding, smaller "sister" of the *gumbrī*; indeed, its name is the feminine form of *gumbrī*. At Dār Bārnū, it would be played for entertainment at evening gatherings. It is described as "comforting" (*ḥanīna*) as it "pulls in" (*yijbid*) the listener. The *nūba* of Bū Saʿdiyya evokes the legend through short vocal phrases sung in a nonprescribed order and often repeated in fragments. The use of the first person in the lyrics blurs the boundary between subject and object; the shifts from Bū Saʿdiyya's narrative to that of the *sṭambēlī* musicians are at times ambiguous and suggestive of their common experiences of displacement and alterity:

W-Allah wild ifrīgiya	O God, a son of Africa
Rānī māshī rawwaḥ	I would return home
Bi-lā sākan	[But I am] without a home
Yā ḥanāna	O Mother
Rānī wild ifrīgiya w-Allah berik	I am a son of Africa, thank God
W-Allah yarḥam jddāy	God bless my ancestors
W-Allah fī mā khallālī	For what they have left me

The song's narrative describes Bū Saʿdiyya's appearance and his welcome presence (that is, for the *sṭambēlī* community) on the streets of Tunis, including the city's slave market (*sūq il-berka*):

W-jlūd dhiyūba	And jackal hides
W-jlūd nmūra	And leopard skins
Fī kūl ith-thniya	On every street
W-Allah salēm ʿalaykum	Greetings [lit. "peace be upon you"]
Jamāʿt il-berka	[To the] slaves [lit. "slave market group"]
Huwwa Bū Saʿdiyya	He is Bū Saʿdiyya

The following two lines, typically grouped together, also blur the line between the legend and the predicament of members of the black community in Tunis, as they may describe Bū Saʿdiyya's daughter as well as the female sub-Saharans in Tunis:

Bint n-nwājaḥ	Favored daughter
W-Allah bint ifrīga	O God, daughter of Africa

Some of the lyrics evoke the close relationship between the black community and the Husaynid regime while also acknowledging awareness of, and connection to, the Moroccan *gnāwa*:

W-Allah wild il-bayya	O God, son of the beys
W-Allah wild il-gnāwa	O God, son of the Gnawa

Bū Saʿdiyya keeps alive the history of trans-Saharan movements of displaced sub-Saharans, not only through the *gambara*-based narratives of Bābā Majīd, but also in possession rituals. The vestments of Bū Saʿdiyya adorn the wall of the performance space at every year's pilgrimage to the shrine of Sīdī Frej. His legend and history are evoked every time *sṭambēlī* musicians perform his *nūba*, and when these vestments are used to adorn a dancer, Bū Saʿdiyya comes back to life, dancing to his eponymous 6/8 rhythm (see chap. 5).

Bū Saʿdiyya is unique in that he is the only member of the *sṭambēlī* pantheon who does not belong to any of the families of spirits or categories of saints. He does not afflict humans or heal them; he does not possess dancers or engender trance. However, his continual presence serves as a regular reminder of the movements of sub-Saharans across the Sahara Desert. While he performs the experience of migration, his legend emphasizes not origins and points of arrival, but the experience of displacement, with its sentiments of loss and suffering as well as its attendant practicalities of healing and transition. Bū Saʿdiyya is an interstitial figure, straddling the line between myth and history, North and sub-Saharan Africas, the longing for a homeland and the immediacy of helping others who are similarly displaced. The narratives of Bū Saʿdiyya evoke several important facets of the history of *sṭambēlī*, including the social organization of the sub-Saharan community, its relationship to the Husaynid ruling regime, and the trans-Saharan slave trade, to which I now turn.

Tunisia and the Trans-Saharan Slave Trade

Although the vast, mostly barren, and virtually waterless Sahara presented a formidable barrier between North Africa and sub-Saharan Africa, it was never an absolute one. Archeological evidence attests to trans-Saharan trade in the late Neolithic period, and it is likely that slaves were part of this commerce as early as 1000 BCE (Boahen 1962: 349). Very little is known about this trade, however, before the spread of Islam to North Africa beginning in the eighth century CE. By this time, several caravan routes provided selective access to destinations on both sides of the Sahara. This difficult and dangerous long-distance commerce mainly concerned traders transporting valuable commodities such as gold, ivory, ostrich feathers, and, above all, slaves. By the tenth century, slave trade by Muslim merchants was regular and relatively organized (Meillassoux 1991: 44–45). The development of these trade routes, fueled in part by a succession of African states boasting a surplus of gold and slaves for export, put sub-Saharan and North Africa into permanent contact with each other.

Due to the relative lack of documentation and the centuries-long time span of the slave trade, estimates of the number of slaves transported across the Sahara remain highly speculative. Unlike the trans-Atlantic slave ship, which was a regulated unit of transport owned by merchant firms with detailed accounting systems, the trans-Saharan caravans were more ephemeral, with varying cargo that could be divided, sold, augmented, or replaced at any of the multiple stops along numerous interconnected routes. The most reliable estimates suggest that from 650 to 1900 CE nearly 9.4 million slaves were forced to cross the Sahara, of which an estimated 7.8 million survived the journey (Austen 1979: 66). This trade intensified over the seventeenth and eighteenth centuries, reaching a peak of 1.2 million slaves making the northward crossing during the nineteenth century (Segal 2001: 56). The sum total of these estimates suggests that the number of slaves transported across the Sahara was nearly equal to that of the shorter and more intensive trans-Atlantic slave trade.

Some of the earliest documented purchases of sub-Saharan slaves in North Africa took place in medieval Tunisia. In about 800 CE, Tunisian ruler Ibrahim I purchased 5,000 military slaves from sub-Saharan Africa, and, in 1016, a subsequent Tunisian regime imported 30,000 (Austen 1979: 31). Indeed, the exploitation of trans-Saharan trade factored in as early as the seventh-century Arab conquest of Tunisia, whose victorious leader, ʿUqba bin Nafiʿ, initially came to the region to develop trade along the trade route leading to Lake Chad (Abun-Nasr 1987: 29). The Tunisian slave trade was most active during the reign of the Husaynid Dynasty (1705–1881), during which far more than 100,000 slaves entered Tunisia. Among its neighbors, only Algeria had fewer during that same period (70,000), compared to much higher numbers in Morocco (520,000), Libya (430,000), and Egypt (800,000) (Austen 1979). A 1789 account written by the British consul to Tunis describes the annual trade in Tunis as consisting of five to six slave caravans, each with up to two hundred slaves. He describes the slave caravan as consisting mainly of female slaves, with far fewer men and boys, and "four or five castrated black Boys, whom [the traders] dispose of, among the principal people here, at a very exorbitant rate" (Limam 1981: 356–357). These eunuchs were mostly destined for the Husaynid palaces, where they would be trained to oversee the harem and prepared for important administrative positions.

Most slaves destined for the markets of Tunis hailed from the Kanem-Bornu region near Lake Chad and the Hausa towns of the Niger River Valley

(Valensi 1967; Takaki 1997). Hausa and Kanuri, the main tongues of the central African source of North African slaves, were thus the two principal languages spoken among slaves in Tunisia (Lovejoy 2004: 2). The interconnected network of caravan routes also brought slaves from many other regions of Sahelian, West, and central Africa to Tunis, either directly or laterally via its North African neighbors (see fig. 4). The often deadly results of these treacherous crossings were captured vividly by German explorer Gerhard Rohlfs's description of the landscape surrounding the route from Bornu: "On both sides of the road . . . we see the blanched bones of the victimised slaves—skeletons still covered by the katoun, the clothing of the blacks. The traveler who knows nothing of the road to Bournou, has only to follow these scattered remains and he will not be misguided" (quoted in Berlioux 1872: 7).

Accounts of spirit possession taking place on trans-Saharan caravans suggest that North Africans not only knew about sub-Saharan spirit possession traditions such as the Hausa *bori*, but also that they valued them highly. In 1906, Swiss explorer Hanns Vischer described the possession of a Baghirmi woman who spoke prophecies that the Arabs and slaves "believed to be a manifestation from the other world" (Vischer 1910: 54). James Richardson's vivid 1853 account of a woman's possession during his crossing of the Sahara, evoking the northward movement of *bori* and the shared beliefs of Arabs and slaves, is worth quoting at length. One of the servants' wives

> was performing *Boree*, the "Devil," and working herself up into the belief that his Satanic majesty had possession of her. She threw herself upon the ground in all directions, and imitated the cries of various animals. Her actions were, however, somewhat regulated by a man tapping upon a kettle with a piece of wood, beating time to her wild maneuvers. After some delay, believing herself now possessed, and capable of performing her work, she went forward to half-a-dozen of our servants . . . and made over them, with her whole body, certain inelegant motions, not to be mentioned . . . and having for a moment thrown herself flat upon the ground, she declared to each and all *their future*—their fortune, good or bad. I did not stop to see the result of the ceremony. The slaves carry these mysteries with them in their servitude, and the practice of such indecent and profane things are tolerated by the Muslims of the coast. The Moors and Arabs, indeed, have great faith in these mysteries, and resort to them to know *their future*. (Richardson 1853: 287; emphases in original)

Although the organized slave trade brought innumerable sub-Saharans to North Africa, there existed alongside it a continuous and "much more casual introduction" of sub-Saharans into Tunisia (Brett 1969: 356). Economic

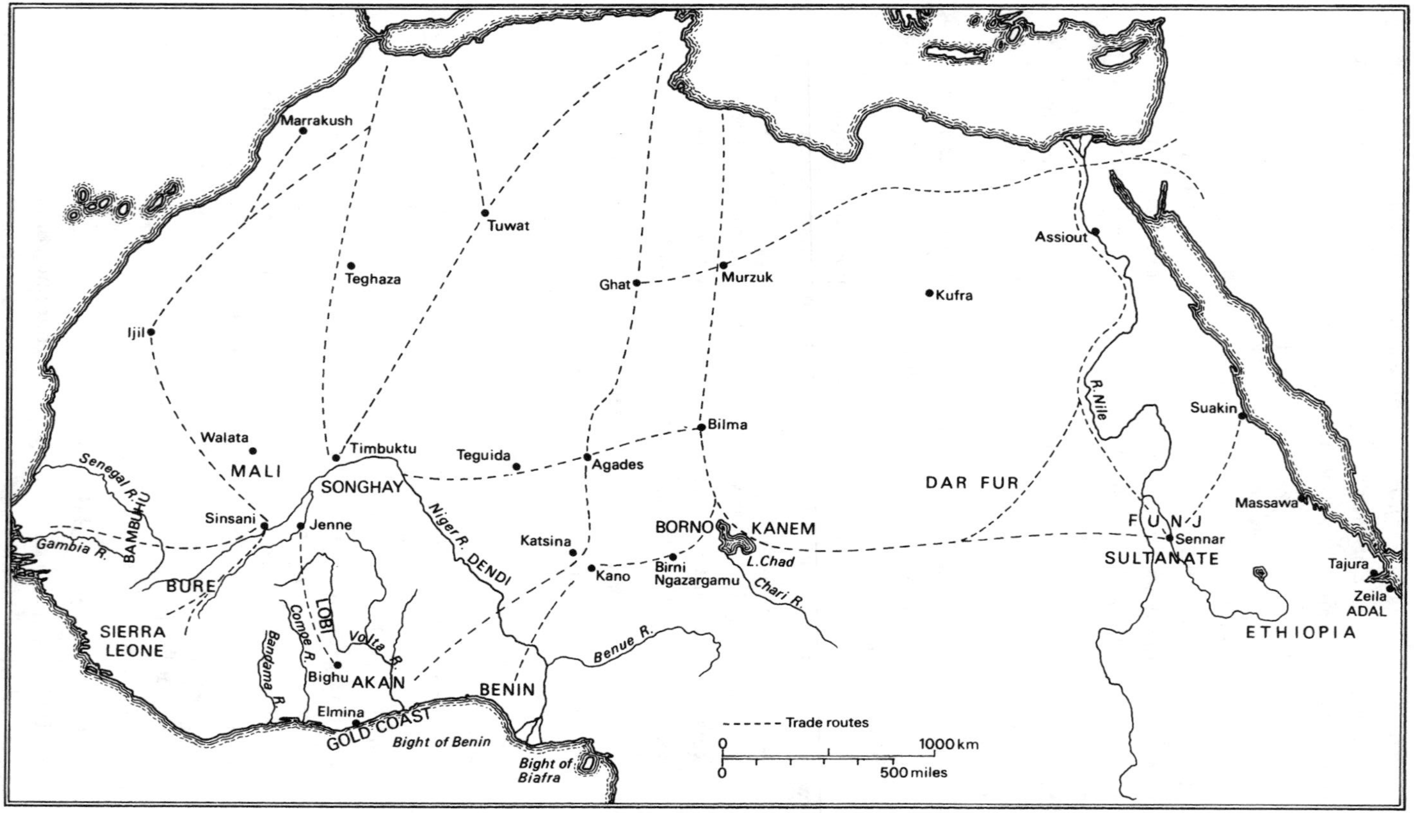

FIGURE 4. The major routes of the trans-Saharan slave trade. From Lovejoy (2000: 27).

migrants, religious pilgrims, and traders would also make the trans-Saharan journey to Tunisia. According to Bābā Majīd, traders would bring ostrich feathers and hides, gems, seashells, and sub-Saharan medicines to sell or trade to blacks in Tunisia, where they would then buy leather shoes, *safsārīs* (traditional women's dress), and red fezzes to sell back in sub-Saharan Africa. Such activities, however, were not without their risks. Intentionally joining caravans, whether for trade or in hopes of escaping colonization or persecution in their home countries, was a dangerous undertaking. Even if the travelers were fortunate enough to survive the crossing, they could still end up sold into slavery. Bābā Majīd describes just such a scenario:

> At the time of their colonization [in sub-Saharan Africa], [the colonizers] would be looking for [escaping sub-Saharans]. But they would not stay put there. They would escape . . . by night. And how, by night? There would be a caravan preparing to go, and one would say, "I'm fleeing" [*rānī ānā nharib*], and the other [in the caravan] would say, "Okay." They would go at night, because they would travel by their own eyes. "At such-and-such a time [*waqt l-fulānī*] you will find me at such-and-such a place [*blāṣa fulāniyya*]." A caravan of camels—there would be one or two following each other, one behind the other. . . . They would travel by the stars. . . . And why would they travel at night? First, for the stars. But second, if they are searching for them, it is harder to see them. . . . There weren't airplanes; there wasn't radar [laughs]. . . . At night, they would follow the route. "Take the path from here, go, be careful, but you will find Gabès, Sfax [Tunisian cities]." But then the Arabs would take them. How? They would buy them. The blacks [*il-akḥal zinjī*] would enter [Tunisia], and [the others] were all white. And they [the whites] would buy what [the traders] had. (Personal communication, 2002)

Some of Tunisia's slaves were destined for agricultural labor in the southern oases. Those who remained on the northward caravan would be put on display at *sūq il-berka*, the slave market established by Yusuf Dey (r. 1610–1637) near the central mosque of Tunis, a centrality that speaks to the importance of slave ownership in the city. There they would be inspected by potential buyers for health, age, and beauty. Some might be sold to slave traders planning to export them to Europe, the Middle East, or the Americas. The majority, however, would be sold to members of the urban elite classes or to the Husaynid court. There, women could expect to enter into concubinage or domestic service as maids, cooks, and servers. Some men would also be put into domestic service, while others served as guards, attendants, and artisans who would make attire such as shoes and red fezzes (*shuwāshī*; sing. *sheshīya*), the most immediately recognizable symbol of Ottoman nobility. Still others were destined for a variety of positions ranging from menial laborer, servant, or foreman to soldier, commander, or government administrator.

The occasional freeing of individual slaves was common in Tunisia, as the tenets of Islam considered freeing a slave—as a reward or after seven years' of servitude—a noble and generous act. Practically speaking, however, while the promise of manumission for good behavior gave slaves hope, it also benefited slaveholders by ensuring a greater degree of obedience. It also enabled the masters to let go of unproductive slaves and force older slaves to look after themselves in their elder years (Meillassoux 1991: 245). Wider-scale manumission also took place before abolition in Tunisia. Upon the death of a member of the Ottoman nobility, it was customary for that person's slaves to be freed collectively. One hundred seventy-seven slaves were freed after the death of a princess in 1823, and six hundred slaves held their freedom papers high as they took part in the funeral procession of the ruling bey upon his death in 1835 (Larguèche 1995).

Aḥmad Bey took the first steps toward the abolition of slavery in 1841 by ending Tunisia's participation in the slave trade, closing down the slave market in Tunis, and eliminating the position of *qaʿīd il-berka*, the official in charge of the market (Brown 1974: 322). The latter measure, however, also meant that slaves who were mistreated by their owners no longer had recourse to the *qaʿīd*, whose responsibilities included mediating such situations, which could result in his demanding that the slave be sold to another master (Brown 1974: 323). After an entire slave family sought refuge in the St. Louis Chapel in Carthage to avoid being sold separately, the bey summoned the family to his court and spoke to each member of the family individually. When faced with the six-year-old boy, the bey told him that he would not allow him to become a slave. This incident, which proved potentially embarrassing for the bey and the French, instigated his 1842 declaration that all children born of slaves were to be free. The bey received accolades for officially abolishing slavery in 1846, two years before the French did the same in colonial Algeria and one year before the Ottoman Empire (Brown 1974: 321). A similar decree followed about a decade later in Libya, but slavery remained in practice, in all three interconnected regions, somewhat more covertly, until the mid-1890s (Anderson 1986: 105), when the prohibition of slaveholding and slave trading became enforced with fixed penalties.[2] Indeed, well after the 1846 abolition, German explorer Gustav Nachtigal reported that as he was leaving Tunis en route to Tripoli, the bey (Muḥammad eṣ-Ṣādiq, r. 1859–1882) "asked me to bring along with me as many little *usfan* (plural of *usif*, Negro) as I could. When the great men of Tunis wish to expand their households by the addition of black servants, eunuchs or domestic slave-girls, they sent to Tripoli and have them purchased there at high prices" (Nachtigal 1971 [1879]: 16).

While abolition provided slaves with the legal status of freedom, socially and economically they continued to suffer from prejudice limiting their opportunities. If it closed the door on the ownership of humans by other humans, abolition also, in the words of Tunisian historian Abdelhamid Larguèche, provided an "open door to social marginalization" (Larguèche 1999: 402). While some slaves returned to their sub-Saharan homes, the vast majority remained in Tunis, continuing to serve as domestic servants for their former masters while others worked as wandering vendors, public bath attendants, mendicants, or prostitutes. Indeed, one of the city's dead-end alleys reserved for houses of prostitution was even named after Bū Saʿdiyya (Larguèche 2003: 337).

The history of the trans-Saharan slave trade reveals the enduring tension between the Sahara Desert as a bridge connecting two worlds and as a barrier separating them. For members of the emergent *sṭambēlī* community of slaves, ex-slaves, other displaced sub-Saharans, and their descendants, these crossings produced enormous loss and suffering. They also, however, necessitated modes for redressing loss, treating suffering, and creating a new space for themselves in Tunisian society. They developed a self-support network of households where they kept alive their sub-Saharan rituals, rituals that also extended into the domain of popular Islamic practices and put Arab and Jewish Tunisians, and the Husaynids into extended contact with Tunis's black population.

Reconstructing Sub-Saharan Identities in Tunis

THE SYSTEM OF COMMUNAL HOUSES

Uprooted, displaced, and dispersed across North Africa, sub-Saharan slaves had their familial, community, and ethnolinguistic bonds destroyed. In urban Tunisia, as well as in many other North African regions, they rebuilt their communities and forged new senses of belonging by creating new modes of social organization that synthesized geocultural and ritual affiliations of sub-Saharan Africa with elements of the religious organization and lineage systems central to identity formation in their host society.

The continual importation of slaves, the various methods of manumission, and the cycle of regeneration through procreation led to an increasingly large and differentiated population of bonded and free blacks in Tunis that included slaves (*ʿabīd*; sing. *ʿabd*), freed slaves (*ʿatīg*; sing. *ʿatg*), children of slaves (*shwāshin*; sing. *shushān*), and servants (*khuddām*; m. sing. *khādim*,

f. sing. *khādima*). The variety of homelands further differentiated the population ethnically and linguistically. In Tunis, this heterogeneous black community established a solidarity that transcended these differences while also maintaining the distinctive geocultural identities slaves brought with them from their different homelands. They organized themselves into a network of "communal houses" (*diyār jamāʿa*), most of which corresponded to, and were named after, ethnolinguistic groups or geographic sites in sub-Saharan Africa. Inside these houses displaced sub-Saharans could find others who spoke their languages, shared their customs and beliefs, and could help them adjust to life in their new setting. To freed slaves, descendants of slaves, and migrants, the houses offered immediate social services such as food, lodging, and help finding work. The houses probably touched the lives of virtually all displaced sub-Saharans. It is "certain," according to French anthropologist Viviana Pâques, "that all the black slaves arriving in a city, be they still enslaved, freed, or escaped, entered one of [these] houses" (1964: 634).

There is a dearth of historical information on the communal houses in Tunis. While "African rituals" held by slaves were reported in the seventeenth century (Takaki 1997), the earliest evidence of the formalizing of communal organization comes from the reign of the bey ʿAlī Bāsha I (r. 1740–1756). He imported thousands of slaves during his reign to serve as soldiers in the military and guards at his palace.[3] He allowed slaves to form ritual associations they called *kūfa*, which were relatively organized religious houses with their own traditions and tribunals (al-Imām 1980: 241–242). The few details we have on the houses in the nineteenth-century come mainly from sporadic and highly polemical accounts decrying the corrupting influence of black "pagan" practices on Arab Tunisian society. Al-Timbuktāwī's diatribe (discussed below), for example, informs us that in 1808 there were at least nine active communal houses, including Dār Bambara, Dār Sīrī, Dār Gwārī, Dār Songhay, Dār Kūfa, Dār Kano, Dār Nūfe (i.e., Barnūfī), Dār Janfara (i.e., Zamfara), and Dār Zakzak (i.e., Ziriyya) (Montana 2004a: 179). British ethnographer and Hausa specialist A. J. N. Tremearne (1914), using the Hausa term *gidan* (lit. "house," but he translates it as "temple") rather than the Arabic *dār*,[4] notes that there were seven main communal houses in Tunis in 1913, providing a partial listing that included Gidan Kūrī (i.e., Dār Bārnū), Gidan Belik, Gidan Aska, Gidan Ziria, and Gidan Yara. Pâques (1964: 625) noted the presence of fourteen (but lists fifteen) houses at the time of independence: Dār Bārnū, Dār Baghirmi, Dār Askar, Dār Waday, Dār Ghademsi, Dār Baday, Dār Debarīn, Dār Tobarga, Dār Songhay, Dār Mel el-Qadīm, Dār Darfur, Dār Makakam, Dār Nefis, Dār Gombra, and Dār Ziriyya. Several subsequent writers, citing Pâques, have also asserted the existence of fourteen houses. Bābā Majīd, however, remembers twenty-one that were active in his lifetime, listing off in almost a single breath a comprehensive list that included Dār Askar, Dār Baday, Dār Baghirmi, Dār Bakaba, Dār Bambara, Dār Bārnū, Dār Bārnūfī, Dār Darfur, Dār Dabarīn, Dār Ghadamsiyya, Dār Guway, Dār Kano, Dār May Takīm, Dār Nafis, Dār Shwāshnā, Dār Songhay, Dār Tubū, Dār Turbēga, Dār Waday, Dār Zgayyat, and Dār Ziriyya.[5]

While the Arabic *dār* translates into the English "house," it is also used to indicate "family," which in the Maghrib is understood to mean a larger patronymic affiliation in which kinship is a relatively flexible and multifaceted association. The house is an objectification of relations of descent, alliance, and patronage with some sense of generational continuity. In addition to patrilineal relations through birth and marriage, it also encompasses a variety of matrilineal relations in addition to numerous "fictive" kinship relations based on patronage, residential proximity, visitation patterns, and other nonbiogenetic alliances (Geertz 1979). The sense of belonging to a *dār* is based on *qaraba* (lit. "closeness"), or "compelling ties of obligations," that are often "expressed as a 'blood' tie, even when no demonstrable lineal ties exist" (Eickelman 1998: 153). Like the traditional Maghribi *dār*, the *sṭambēlī dār* is a material dwelling that represents an identifiable social unit bound together by descent, individual ties, and common interests and obligations. Relations among members are presented in kinship terms so that all members share a familial identity. The association of genealogical belonging is a central factor in determining social identity in Tunisia. Bābā Majīd emphasized the surrogate genealogical function of the houses, telling me that, in response to the question "Who is your family?" (*wulad shkūn?* lit. "Who were you born to?"), a member of Dār Waday would simply reply, "I am from Dār Waday." These houses, then, provided slaves and other migrants not only with a family-like support structure, but also with a new genealogy of belonging, sometimes with new surnames such as Barnāwī or Baghirmī.[6]

Since blacks were prohibited from owning homes in Tunis, the communal houses they inhabited were rented from Arab Tunisians (Bābā Majīd, personal communication; Tremearne 1914: 70). This arrangement meant that from time to time communal houses would need to be moved, whether through eviction or the volition of the house's members. This potential mobility meant that the identity of a communal house was not necessarily tethered to specific buildings, but rather defined by its inhabitants, their activities, the shrines they built, and the ritual paraphernalia those shrines housed. In some situations, such as irreconcilable internal disagreements, a single house could create offshoots, resulting in, for example, "Little" Dār Bārnū and "Big" Dār Bārnū. Furthermore, a single building could host several communal "houses." At various times, Dār Bārnū also housed Dār Debarīn, Dār Waday, Dār Baghirmī, Dār Shwāshnā, and Dār Askar. These latter two houses referred not to ethnolinguistic or geocultural identities, but rather to the role of certain blacks in Tunisian society. Dār Askar (*askar* is Arabic for "soldiers") congregated slaves who had served in the military, while Dār Shwāshnā (*shwāshnā* is Arabic for "our children of slaves") served the offspring of slaves.[7]

The importation of Hausa *bori* practices and beliefs not only provided a more or less shared ritual tradition that provided a sense of historical continuity for displaced sub-Saharans, it also provided an additional structural force in the organization of the community itself. Just as the houses were differentiated according to the regional origins of its slaves, they were also associated with particular spirits, honored in each house by small shrines. As noted earlier, this feature of the houses was so important that Tremearne did not call them houses but rather temples. Dār Bārnū accords primacy of place to the spirit Kūrī, who is understood as originating in Bornu. Indeed, Tremearne referred to Dār Bārnū as Gidan Kūrī. The Water spirits (Baḥriyya) were most important to Dār Gwārī and Dār Bambara, which had shrines to Sārkin Gwārī and Sārkin Gīda, respectively. Many of the communal houses cultivated distinctive musico-ritual practices originating in their specific regions of origin in sub-Saharan Africa. According to Bābā Majīd, some houses, such as Dār Bambara, played a small *gambara*, while others, such as Dār Songhay, used a large *gambara*. The *gūgāy* was the instrument of choice for many houses.

At the same time, the houses routinely engaged in community-wide ceremonies, thus creating an environment in which members of any one house encountered the traditions of the other houses, thus contributing to the consolidation of the *sṭambēlī* tradition. The houses came together for annual rituals such as the *difāʿ it il-bilā'*, or "defense against misfortune," which took place at the shrine of Sīdī Ghrīb at Bēb el-Khadra (one of the ancient gates of the medina's perimeter). It reportedly first became a ritual in about 1900 after an ailing *ʿarīfa* at Dār Bārnū dreamed that she would be cured after making a sacrifice there. Her full recovery after house members made the sacrifice so impressed the rest of the community that they made it an annual tradition that included possession dances as well as the *takai* dance (Tremearne 1914: 192).[8] The shrine of Sīdī Ghrīb, according to Bābā Majīd, was a site of visitation especially among migrants and exiles (*ghrīb* literally means "strange" or "foreign"), and the *difāʿ it il-bilā'* was a means of protecting a vulnerable nonnative population from adversity.

The presence of communal houses was not unique to Tunis. They existed in other Tunisian cities such as Sousse, Beja, Bizerte, and Gabès (Bābā Majīd, personal communication). In other areas of the country, the black communities were organized around the shrines of saints: in Sfax, it was organized around Sīdī Manṣūr (Dubouloz-Laffin 1941), and in the southern oasis of Nefta, it was organized around the *zāwiya* housing the tomb of Sīdī Marzūg (Pâques 1964). Outside Tunisia, Tripoli and Algiers both had similar systems of social organization in place (Tremearne 1914; Andrews 1903). J. B. Andrews noted the seven houses associated with the Seven Springs in Algiers: Dār Bambara, Dār Songhay, Dār Tombū, and Dār Gūrma were the houses of the "west," the part of Algiers under French control, while Dār Katchena, Dār Zūzū, and Dār Bārnū were the houses of the "east," under English control (1903: 16–17). In the early 1950s, Dār Baḥrī, Dār Bārnū, and Dār Hausa remained active in Biskra and Constantine, the latter of which also hosted Dār Tumbuktū (Dermenghem 1954). The presence of Dār Bārnū, Dār Hausa, and Dār Bambara was also recorded in the 1960s in the major cities of Algeria and the Fezzan area of Libya (Pâques 1964).

ADMINISTRATION AND RELATIONSHIP TO THE HUSAYNID STATE

The communal house system experienced by Bābā Majīd in the twentieth century involved a hierarchy of titled administrative and ritual positions. Each house was led by a *galadīma kbīr*, who was responsible for making decisions that affected its members, coordinating events, aiding newcomers in finding work, and arbitrating disputes. Under the *galadīma kbīr* was a *galadīma sghīr* (lit. "small chief"), or deputy, who supervised the *serki samari* (attendant and cook), the *muqaddim* (treasurer), and the *ʿarīfa*. The *ʿarīfa* was a position typically held by a woman, although there were (and are) several men who held the role, with no change to the feminine title (see chap. 8). The *ʿarīfa* was responsible for diagnosing new patients, divining which (if any) of the *sṭambēlī* spirits was responsible for the affliction, and determining which medicines and ritual procedures were required to placate the spirits. She was a conduit for the spirits, becoming possessed during rituals. She was also a caretaker for her patients, attending to them before, during, and after their own possessions. *Sṭambēlī* musicians also held titled positions. The *yinna* was the leader of the musicians and by definition played the *gumbrī* and, when necessary, the *ṭabla*. All the other musicians, referred to collectively as the *ṣunnāʿ* (lit. "workers" or "craftsmen"), were responsorial singers who played the *shqāshiq* and various other percussion instruments as needed. With the exception of the *ṣunnāʿ*, these were all official positions, complete with identification cards issued with the permission of the *gaʿīd*, and recognized by local authorities.

The *ga'īd* reported to the Husaynid palace's *bash agha*, a black African slave eunuch responsible for watching over the court's harem and for carrying out important administrative and fiscal duties. He was not only the head of the court's slaves, but also of the black community in general; thus, he was also known as "governor of the black skin (*ḥākim fel-qechra es-sūdā*)" (Zawadowski 1942: 147). According to Bābā Majīd, the *bash agha* "managed the bey's wives; he would accompany them and watch over them. He was distinguished. You would find two or three at the house of the bey. Where was he from? He came from Turkey. You find him in his [Turkish] clothes, with a *sheshiyya*. As for the blacks here, [the bey would] tell him, 'Watch over them.' How would he do that? Through the ga'īd. [The bey would tell the *bash agha*,] 'Go find one in the group who is trustworthy and knows them well. He is the one I want. Recruit him, and bring him back to me'" (personal communication, 2002).

In his *Histoire de Tunis*, Louis Frank describes the role of the *bash agha* and the protection he accorded the slaves: "The agha, the primary eunuch of the bey, is the head or rather the representative and judge born of the Negroes, and this jurisdiction is all the more necessary as many of them know only very imperfectly the language of the country. . . . It is he who has the right to settle disagreements that arise among them and to hear their complaints. If a slave finds the means of taking refuge at his place, the owner can only reclaim his slave with a payment of six piastres to the head eunuch" (cited in Larguèche 1999: 400).

Bābā Majīd told me that the blacks in Tunis referred to the *bash agha* as *el-mḥarrak* (the mover, or the instigator) because he had a great deal of influence with the bey in matters concerning the black community. It was the *bash agha* who was responsible for scheduling the annual pilgrimage to the shrine of Sīdī Sa'd, and for granting permission for other large *sṭambēlī* gatherings. He also made sure that *sṭambēlī* troupes were invited to perform at the bey's palace during holidays. While it was well known that one of the cousins of the bey even had his own *sṭambēlī* "temple" (Tremearne 1914), the bey himself would host *sṭambēlī* performances in his palace during holidays. *Sṭambēlī* musicians from all the houses would gather together to perform for the bey, who would reward them with money, food, and clothing. According to Bābā Majīd, "During holidays—Ramadan—they would go to the bey with a big *gambara*. They would begin to play 'dij-tek, dij-tek' and sing "Allah w-nabīnā, Allah ḥāya" [God and our Prophet, God lives]. They would begin to dance, and play; they would play very well. . . . They would wish the bey a happy holiday—this was before Bourguiba—and he would have food prepared for them. He would give them *'asīda* [a sweet dessert traditionally served on religious holidays], and he would give them money" (personal communication, 2001).

The relationship between the Husaynid regime and the black community in Tunis was complex and not reducible to a simple master-slave dichotomy that overlooked the agency and influence of slaves and their nuanced relationships with slaveholders. Like the slaves of Morocco's preprotectorate Makhzen (Ennaji 1999: 91–93), slaves at the court in Tunis held a wide range of positions, from menial laborers living in squalor to administrative aides to the bey who dwelled in relatively luxurious conditions. After the abolition of slavery, many continued to perform the same duties at the court in exchange for room and board or nominal wages.[9]

The *sṭambēlī dār* system also had much in common with the trade guilds that organized urban professions in precolonial North Africa. The guilds had a hierarchical structure that patterned the division of labor and the status of members; they performed cultural, social, and welfare functions in addition to economic ones; and each guild had its own patron saint (Stambouli and Zghal 1976: 8–9). The main economic activity of the *sṭambēlī* communal houses was the performance of ritual healing. The houses provided—to members and local Tunisians alike—therapeutic services through the performance of possession trance ceremonies. These ceremonies operated on a number of different levels to provide a means by which the community could claim a place for itself in Tunisian society. First, they generated crucial income for the houses. This enabled the houses to attain a certain degree of autonomy and self-dependence. It also ensured the maintenance of the role of professional ritual musician. Second, by performing rituals that were in high demand by Arab Tunisians, sub-Saharans gained a level of social acceptance by filling an important niche in Tunisian society. Third, the ceremonies provided a sense of historical continuity that enabled sub-Saharans to define their encounter with Tunisians on their own terms, without having to succumb to total assimilation. The paradox of this arrangement was that it served to both integrate and further marginalize the black community, as well as further solidify its association with misfortune.

A Problematic Presence

As the Tunisian slave trade reached its peak during the reign of the bey Ḥammūda Pāshā (1782–1814), there was a growing concern that the expanding and increasingly organized black community could pose a threat to state security, and that its ritual activities, which attracted participants from various sectors of Tunisian society, threatened Tunisian morality. Ḥammūda Pāshā took severe measures to prevent a critical mass of blacks from congregating together and condemned their music and trance ceremonies, which were at the heart of what he called "harmful black activities" (*nashāṭāt al-*

sūdān al-musī'at) responsible for corrupting the religious sensibilities of its citizens (al-Imām 1980: 242).

A major catalyst for Ḥammūda Pāshā's denouncement and eventual suppression of these ceremonies was a letter he received from a visiting Muslim cleric from Timbuktu in 1808. The cleric, Aḥmad ibn al-Qāḍī al-Timbuktāwī, conveyed his outrage over the continued practice of "pagan" spirit possession rituals by blacks in the Islamic context of Tunisia, home to Kairouan, one of the holiest cities in Islam. Noting the presence of similar ritual groups and activities in Morocco, Algeria, and Libya, al-Timbuktāwī singled out Tunisian slaves as the "strongest amongst them in their unbelief (*kufr*) and mischief" (Montana 2004a: 174). Assuming that the religious and political leaders of Tunis were unaware of these practices, he wrote: "I found that the notables, the pious, and the learned men [of Tunis] were not aware about this dissension (*fitna*), because this dissension was neither the deeds of the Unbelievers, the Jews and the Christians, but was the behavior of the Unbelievers of our native land, the *sūdān* [black Africa]." (Montana 2004a: 184).

Al-Timbuktāwī called for the destruction of *sṭambēlī* musical instruments and the suppression of black musical practices in public (Montana 2004a: 191). He also proposed returning freed slaves to slavery, elucidating the orthodox interpretation of slavery based solely on belief: "And if a sayer says to me: 'on what grounds do you label them [i.e., the blacks of Tunis] slaves and they are emancipated, and an emancipated person is free?' My reply to him is: because they returned to the source of slavery, which is unbelief (*kufr*)" (Montana 2004a: 193).

Ḥammūda Pāshā had already been confronted by Wahhabi denouncements of Tunisian religious practices involving Sufism and the veneration of saints. L. Carl Brown notes that after a Wahhabi letter decrying Sufism and other mystical practices reached Ḥammūda Pāshā, he called on Tunisian religious leaders to respond. Apparently, Tunisian Islamic scholars were "unimpressed by the Wahhabi theological arguments, were scandalized by the sack of the Holy Cities (in 1804 and 1806) and rejected a doctrine authorizing warfare against fellow Muslims" (Brown 1974: 175, n70). But since Ḥammūda Pāshā already viewed the blacks of Tunis as a threat to both security and morality, it appears he was willing to act on the advice of al-Timbuktāwī. According to Tunisian historian Rashād al-Imām, al-Timbuktāwī's letter instigated the bey to command his troops to target the city's black population (1980: 242). He ordered communal houses destroyed, prohibited blacks from congregating, issued a decree demanding that they conform to Islamic precepts, and broke up black families, distributing their members across the country (Larguèche 2003; al-Imām 1981). In a subsequent letter to the Moroccan authorities, al-Timbuktāwī implored the Moroccans to follow the example of Ḥammūda Pāshā in this regard (Montana 2004a: 189). It remains unknown exactly how many communal houses were in operation at this time, and how many, if any, were actually destroyed by the bey during this effort. Bābā Majīd's knowledge of twenty-one houses provides evidence of the resilience of the system and the tenacity of the sub-Saharan diaspora in Tunis, and suggests that Ḥammūda Pāshā was unable to permanently dismantle the social and ritual system created by the city's black community.

Sṭambēlī at the *Zāwiya*: Accommodation and Resistance

Just as it had sometimes encouraged the communal houses, the Husaynid regime was also implicated in *sṭambēlī* practices at the shrines of saints. The founding ruler of the Husaynid state, Ḥusayn ibn ʿAlī (r. 1705–1725), built a forty-room *zāwiya* in honor of Sīdī Saʿd, an emancipated slave from Bornu. Although it is believed that the shrine of Sīdī Frej, in the Sūkra region north of Tunis, is older than that of Sīdī Saʿd, the latter was a more popular pilgrimage site, attracting thousands of slaves from around the country (Pâques 1964: 494; Montana 2004b: 92). Sīdī Saʿd, who was considered the patron saint of the black community of Tunis, was also venerated by Arab and Jewish Tunisians, many of whom also took part in the *sṭambēlī* ceremonies held there.[10] During the nineteenth century, the shrine of Sīdī Saʿd was considered one of the most important sacred sites in the greater Tunis region (Montana 2004b: 92). Sīdī Saʿd was also venerated by many in the Jewish community, especially by those who participated in *sṭambēlī*: "The passion for *sṭambēlī* of so many Jewish families at one time in Tunisia is remarkable. In Tunis, in La Goulette, in Ariana, the Jews often resorted to the 'therapy' of *sṭambēlī* and found it natural to dedicate a certain devotion to Sidi Saʿd, who is considered to be the 'patron saint' of the brotherhood" (Ben Abdallah 1988: 164).

Tunisia's Jewish minority was highly active in *sṭambēlī* before 1948. Although many Tunisian Jews were as vehemently anticolonial as their Muslim counterparts, the use of Islam in anticolonial campaigns, which tried to speak to one of the few shared identities among the majority of Tunisians, contributed to their exclusion (Perkins 2004: 144–145). This, combined with the establishment of the state of Israel in 1948 and the subsequent anti-Zionist demonstrations in Tunis in a show of solidarity with displaced Palestinians, created an unfavorable climate for the country's Jewish population, which dwindled from nearly one hundred thousand after World War II to only five thousand in the late 1970s (Anderson 1996: 113).

Jews also created for themselves a distinctive form of *sṭambēlī* experience and interpretation.[11] According to Bābā Majīd, major *sṭambēlī* rituals held for the Jewish community involved the copresence of three different musical ensembles from three distinct musical communities. The *sṭambēlī* group would utilize the *gumbrī dhaʿīf* (lit. "weak *gumbrī*," a smaller and more portable version of the gumbrī), the *shqāshiq*, and the *kurkutūwāt* (small kettledrums played with sticks).[12] The Jewish *rbabiyya* group, in addition to the *rebāb* fiddle from which it takes its name, would include a *darbūkka* (clay goblet drum) and a *ṭār* (tambourine). The *awlēd iz-zāwiya* (lit. "sons of the *zāwiya*") would play praise songs to the saints on the *mizwid* (a North African bagpipe) or the *zukra* (a double-reed aerophone or *shawm*) along with the *bendīr* (frame drum with snares) and *darbūkka*. The groups would usually perform in separate rooms or areas.[13]

The Arab Muslims of Tunis also sought out the *sṭambēlī* community for musico-spiritual interventions at shrines. The popular shrine of Sīdī Belḥassen, for example, known for its weekly Sufi ceremonies, also hosted occasional *sṭambēlī* rituals. In times of drought, the Arab Tunisian community often looked to the black community to perform rituals aimed at procuring rain. At these times, all the houses, each with its own flags and musicians, would gather to march in procession through the city to the hilltop shrine of Sīdī Belḥassen, one of the most visited sacred sites in Tunis and home to the Shādhiliyya Sufi order. Possession ceremonies would be held on the flat areas on the side of the hill, while at the very top the *takai* would be performed by the members of Dār Ziriyya (Tremearne 1914).

While the space of the *zāwiya* provided an arena within which sub-Saharan people and spirits interacted with their Maghribi counterparts, it was precisely this interaction within a sacred space that elicited the hostility of critics such as Ṣādiq Rizgī. A businessman and lay intellectual with a religious education, Rizgī studied at the Qur'ānic school at the mosque of Sīdī ʿAtīq and at the *zāwiyas* of the Raḥmaniyya and ʿAzūziyya brotherhoods. His book *Aghānī al-tūnisiyya* (Tunisian song) is still widely considered one of the most authoritative accounts of Tunisian music. It includes a short chapter, "The Doings of the Blacks at the Shrines," in which he describes a community of internal others using Tunisian popular Islam as a smoke screen to cover up their "outrageous," "superstitious" activities: "Their customs became more and more concealed by being performed under the name of the *zāwiya* of Sīdī Saʿd, where [they practice] paganism and a clear return to their savage state [*tawaḥḥush*]. Among the most important of their convictions is the passing of the spirits of various "holy ones" [*ṣālḥīn*] and 'lords of the jinn' [*sulāṭīn al-jinn*] into their human heads and into some other living creatures, too" (Rizgī 1989 [1968]: 156).

The music barely merits mention in this account, for it is seen as illegitimate, as are the rituals it animates. Rizgī views *sṭambēlī*'s social impact as corrosive and contagious; Muslims and Jews, he asserts, are being fooled into believing in this false magic. Tunisian blacks are seen as outsiders to Islam, for their ceremonies are performed in their own language (not in Arabic, the language of the Qur'ān), they prostrate themselves before images, and they drink animal blood:

> Their activities include playing and making an annoying clamor, with just a little bit of praise singing [*madīḥ*] in their language, but if that banging in their ears takes them to the *nubā*s of the spirits, it makes them dance solemn dances and they are then permitted to speak (from their conscience). They then prostrate themselves before the *ʿarīfa* and to that image they had made, and they slaughter the billy goat in order to drink its blood and grill its meat. And their beliefs have influenced some of the Muslims and even the Jews. When they become afflicted, they [the blacks] come to them to perform the *nubā*s on the pretext that the sickness is "by the hands" of one of the spirits and cannot be eliminated except by the "Dār Kūfa" group. . . . Their disorganized processions mix together women and men, and accompanying them is a billy goat adorned in silk vestments. . . . The prestige of these foolish acts has begun to decline in the minds of the general public . . . and may God lead them down the correct path. (Rizgī 1989 [1968]: 157–158)

The problematic border crossing encouraged by *sṭambēlī* was not only in the realms of race and religion; a major concern of *sṭambēlī*'s critics was the involvement of Tunisian women. While critics accused *sṭambēlī* of leading Tunisian women away from Islam, it appears that the major concern was maintaining male control over women. Rizgī bemoaned the high status and influence of female officiants and also complained that *sṭambēlī* ceremonies allowed men and women to intermingle (Rizgī 1989 [1968]). A century earlier, al-Timbuktāwī expressed his concern that Arab Tunisian women involved with *sṭambēlī* were not only stealing money from their husbands to finance their ceremonies, but also relinquishing their reliance on their husbands and men in general. He also claimed that as Tunisian women "exchange . . . their menfolk for slave women," they become involved in lesbianism (*al-musāḥaqa*), an accusation that appears to equate the prominent role of women in *sṭambēlī* with sexual deviance (Montana 2004a: 190–191).

While Husaynid policy supported the veneration of saints as a means of integrating (and exerting influence over) a diversity of communities in Tunisia (Clancy-Smith 1994; Montana 2004b), the first postcolonial regime in Tunisia, which deposed the last bey in 1957, would exhibit a far different relationship with the institution of the *zāwiya*. Under Habib Bourguiba, the country's first postindependence president, the Tunisian government opted instead to attempt to eliminate the social institution through the closure, reappropriation, or destruction of *zāwiyas* across the country. While this measure reflected the president's firm belief that saint veneration and the healing practices associated with it were incompatible with the modernizing project, it also served as a preemptive strike against the congregation of potentially oppositional groups. Sīdī Sa'd was closed in 1958, not to reopen until a decade later to coincide with efforts to document *sṭambēlī* as folklore (see chap. 8).

It should also be noted that a *zāwiya* also provided the main performance context and base of operations for a distinctive *sṭambēlī* tradition in Tunis that developed independent of the network of communal houses. At the *zāwiya* of Sīdī 'Alī el-Asmar (i.e., Sīdī 'Alī "the brown-skinned" or "mestizo"), the *sṭambēlī* troupe is traditionally black while its clients are Arab Tunisians (Pâques 1964: 627). By the 1960s, the troupes at Sīdī 'Alī el-Asmar (led by Jelūl Sūdānī, who passed the torch to Ḥamādī Bīdālī) and Dār Bārnū (led by Jelūl's brother Sālaḥ until Bābā Majīd inherited the role of *yinna*) represented the two largest and most active *sṭambēlī* traditions in Tunis (Lapassade and Ventura 1966). The relationship between the two traditions has become increasingly antagonistic, so much so that they seem to define themselves against each other (see chap. 8). A major difference between the two traditions is in the role of the *'arīfa*. Unlike trance in the tradition of Dār Bārnū, where clients engage in their own possession trance by their spirits, here it is only the *'arīfa* who becomes possessed on behalf of her clients, who remain relatively passive participants of the ritual.

The Sahara as Barrier and Bridge

While it was their sub-Saharan origins that marked black Africans as targets for the violence of slavery and servitude, it was precisely this sub-Saharan identity that they embraced in order to make their new lives manageable, to establish some form of historical continuity, and to claim space in Tunisian society. Although the long-term maintenance of sub-Saharan languages, methods of subsistence, and social structures in their new home was impractical or impossible, the rituals and music of *sṭambēlī* were not only possible to maintain, but, due to an ever-increasing demand by local Tunisians, their development was also in the slaves' best interest socially, spiritually, and economically. *Sṭambēlī*'s integration—its niche in Tunisian society—was predicated on its place at the margins, defined by otherness, but an otherness that overlapped with certain Tunisian religious beliefs and practices. Nevertheless, the predicament of displacement and alterity created a need for a new system of social organization and support to replace the ones slaves were forced to leave behind, and to address the new needs that arose in their new situation. As a toponymic signifier of connections to other, distant places, the communal house is an imaginal space of remembrance. As a place where the harsh realities of suffering and loss associated with displacement were addressed with empathy, practical support, ritual treatment, and new genealogies of belonging, it is also a site of emplacement. Moreover, its position within a larger network of other communal houses, similarly anchored within a landscape referring to meaningful places across the Sahara and beyond, highlights the ways in which emplacement concerned the creation of new places that embody the histories of displacement.

I have argued that the Sahara Desert has proven to be both a barrier and a bridge between the constructed worlds of sub-Saharan Africa and North Africa. Integration, however, does not exclude exclusion; rather, the two are different sides of the same coin. The diasporic sub-Saharan community of Tunis built a network of support that was both unique and creative. Consider, for instance, the title of *galadīma kbīr*, a term that combines a Hausa noun with an Arabic adjective in order to denote a position without an exact equivalent in either Hausaland or in Tunisia. It, like the network within which it functioned, was informed by elements sub-Saharan and Tunisian but corresponded fully to neither. *Sṭambēlī* became a style of being-in-the-world, in which hybridity, in Homi Bhabha's terms, is not about being "able to trace two original moments from which the third emerges," but is instead "the 'third space' which enables other positions to emerge" (Bhabha 1990: 211). While its name refers to a specific sub-Saharan empire, Dār Bārnū is more usefully seen as a node in a network, a landing point for a diversity of dislocated persons. The house is itself a way to move; its courtyard, a space for performing the rituals of *sṭambēlī*, allowing sub-Saharan music, migrants, and spirits to arrive and claim space by taking an active role in redefining the terms of their encounter with their others.

CHAPTER THREE

Black Spirits, White Saints

GEOGRAPHIES OF ENCOUNTER IN THE *SṬAMBĒLĪ* PANTHEON

Each member of the *sṭambēlī* pantheon has its own *nūba* (pl. *nuwab*, sometimes *nūbēt*), or tune.[1] *Nūba* (from the classical Arabic *nawba*) literally means "[one's] turn," and to do things *b-nūba* is to do them in succession.[2] *Sṭambēlī* rituals entail the successive performance of numerous *nūba*s—and thus the invocation of their corresponding saints and spirits—involving up to several dozen in a single performance. With very few exceptions (such as Ṣlāt in-Nabī, or Prophet's prayer), the name of each *nūba* is simply the name of the corresponding spirit or saint. The *nūba* is how a spirit's potentiality for presence, and thus its existence, is recognized. This metaphorical relationship is often verbally manifested; if somebody wishes to know which spirit possesses a patient, one simply asks, "What is her *nūba*?" (shnīya nūbit-hā?).

No *nūba*—and thus no saint or spirit—stands alone; each is situated within a larger framework of relationships. Performance of one *nūba* immediately opens up possibilities for the next *nūba* while eliminating others. The *nūba*s are nested within larger structures called *silsilēt* (chains; sing. *silsila*), which are loosely prescribed sequences of *nūba*s corresponding to different subsections of the pantheon. *Silsila*s are most often played in hierarchical order, from the strongest or oldest spirit in the family to the weaker or younger. Although each *silsila* is theoretically discrete and robust, there is a certain amount of room for improvising the ceremony's structure through song. The musicians may skip or repeat certain *nūba*s, or even play some in a nonnormative order, depending on the type of ceremony, the composition of the ritual gathering, and the relative rank of the spirits involved. As certain attendees are also affiliated with particular members of the pantheon, the placement and timing of a *nūba* may reflect the dynamics of patronage and social relations; in a private *sṭambēlī*, for example, the host's *nūba*(s) will be performed most often and may lead to increased amounts of monetary offerings to the musicians.[3] The malleability of the *silsila*, and indeed of each *nūba* within it, gives the ceremony a certain sense of spontaneity and unpredictability. In any case, the *silsila* structure connects certain *nūba*s to each other, musically and thus conceptually.

I am convinced that this music does not merely allude to or represent an abstracted pantheon of spirits. *Sṭambēlī* is a system of knowledge that is performed and embodied. There are no formal recited or written texts to represent the structure of the pantheon, nor are there any social institutions or pedagogical practices dedicated to the process of transmitting such knowledge as an abstract set of information. Rather—and this is crucial—the *sṭambēlī* pantheon exists only through its musical performance. Through performance, the music produces, reproduces, and reworks the organization of the *sṭambēlī* pantheon of saints and spirits and the interrelationships among its members.

Sṭambēlī musicians must "go" from one *nūba* to another by adhering to certain ritual obligations based on the relationship between saints and spirits and among the families within those categories. As proper musical navigation through the pantheon is a crucial condition for ritual efficacy, musicians must learn not only the entire repertoire of *nūba*s, but also the relationships between members of the pantheon. Taken as a whole, these musical routes constitute a progressive disclosure of the *sṭambēlī* pantheon, the members of which provide the geocultural and historical references that direct participants into fields of meaning. It is only through music that these unseen beings arrive, and therefore it is only through music that the histories and meanings they evoke are manifested in front of witnesses in a systematic, public way.

For *sṭambēlī* musicians, deep knowledge of the spirits and the relationships among them is far more important than knowledge of the specifics of a patient's affliction. It is often sufficient for musicians simply to know which spirit or saint is afflicting the patient, as this suggests particular routes through the pantheon that will be efficacious in getting the spirit to descend, dance until it is placated, and please other spirits in the pantheon, some of whom must be invoked, even if none of their hosts are present to dance, in order for the ceremony to be successful.

Ethnographic studies of sub-Saharan spirit possession traditions, such as Adeline Masquelier's (2001) work on *bori* in Niger and Janice Boddy's (1989) study of *zār* in Sudan, have been increasingly concerned with the trance experience, providing highly illuminating accounts of select spirits and their human hosts. While these studies convey powerfully, among other things, the experience of particular individuals who undergo profound personal and social transformations through spirit possession, it should be noted that each host typically interacts with a relatively small segment of her spirit pantheon.

Such experiences, however, at least in the context of *sṭambēlī*, would not be possible were it not for the musicians' expansive knowledge of the entirety of the pantheon, and thus, I hope to complement such studies with my focus on musicians and the pantheon as a whole. By invoking the unseen characters of the pantheon, musicians orient participants within a system of cultural references characterized by border crossing and transformative potentialities. As they appear in ritual—in succession yet not always entirely predictably—members of the *sṭambēlī* pantheon evoke and engage with social, historical, and religious contexts and encounters, both past and present.

It must be emphasized from the outset that there is no single, definitive *sṭambēlī* pantheon. While there have undoubtedly been changes over time in pantheon membership, diachronic variations are difficult to assess, due to the fact that previous scholarship has failed to note synchronic variations, that is, between different *sṭambēlī* troupes. Taxonomies of *sṭambēlī* spirits by Treamearne (1914) and Ahmed Rahal (2000) downplay or simply ignore the differences among various local *sṭambēlī* troupes. Three main problems arise from such categorical assertions. First, they result in a rather monolithic interpretation of *sṭambēlī* and a related, overdetermined sense of a unified "black community" in Tunis, a context that is more accurately characterized by antagonism between troupes, exacerbated by competition for what is perceived as a diminishing potential clientele. Second, they overlook the particular meanings attached to certain saints and spirits by clients and practitioners of different *sṭambēlī* traditions. Third, they ignore the fundamental flexibility of ritual knowledge and the variegated, highly localized interpretations and refigurations that are defining features of spirit practices throughout the African diaspora.

This last point is highlighted by Andrew Apter's (1992) consideration of the widespread variation in the membership of orisha pantheons and the relationships between deities therein throughout Yorubaland, where ownership of ritual knowledge and the secrecy surrounding it create a space for revision and transformation, the forms of which are shaped more by a possession troupe's specific histories and sociopolitical contexts than by adherence to any fixed and shared content. Extending this argument to Haitian vodou, Apter shows that behind the public identities of vodou deities as European Catholic saints lies a secretive and more powerful African incarnation that initiates, through deep knowledge claims, may invoke and manipulate in ritual (2002: 238). The categorical opposition between Rada ("cool" spirits associated with Africa and authority) and Petwo ("hot" spirits associated with Creole and power) is essential to the practice of Haitian vodou precisely because the boundaries between them can be blurred and the categories inverted; a Petwo spirit in one town or region may serve as a Rada in another (2002: 248). While the *sṭambēlī* pantheon is broadly divided into saints ("the Whites," generally associated with Islam and North Africa or the Middle East) and spirits ("the Blacks," generally associated with sub-Saharan Africa), these are not oppositional categories that are pitted against each other or undergo ritual reversals as in the Haitian or Yoruba cases. There is also no dualistic (re)interpretation of the dominant religion's spiritual personalities as sub-Saharan deities, as one finds throughout the Caribbean. However, Apter's suggestion that it is precisely the potential for refiguration that endows spirit possession practices with their power and continual relevance applies as meaningfully to *sṭambēlī* as it does to the traditions of sub-Saharan Africa and its diaspora in the Americas.

Spirit Possession as Social Encounter

Spirit possession is not only about human-spirit interactions. Throughout Africa, spirit pantheons and the embodied ritual appearance of their members reveal, reflect, and reshape histories of social encounter (Besmer 1983; Boddy 1989; Echard 1989; Emoff 2003; Kramer 1993; Makris 1996, 2000; Stoller 1989). Spirits are often grouped into families or societies with meaningful identities corresponding to neighboring ethnolinguistic groups, immigrant populations, local ancestors, colonial officials, religious leaders, and others connected to heavily freighted sociohistorical encounters. Among the Songhay of Mali and Niger, for example, each spirit family represents a particular period in Songhay history. The Tooru are ancestors and founders of the Songhay kingdom, while the Black spirits represent the first inhabitants of the land. The White spirits are Muslim clerics, representing the first encounters with Islam. The Hausa spirits arrived with the mass migration of Hausa to Songhay regions starting in 1911, while the Hauka first appeared in 1925 in response to French colonization (Stoller 1997: 62; 1989: 30). Most recently, the Sasale spirits, representing "social deviants" such as prostitutes, appeared in the 1960s, amid government reforms based on scripturalist interpretations of Islam (Stoller 1989: 175). In addition to bringing the past to bear on the present by "embodying cultural memory" (Stoller 1989), spirits can also influence political life more directly. As spirits did in the former Rhodesia's fight for independence (Lan 1985), Hauka spirits encouraged acts of resistance such as the refusal to pay taxes, participate in forced labor, or answer to local chiefs (Masquelier 2001: 165). In the Kurfey region of Niger, parallel French colonial spirits called Babule also appeared in *bori* rituals, where they arrived almost daily throughout much of the year in 1926 (Echard 1989).

Zār rituals in northern Sudan evoke a history of encroaching others through drummed "threads" that organize the *zār* spirits into distinct "societies" including founders of Islamic orders, Ethiopians, Arab nomads, Europeans, Ottoman rulers, Gypsies, West Africans, and slaves (Boddy 1989: 275–301). Elsewhere in Sudan, some of the same spirit groups are invoked through ritual music, but alternative meanings are ascribed to them. While the *zār* is performed mainly for and by descendants of freeborn Arabs in the Sudan, a related possession tradition called *ṭumbura* is practiced by descendants of slaves in southern regions and in the ghettos and shantytowns of Khartoum. While the Black and Sorcerer spirits represent foreign others in the northern Sudanese *zār* context, they represent in the *ṭumbura* pantheon the autochthonous or indigenous identities of devotees' ancestors before the violence of slavery and war plagued the region (Makris 2000).[4] In a similar vein, "Arab" spirits are admired by the Islamicized Swahili, but for the neighboring Giryama people, the same Arab (as well as Swahili) spirits are feared (Kramer 1993: 99). Thus, even when spirits are "shared," they are nevertheless arranged into systems that relate to particular traditions' historical encounters, and may be interpreted differently, or take on new identities and lives.

While there is indeed a "remarkable" continuity of *bori* spirits found throughout Hausaland (Besmer 1983: 62), there is an equally remarkable distinctiveness to the pantheons in different parts of the region that reflects local histories and relations. In Kano, Nigeria, spirits are associated with certain local occupations, physical handicaps, and animals, as well as with religious or geocultural others including Fulani, Tuareg, Muslims, and pagans (Besmer 1983). In the Kurfey region of Niger, *bori* spirit families include Peul, Zarma, Muslim, Asna (spirits of the indigenous animist religion of the region), Tuareg, Mossi, and European. In nearby Ader, Sorcerer spirits first appeared in *bori* rituals as a major famine began in 1967 and did not stop multiplying until 1973, when the famine ended.[5] Further afield and more recently, during the first Gulf War new spirits named Georges Klinsky (a composite of George Bush and Bill Clinton) and Sadam Hoseny appeared in *tromba* possession rituals on the east coast of Madagascar (Emoff 2003).

In addition to this diversity of content, differing social and geographic contexts mean that the societal position of spirit possession practices are variable from location to location. *Bori*, as Nicole Echard (1989) has shown, is very diverse in content, context, and membership across Niger and beyond. In some areas, it is interpreted as central to a village's social organization (as Echard has shown for Ader, Niger), or perceived as peripheral (as Fremont Besmer has shown in Kano, Nigeria), or "virtually absent," since only some women are adepts (as Jacqueline Monfouga-Nicolas has shown in Maradi, Niger). However, as Masquelier (2001) deftly shows in her study of *bori* among the Mawri of Niger, even where *bori* appears "peripheral" (less than 2 percent of the population is not Muslim), its importance and relevance, while elusive (due to public attitudes and spoken discourse of the majority Muslim population), resonates well into the "dominant" sectors of society.

Islam, Spirit Practices, and Geographies of Encounter

A common denominator shared by most of the above examples is the encounter with the increasing influence of Islam. Several recent studies of sub-Saharan possession practices have shown that while the encroachment of Islam has met with differing degrees of confrontation or accommodation, these encounters are often much more nuanced and situational than the oppositionality expressed publicly might otherwise suggest. In regions where *bori* is more or less indigenous, Muslims may interpret *bori* as manifestations of the *jinn* (spirits that are recognized in textual authorities including the Qur'ān), while others may accept the reality of *bori* spirits but disapprove of interacting with them (which is often cited as "magic" and thus antithetical to Islamic precepts), and still others may see little contradiction at all in participating in both domains of practice (Echard 1989; Masquelier 2001; Danfulani 1999). Issues of gender and the public sphere further complicate any possession-Islam dichotomy. While *zār* in Hofriyat may constitute a counterhegemonic women's practice vis-à-vis a male-dominated Islam, it does not ritually challenge or oppose Islam per se. *Zār* ceremonies begin with songs in praise of the Prophet and several Muslim saints, and during important life-cycle rituals such as childbirth, *zār* spirits and Muslim saints are both invoked (Boddy 1989: 16). For Hofriyati women, Islam is "commensurate with vernacular knowledge," of which *zār* is central, and while men may publicly bemoan the practice of *zār*, in private they often find it necessary to give in to the demands of their wives' spirits (Boddy 1989: 7). The experience of internalizing both Islam and indigenous spirit possession systems is analyzed eloquently by Michael Lambek in the following passage on these overlapping domains in the context of Mayotte: "Neither possession nor Islam are unified phenomena nor is peoples' commitment to each of them all of a piece. . . . The critical time dimension for the individual is not necessarily one of major biological shifts, of conversion, as it were, but rather of a more subtle shifting of perspective on a daily basis. Phenomenological perspective is deeply embedded in practice. To receive a diagnosis of possession is to shift perspective and interest just as the annual passage through Ramadan shifts the intensity of Islamic interest" (Lambek 1993: 62).

The dynamics between Islam and spirit practices, then, are multiple, situational, and shifting. The foregoing illustrates vividly Michael Taussig's

(1993) suggestion that spirits often represent difference itself. It follows, then, that rituals of possession can provide a means of negotiating that difference. While the above examples provide useful starting points for gaining access to *sṭambēlī*'s roles and meanings in Tunisian society, there are important differences that first need to be accounted for, given the particularities of *sṭambēlī*'s history. Whereas the foregoing *bori* and *zār* examples mainly deal with histories of contact with incoming others, *sṭambēlī* recreates its own movement—the movement of the racialized and displaced body—across the Sahara and its ensuing historical encounters in North Africa. This has important implications for the ways in which *sṭambēlī* participants situate their own cultural histories in relation to the movements of the spirits and saints, as well as for the way *sṭambēlī* is perceived within Tunisian society.

The *sṭambēlī* pantheon does not reproduce a systematic and linear narrative of a people's history and its moments of social crisis (as does the Songhay pantheon) or a comprehensive inventory of sociocultural or religious others (as does the *zār* pantheon). Yet it is no less evocative of historical and sociocultural meanings. The *sṭambēlī* pantheon, as performed in ritual, reveals symbolic and practical links to sub-Saharan Africa while simultaneously revealing a common ground or compatibility between the two. *Sṭambēlī*'s trajectory from sub-Saharan Africa, where such spirit possession practices were indigenous, to North Africa, where Islam is considered the indigenous religion, leads to specific social dynamics, different from *bori* in Niger, for example, where Islam is understood to be an imported religious tradition. Yet while perceived as radically other, *sṭambēlī* also espouses an ethos of inclusiveness; as the aesthetics of the structuring of the ceremony indicate, the *sṭambēlī* body is equally comfortable interacting with sub-Saharan spirits and North African saints, all of whom respond to the distinctive aesthetics of *sṭambēlī*. It is the purpose of the remainder of this chapter to describe the salient categories, identities, and relationships among these members of the *sṭambēlī* pantheon as they are recognized at Dār Bārnū.

Black and White

As a considerable amount of traffic in spirits accompanied the trade in humans across the Sahara, the members of the *sṭambēlī* spirit pantheon (literally) embody the encounter between sub-Saharan and North Africa. Like humans, the spirits adapted to social and historical change, and just as displaced sub-Saharans took part in new forms of alliance, dependence, and genealogies upon landing in North Africa, so too were the spirits' relationships transformed from a framework of social relations salient in sub-Saharan Africa into kinship terms having currency in North Africa.

Sṭambēlī communicates with two categories of the invisible world: the

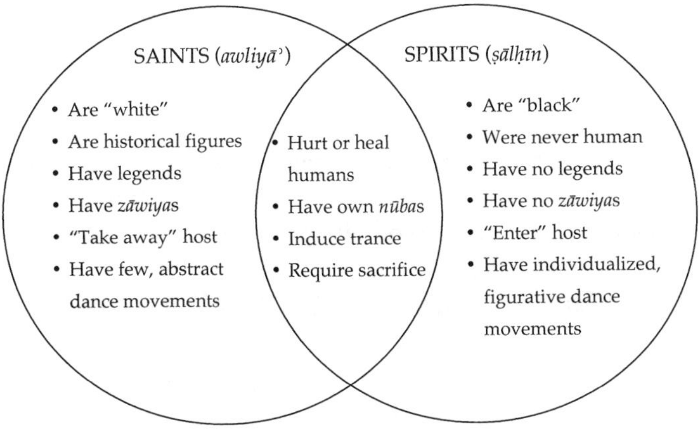

FIGURE 5. The *sṭambēlī* saints and spirits: commonalities and differences.

"Whites" (*abyāḍ*), also called the "saints" (*awliyā'*; sing. *walī*), and the "Blacks" (*kḥūl*), who are sub-Saharan spirits (*ṣālḥīn*, lit. "holy ones"; sing. *ṣāliḥ*) and may be either Muslim or Christian. The *sṭambēlī* saints and spirits are named, social beings with humanlike characteristics and with the same power to disrupt or enrich another's life. The distinction between the categories of Black and White, and the way they are mobilized in ritual, however, is essential to understanding the ontological foundations underpinning the therapeutic and cultural "work" of *sṭambēlī*.

In West Africa, the distinction between black and white spirits often corresponds to changes in habitat and religious identity, such that white spirits and black spirits alike originate in the bush, but only the white spirits leave the bush to enter towns and convert to Islam (Kramer 1993; Masquelier 2001).[6] In contrast, the Black-White distinction in *sṭambēlī* is an ontological one, since the Black spirits were never human. The Whites, however, were once living beings, recognized Muslim historical figures, and have lived in North Africa or the Middle East.

The ontological differences between the Blacks and Whites is also perceptible to the local observer in the modes of interaction with their human hosts (see fig. 5). While members of both categories compel their hosts to "dance" (*yashṭaḥ*), they do so in different ways. The Blacks "enter" their hosts' bodies, causing possession trance. The Whites, in contrast, do not possess their hosts, but rather "take them away" from their bodies, engendering nonpossession trance (*jedba*, lit. "attraction"). Each of the Blacks has his or her own distinctive dance movements, as well as certain attire and other ritual paraphernalia such as walking sticks, spears, knives, or rods, which they will sometimes use to hit their hosts. In Gilbert Rouget's terms, these dances for the Blacks are "figurative" or "mimetic," while those of the Whites, in contrast, are "abstract" (Rouget 1986: 114–115). The Whites, in *sṭambēlī*, put their hosts' bodies through vigorous, repetitive dance movements selected from a very small, stock repertoire of movements basically limited to bending forward and back at the waist or, if on all fours, swinging the head vigorously to and fro. These movements are virtually identical to those one might find at other, non-*sṭambēlī* rituals held at many saints' shrines across the Maghrib. The vocabulary of spirit possession (e.g., *maskūn*, "inhabited") does not apply to affliction by the Whites, just as the vocabulary of saintliness (e.g., *baraka*, "blessing," or *zāwiya*, "shrine") does not apply to the Blacks.

These distinctions are essential to understanding how, even for the uninitiated local observer, *sṭambēlī* ritually connects sub-Saharan African possession practices and North African Islam. While the categorical distinctions between Black and White (and by extension, possession and nonpossession trance; see chap. 6) are fundamental to understanding *sṭambēlī*, it is also the unification of the two within the same ritual-aesthetic space that suggests *sṭambēlī* can provide a performative commentary on the relations between sub-Saharan and North Africa as experienced by the *sṭambēlī* network's members. The boundaries between Black and White can be transcended in ritual, where, for example, Whites may appear during the Black part of the ceremony, resulting not in a blurring of boundaries but rather in a performative and embodied interaction between Black and White.

Il-Abyāḍ ("the Whites")

The White half of the pantheon is populated by Islamic historical figures. At the top of this hierarchy are the Prophet Muḥammad and his companion Bilāl, an emancipated African slave who became Islam's first caller to prayer. These two figures are considered closest to God, and thus furthest from the human realm; unlike most other members of the pantheon, they do not interact with humans through ritualized trance. The remaining members of this category are Muslim saints known for their healing and mystical powers and whose notoriety or veneration may be pan-Islamic, regional, or local in nature. The "White" designation, it is worth reiterating, is not a racial referent; Bilāl, as well as some of the most powerful *sṭambēlī* saints, were of sub-Saharan origin.

THE PROPHET AND BILĀL

Dār Bārnū *sṭambēlī* rituals always begin with two *nūba*s that are "tied together" (*murābiṭ mabīnhum*): Ṣlāt in-Nabī (lit. "Prophet's Prayer") and

Jerma. The idea of being tied together is an important and highly symbolic concept in *sṭambēlī*: musically, it means that the *nūba*s are played in succession without stopping, a performance of the idea that they are tied together not only aesthetically, but also conceptually and historically. While Muḥammad is the Messenger of God, chosen to receive the revelation of the final, inviolable words of God that became the holy Qur'ān, in much popular Islamic practice, and especially certain paths of Sufism, the Prophet himself has also been the object of veneration, and prayers often ask for his intercession with God (Trimingham 1971: 27).

Ṣlāt in-Nabī, as a rule, segues directly into Jerma. Jerma refers to a sub-Saharan ethnolinguistic group situated near the Bornu region.[7] Within the *sṭambēlī* community, however, Jerma is also the *ʿajmī* name for the important Islamic figure named Bilāl bin Rabāḥ (also known as Ibn Ḥamāma). Of African heritage and born into slavery in Mecca, Bilāl became one of the first converts to Islam. His conversion, which was not widely tolerated at the time, resulted in severe punishment by his master. When the Prophet's companion Abū Bakr heard of his piety and stoicism, he purchased Bilāl from his former master. Bilāl joined the Prophet in the emerging Muslim community of Medina, where he accompanied the Prophet in various capacities, including steward, servant, and soldier (Arafat 1960). Most important, Bilāl was the one chosen by the Prophet to become Islam's first caller to prayer (*mu'adhdhin*), responsible for chanting the melodious *adhān* (call to prayer) throughout the city before each of the five obligatory daily prayers. As a slave of sub-Saharan origin whose piety and exceptional vocal abilities were recognized by the Prophet, the figure of Bilāl provides a strong historical link between sub-Saharans and the very origins of Islam. Indeed, ritual communities of sub-Saharans in North Africa claim, in varying degrees, spiritual descent from Bilāl.

The connection to Bilāl also reinforced the social roles that black African Muslims would play in their new settings, namely, as musicians and mediators. Viviana Pâques recorded the following legend from the Sīdī Bilāl community of Algeria. Here, Bilāl performs the role of intermediary, healing and problem-solving through music and dance: "A quarrel separated the two spouses [ʿAlī and Fāṭima], and Fatima (the daughter of the Prophet) locked herself up and refused to see her husband. Bīlāl appears in front of Fatima's room and starts to play the *qraqeb* [*shqāshiq*] and begins to dance, whirling around while squatted down on his heels, according to the dance characteristic of the blacks of the oases. Fatima starts laughing and follows Bīlāl, attracted by the dance. The Negro leads her back to her husband" (Pâques 1964: 479).

Bilāl became an important, if not central, spiritual figure of veneration among some of these communities, some of which, especially in neighboring Algeria, refer to themselves as *awlēd sīdī bilāl* (children of Saint Bilāl), and to their rituals as *dīwān sīdī bilāl* (Sīdī Bilāl's assembly) (Dermenghem 1954; Pâques 1964). Further west, in Essaouira, Morocco, the Gnāwa have built a shrine in honor of Bilāl. At Dār Bārnū, however, Bilāl is not remembered through such stories, nomenclature, or shrines. Moreover, even his identity in *sṭambēlī* is cloaked by naming his *nūba* Jerma, a Songhay name unknown to Tunisians outside the *sṭambēlī* network.[8] Although he is an important figure in the *sṭambēlī* pantheon, as evidenced by his *nūba*'s being situated second only to that of the Prophet, it would be misleading to interpret Bilāl's role in *sṭambēlī* simply as a strategy for legitimizing *sṭambēlī*'s location within Islamic history. In contrast to the aforementioned Moroccan and Algerian examples, in Tunisian *sṭambēlī* the figure of Bilāl is comprehensible only through the transnational routes that brought him into sub-Saharan African spirit pantheons such as that of the Songhay of Niger.

Among the Songhay, Bilāl is the head of the Jerma spirits, who, through their ability to bring or withhold rain, wind, thunder, and lightning, are the most powerful and feared family of spirits. He is also considered the chief of the Hauka spirits (who arrived via the Red Sea from Mecca), as well as "the mystical alter-ego of Dongo (the deity of thunder), [who] possessed the power to burn villages and kill villagers without remorse" (Stoller 1995: 115; 1989: 160). In Sudan, Bilāl is also the legendary figure who gave Sudanis the first *ṭumbura*, the stringed instrument played by descendants of slaves in their possession ceremonies (Makris 1996: 169).

While in *sṭambēlī* Bīlāl suffers from none of the dangerous or negative connotations found among the Songhay, the lyrics of his *nūba*, which welcome him, preserve some words in the Jerma language: *ka*, for instance, is a call for someone to come. The words are

Wayay wayay jerma	Truly, truly, Jerma,
Kakabilāli bābā	Come, come, Bilāl, father
Jadiy irḥam	Welcome him, grandfather
Kakabilāli bābā	Come, come, Bilāl, father

Although at times there is a certain malleability to the aesthetic structuring of *sṭambēlī* ritual, the performance of Ṣlāt in-Nabī and Jerma, in succession, at the start of the ceremony, is absolutely obligatory. By tying Bilāl's *nūba* to that of the Prophet, *sṭambēlī* aesthetically performs a historical relationship of profound significance. The two inseparable *nūba*s mark the *sṭambēlī* body as connected, via sub-Saharan Africa, to the very source of Islam, demonstrating not only the compatibility, but moreover the inseparability, of the sub-Saharan body and the history of Islam. The special status

TABLE 1. The *silsila* of the saints

Ṣlāt in-Nabī (Prophet's Prayer)	Sīdī Marzūg	Sīdī Beshīr
Jerma (Bilāl)	Sīdī Manṣūr	Sīdī Ḥammūda
Bū Ḥijba	Sīdī Bū Ra's el-ʿAjmī	Lilla Malīka
Sīdī Saʿd	Sīdī ʿĀmr	Sīdī Belḥassen
Sīdī Frej	Sīdī ʿĀmr Bū Khatwa	Sayda Manubiyya
Sīdī ʿAbd el-Qādir	Sīdī Amār	Sīdī Ben ʿĪsā
Sīdī ʿAbd es-Salēm	Sīdī ʿAmawī	Bābā Baḥrī

of the Prophet and Bilāl is also evoked through the conspicuous *absence* of embodied interaction with participants: there is never any trance during the *nūba*s for the Prophet and Bilāl. They, like God above them, are too distant and too divine to interact with humans in such visceral ways. This does not mean, however, that there is no communication; performing these *nūba*s is a means of praising them in hopes of attaining some of their blessing, and it also pleases other saints and those spirits who appreciate Islamic prayers and offerings.

THE SAINTS

The saints, usually identified by the honorific "Sīdī" (lit. "my lord"; fem. "Sayda" or "Lilla") preceding their names, were all living, historical figures recognized for their exceptional piety and/or mystical powers (see table 1). They are honored in dedicated shrines (*zāwiya*s) that may house the saint's tomb and are often distinguished by a domed roof (*qubba*), the reason they are sometimes also collectively referred to as the *qubbaniyya*, or "those with a domed shrine." More commonly, however, they are called *awliyā'*.[9] These shrines, sacred sites infused with the saint's *baraka*, host religious rituals ranging from private prayers and supplications to the chanting of praise songs or the *dhikr* to dramatic healing trance rituals. A saint's spiritual power can be ambivalent. While humans can receive some of a saint's *baraka* through offerings, prayers, and pilgrimages, they can also be hurt by a saint. In such cases, a person is said to be "hit" or "struck" (*maḍrūb*) by the saint.[10]

The saints in the *sṭambēlī* pantheon are, for the most part, considered local—having lived or died in Tunisia or its North African neighbors. They may be venerated far outside their towns or only very locally, with most having a presence limited to Tunisia and its Maghribi neighbors. Sīdī ʿAbd el-Qādir is one exception, as he is recognized throughout the Islamic world and venerated in rituals from Morocco to Indonesia. Only some *sṭambēlī* saints, such as Sīdī Frej and Sīdī Saʿd, are of sub-Saharan origin, but they constitute some of the most powerful entities in the pantheon. In addition to these two saints, *sṭambēlī* at Dār Bārnū also accords a prominent place to Sīdī Marzūg, who lived in Nefta (a desert oasis town in the far southwestern corner of Tunisia), as well as to Sīdī Manṣūr, who lived in the coastal city of Sfax, where a group of black sailors would congregate for *sṭambēlī*. These two saints have similar functions to those of Sīdī Saʿd and Sīdī Frej in their own locales: the shrines of both Sīdī Manṣūr and Sīdī Marzūg are sites of group pilgrimages each year. Other *sṭambēlī* saints include Sīdī Bū Ra's el-ʿAjmī, Sīdī ʿAmr, Sīdī ʿAmr Bū Khatwa, Sīdī ʿAmawī, Sīdī Beshīr, Sīdī Ḥammūda, and Lilla Malika.

Still other saints, while not technically part of the White *silsila*, have been introduced into this part of the ceremony. Sīdī Belḥassen, Sīdī Ben ʿĪsā, and Sayda Manubiyya are not *sṭambēlī* saints per se, yet they have *sṭambēlī nūba*s that may be performed "on demand." This means that they are not technically part of the *sṭambēlī* pantheon, since their *nūba*s are not obligatory parts of the *silsila* and they are not divined by *sṭambēlī* healers as entities afflicting a potential client. Moreover, unlike the saints of the *silsila*, whose *nūba*s will conventionally be performed whether or not someone present dances, these three *nūba*s are rarely performed unless someone present requests it. Sayda Manubiyya, Sīdī Ben ʿĪsā, and Sīdī Belḥassen are not of sub-Saharan descent and do not have the special status of certain non-sub-Saharans such as Sīdī ʿAbd el-Qādir. What is special about these saints, however, is that they are local or regional saints active in treating their followers' ailments through trance and possession. Sīdī Ben ʿĪsā was a sixteenth-century Moroccan saint who founded the ʿĪsāwiyya Sufi order, which quickly spread across the Maghrib to become one of the most popular Sufi organizations in Tunisia. Some branches of the ʿĪsāwiyya in Tunisia are credited with preserving and developing *ma'lūf*, the Arab-Andalusian classical music that would later become, in a "modernized" guise, the country's official "national" musical heritage (Davis 1997; Jones 1977). But the ʿĪsāwiyya are most renowned for their dramatic music and trance ceremonies, which involve acts of self-mortification such as eating glass and nails, falling on cactus husks, and dancing with fire. While ʿĪsāwiyya ceremonies mainly involve men, women flock to the *zāwiya* of Sayda Manubiyya for its popular weekly healing ceremonies, geared mostly toward women with marital or fertility problems (Boissevain-Souid 2000; Larguèche and Larguèche 1992). The *zāwiya* of Sīdī Belḥassen also hosts women's trance and possession ceremonies, but of a much different nature. The official followers of this order are men, generally from the petit bourgeoisie, who consider their weekly *dhikr* ceremony to be the most "orthodox" of activities. What is remarkable is that in an adjoining room, closed off from the men, women become possessed by *jinn* and enter trances to the music of the men's *dhikr* (Ferchiou 1972, 1991). By acknowledging these saints and their followers by performing their *nūba*s, *sṭambēlī* fosters connections with the other most influential trance and possession practices in the greater Tunis area.

In *sṭambēlī*, the trance movements of the saints are comparable to those characteristic of other trance practices associated with Muslim saints in Tunisian *zāwiya*s. These movements usually involve vigorous and continuous forward bends or swaying of the head. It is only during the *nūba*s for the saints that uninitiated participants may enter into trance.[11] Thus, one of the salient forms of *sṭambēlī* ritual dynamics, especially for noninitiates and other outsiders, involves the performed congruence between the familiar (trance movements) and the alter (*sṭambēlī* musical aesthetics) that generates the conditions for those trances.

The saints typically begin with a seamless transition from Jerma to the *nūba* of Bū Ḥijba. At Dār Bārnū, little biographical information is known about Bū Ḥijba (a shortened version of Sīdī Ṣālaḥ Bū Ḥijba), though he may be Bū Ḥajba, the barber venerated in the interior town of Gabès (Pâques 1964). That so little is remembered about him may appear to belie his prestigious position following the *nūba*s of the Prophet and Bilāl. That he is "tied" to Bilāl's *nūba* may explain why a saint who has fallen out of favor (as most of the clients who trance to his *nūba* have passed away) continues to appear in such a prominent place in the ceremony. Another important factor is that this *nūba* was one of Bābā Majīd's favorites on which to improvise.

Unlike the first three *nūba*s, which are tied together, the remaining *nūba*s of the White section of the pantheon are most often performed in a singular fashion as individual *nūba*s with clear endings and extended pauses before beginning the next *nūba*. There remains, however, a loosely prescribed sense of hierarchy in which some or all of the most powerful saints—the Shaikhs—are performed following Ṣlāt in-Nabī, Jerma, and Bū Ḥijba, and before any others.

THE SHAIKHS

Four saints—Sīdī Frej, Sīdī Sa'd, Sīdī 'Abd es-Salēm, and Sīdī 'Abd el-Qādir—collectively known as the "Shaikhs" (*mashāyikh*) constitute the most active and powerful *sṭambēlī* saints. Sīdī 'Abd es-Salēm and Sīdī 'Abd el-Qādir are transnational in their reach, as they or their followers founded well-known Sufi orders (the Sulāmiyya and the Qādiriyya, respectively), while Sīdī Frej and Sīdī Sa'd, two emancipated slaves of sub-Saharan origin, are highly localized to their neighborhoods in the Tunis vicinity (though *sṭambēlī* groups throughout the country recognize them both), where they are venerated by black and Arab Tunisians alike.

Sīdī ʿAbd el-Qādir el-Jīlānī was a twelfth-century Persian theologian who lived most of his life in the city of Baghdad. A wandering ascetic for twenty-five years, he is remembered for reconciling Sufism with the precepts of Hanbali religious jurisprudence in his teaching, although scholars disagree over whether he actually became a Sufi himself (Braune 1960; Trimingham 1971).[12] His sermons, often geared toward large non-Sufi audiences, extolled the virtues of living as a saint, which he presented as an ideal type capable of conquering the self's desire for earthly pleasure, overcoming the fear of fate and death, and recognizing in all things the will of God (Braune 1960: 70). After his death, ʿAbd el-Qādir became the subject of numerous hagiographies enumerating a lifetime of miracle making, crediting him with the capacity to move mountains, dry seas, raise the dead, and punish sinners and aid the oppressed from afar. He is characterized as held in esteem by angels, the *jinn*, and even the Prophet (Braune 1960: 70). The Qādiriyya, the Sufi order that carries his name, was not established by his descendants until the fourteenth century. Since he did not preach mysticism and had no *ṭarīqa* (and thus no disciples), and the first of these treatises was not written until a century after his death, his immense transnational popularity and association with Sufism remain unsatisfactorily accounted for by scholars of Sufism (Trimingham 1971). Nevertheless, in Tunisia as well as the rest of the Islamic world, he is called the *sulṭān ij-jinn* (master of the jinn) or *sulṭān iṣ-ṣālḥīn* (in the context of *sṭambēlī*, master of the spirits), as he is considered one of the most powerful spiritual entities capable of intervening on behalf of his supplicants, if not the most powerful. In ritual, his host typically wears a green *kashabiyya* and holds a walking stick.

Sīdī ʿAbd es-Salēm el-Asmar (d. 1573) founded the Sulāmiyya Sufi order in what is now Libya, from where it spread across the Maghrib. The first *zāwiya* built in his honor in Tunis did not appear until 1850, but by the end of the nineteenth century the city hosted no fewer than six shrines for Sīdī ʿAbd es-Salēm (Zeghonda 1991: v). (The neighborhood known as Bēb Sīdī ʿAbd es-Salēm—"Sīdī ʿAbd es-Salēm's Gate"—referring to an ancient entryway on the city's walled perimeter, is named after one of these shrines located a short distance from Dār Bārnū.) Sīdī ʿAbd es-Salēm wrote much of the poetry that constitutes the lyrics of the Sulāmiyya's collective rituals, which are performed with only vocals and percussion. When invoked in *sṭambēlī*, Sīdī ʿAbd es-Salēm wears a white *kashabiyya*, dances with fire, and may lead the group in reciting the *fātiḥa*.

In contrast to Sīdī ʿAbd el-Qādir and Sīdī ʿAbd es-Salēm, who are associated with formal teachings and institutional Sufism, lived outside Tunisia, and have regional and transnational reach, Sīdī Frej and Sīdī Saʿd have a mostly local presence in the Tunis area, did not found or inspire any Sufi institution, and are defined in large part by their sub-Saharan origins and trans-Saharan movements. Both came to Tunis from Bornu as slaves, demonstrated their *baraka* through various miracles, and had shrines built posthumously in their honor by 1728 at the latest, attracting supplicants making small visits as well as large, communal, annual pilgrimages (see chap. 7). While Sīdī Frej's trance movements consist of the typical repetitive motions, Sīdī Saʿd may beat his host with two wooden clubs, hitting both legs, then the head, with each beat. If there are no clubs present, he will sometimes grab a pair of *shqāshiq* to do the same.

That all four saints, each with varying degrees of local, regional, and transnational movements and influences, are considered the most powerful of *sṭambēlī* saints and have no hierarchy among them highlights the remarkable integrative capacity of *sṭambēlī*'s spiritual constitution. As does the linking of Bilāl and the Prophet, the copresence of Sīdī Frej, Sīdī Saʿd, Sīdī ʿAbd es-Salēm, and Sīdī ʿAbd el-Qādir connects sub-Saharans—more specifically, ex-slaves—in Tunisia with venerable spiritual personalities and institutions recognized and respected far beyond the context of *sṭambēlī*. Sīdī Saʿd and Sīdī Frej are powerful examples of sub-Saharans in Tunisia who were accorded the highest form of respect in the context of Tunisian popular Islam. Even within the "White" *silsila*, we have a sub-Saharan–North African Islamic border crossing of profound significance for the integration of slaves into the fabric of local religious praxis.

Il-Kḥūl ("the Blacks")

It may be useful to begin with what the spirits are not, at least in how they are understood within the *sṭambēlī* context, and, more specifically, at Dār Bārnū. They are not the spirits of "African" ancestors. In fact, they are not of human origin. They are not the anthropomorphic spirits of objects and places, nor are they the totems of "clans," although several spirits imported from the *bori* system bear names that identify them as part of the totemic system of the Hausa-speaking Magazuwa. While many *sṭambēlī* spirits are related to those of the Hausa *bori* pantheon, a relationship made explicit by *sṭambēlī* participants themselves, they were not simply relocated to Tunisia. Some spirits disappeared, while others emerged. The latter, as well as those that remained, were reinterpreted within a new cosmological framework. While there are certain continuities with the *bori* ritual system, new functions and meanings associated with the spirits emerged in the Tunisian context.

Most important, in terms of *sṭambēlī* practitioners' religious sensibilities, the spirits are also not the *jinn*, or *jnūn*, of which the Qur'ān speaks, whose existence was acknowledged by the Prophet. The *jinn* are mostly nameless beings born of fire who seek to bring calamity on humans. While they are exorcised in rituals across the Islamic world, engaging in such rituals is often considered sacrilegious. Within the *sṭambēlī* community, the *jinn* are understood as "working for the devil," and willfully interacting with them would thus constitute *shirk*, the polytheistic act of creating or supporting one of God's rivals. In contrast, *sṭambēlī* spirits and saints all "work for God" in a relationship often described as analogous to that of ministers serving their president. A telling example of the importance of the distinction between *sṭambēlī* spirits and the *jinn* is found in the instructions given to a client who is starting her *sṭambēlī* healing process. While Muslims often utter the word "bismillāh" (in the name of God) to protect themselves from the *jinn* in transitional situations (such as upon entering a room or lighting a fire or incense), *sṭambēlī* clients are carefully instructed *not* to say "bismillāh" before lighting their incense because the spirits might be offended by being confused with the *jinn*. *Sṭambēlī* cannot heal those afflicted by the *jinn*, and its practitioners readily acknowledge the existence of spirits such as the *jinn* that are beyond their ritual reach.[13]

The *sṭambēlī* spirits are referred to in a variety of terms. At Dār Bārnū, the collective terms in use are (1) *in-nās il-ukhrīn*, or "the other people"; (2) *iṣ-ṣālḥīn* (sing. *ṣāliḥ*), or "the holy ones";[14] and (3)*il-kḥūl* (sing. *ākḥal*), or "the Blacks." While the terms are often used somewhat interchangeably, each one points to a nuance of identity that no single term alone can encompass. The first term, *in-nās il-ukhrīn*, is the most general of the three and indicates that the spirits are humanlike actors. Indeed, they are understood to be like humans in many ways. Each has a distinct personality with certain tendencies, desires, and idiosyncrasies. Their behaviors, like those of humans, can be surprising, even to their hosts. They are gendered, have spouses and offspring, and are organized into families. The second term, *iṣ-ṣālḥīn*, is slightly more specific, and defines the spirits as distinct from both the *jnūn* and the *awliyā'*. With regard to the latter, however, *iṣ-ṣālḥīn* also situates the spirits on the same level of power and respect as the saints. To be called a *ṣāliḥ* is to be considered a spiritual power within the socioreligious framework of Tunisian society. This term thus situates the spirits on equal footing with the saints. The third term, *il-kḥūl*, is more specific still. It marks the spirits as "Black," in contradistinction to the "White" saints. The spirits, as opposed to the saints, are unequivocally sub-Saharan and Black. Through this terminology, we see that the spirits are holy, they are Black, and they are other.

The main categories of *sṭambēlī* spirits in the Dār Bārnū tradition are Banū Kūrī (Kūrī's Children or Kūrī's Tribe), Baḥriyya (Water spirits), and Bēyāt (Royalty). There are two other groups, the Brāwna ("from Bornu") and the Sghār (Children), which are composed of spirits that are often subsumed under the Banū Kūrī and the Bēyēt, respectively. While all the categories of spirits are understood as originating in sub-Saharan Africa, each one represents a different set of relations between sub-Saharan and North Africas. The "blackness" of Banū Kūrī is emphasized in ritual, they are understood to be Christian, and, as they have no parallels in Tunisian cosmology (as do the Baḥriyya) or references to official Tunisian history (as do the Bēyēt), are the most other of the groups. The Baḥriyya reveal parallels between the sub-Saharan and North African conceptions of spirits: these water spirits of sub-Saharan Africa required little or no modification to enter into the cosmological framework of North African Islam, which holds similar assumptions about the presence of potentially malevolent spirits in and around water. Finally, the Bēyēt provide a powerful commentary on Tunisian history: the arrival of the Bēyēt spirits corresponds directly to the decline of the Husaynid regime that ruled Tunis and the subsequent suppression, after their departure, of *sṭambēlī* and other popular spiritual practices under nationalist regimes. It is not my aim to present an exhaustive inventory of spirits, but rather to sketch the main characteristics of the groups and how they signify in the *sṭambēlī* context, since musicians must act upon this knowledge as they progressively disclose the pantheon membership, with its historical and geocultural referents, to their clients and other members of the ritual gathering.

A caveat is in order before moving on to the organization of the spirits of the pantheon. While each spirit group has a few core members whose identities are definitive of their group, the categories can be somewhat porous or overlapping. While in some instances this apparent flexibility may simply be the product of informants' varying levels of knowledge, generally speaking it highlights the fact that spirits (and some saints, for that matter), may have multiple memberships in different categories. It is the relationships among spirits that are performed in the *silsila*s, rather than strict adherence to a single, rigid order. For example, Ummī Yenna is often described as a member of the Baḥriyya, but Bābā Majīd usually performs her *nūba* with those of her husband Kūrī's family in the Banū Kūrī, while others situate her along with her daughters in the Bēyēt. Moreover, specific spirits may have differing attributes specific to the particular *sṭambēlī* troupe's tradition. This is not to suggest that the spirits are open to any interpretation, or rather, that alternative interpretations are not contested. In an interview filmed in the documentary *Stambali: Un rite Africain en Tunisie*, a male *ʿarīfa*, possessed by May Gājiya, describes her effect on him: "She is a lunatic woman. She makes me act crazy." The Dār Bārnū folks see this as indication of the illegitimacy of this *ʿarīfa*'s work. "May Gājiya cannot act like that," I was told, "because she is one of the Bēyēt. They are good and proper."

TABLE 2. The *silsilas* of the spirits

Banū Kūrī	*Brāwnā*	*Baḥriyya*	*Bēyēt*	*Sghār*
Sārkin Kūfa	Gindīma	Ummī Yenna	Maʿllem Sofū	Sayyed
Dundurūsū	Yakba	Jawayay	Lawra	May Nasra
Ḥaddād	Jato	Bābā Mūsa	Bābā Ndūzū	Miryamū
Garūjī	Ubāna	Mūlay Brāhīm	May Gājiya	Nana ʿAysha
Dakākī	Guwaray	Sārkin Gārī	May Ftīla	Sīwa
Kūrī	Megrū	Baḥriyya	Jījī	
Yā Arnawēt	Tatanī	Bakaba	Sīdī ʿAlī Dīwān	
Migzū	Baybay	Derna	Irzīqī	
Jamarkay	Sīwa	Badaydū	Yā Rīma	
Bābā Magojay		May Saderwa	May Aska	
Nikīrī			Badawrī	
Kūmār Karkajī				
Wada				
Yarga Yarga				
Danīlya				
Jīgū				

BANŪ KŪRĪ: CONNECTING DĀR BĀRNŪ TO BORNU

The Banū Kūrī family's membership (see table 2) reveals a direct link to Hausa *bori* traditions in sub-Saharan Africa. These spirits, like a large proportion of slaves that landed in Tunis, are from the Bornu region of sub-Saharan Africa and, like their displaced human counterparts from that region, have been especially active at Dār Bārnū.[15] There is also a subsection of this group that is referred to specifically as Brāwna (the plural of *barnāwī*). Because of this close relationship with the Dār Bārnū tradition—and because they afflict certain members of the Dār Bārnū household—the Banū Kūrī must be invoked in all ceremonies performed by the Dār Bārnū troupe, even if there is no adept afflicted by one of the spirits in the group. The Banū Kūrī spirits are all Christians (*masīḥiyyīn*) and must be invoked after sunset, ideally after midnight. Black is of high symbolic import: something black (usually *mlūkhiyya*, a dish characterized by its dark-colored sauce made from powdered jute) must be eaten, and the dancer must wear a hooded black cloak (*kashabiyya*). These spirits can be violent, and several beat their hosts with rods or clubs. Collectively, they are considered the most powerful of the spirits at Dār Bārnū; indeed, one room at Dār Bārnū traditionally houses ritual paraphernalia dedicated to Kūrī.

The *silsila* typically "opens" with the *nūba* for Māshī (also called Istiftāḥ il-Kḥūl, lit. "opening of the Blacks") before invoking Sārkin Kūfa, a spirit as dangerous and unpopular today as he was when Tremearne (1914: 298–299) described him as such nearly a century ago. Bābā Majīd characterized Sārkin Kūfa as "intolerant," and, although *sṭambēlī* musicians are obliged to play his *nūba*, I did not encounter a single instance of anyone possessed by Sārkin Kūfa in my eight years of studying *'sṭambēlī*. Dundurūsū (Hausa: "hammer") and Ḥaddād (Arabic: "blacksmith"), both identified as blacksmiths, come next, followed by Garūjī, originally a Hausa *bori* fighting spirit (Tremearne 1914: 360).

The following spirits, namely, Dakākī, Kūrī, Migzū, Jamarkay, and Bābā Magojay, are the definitive spirits of the Banū Kūrī. They possess more initiates than do other spirits in the family, and in some ceremonies I attended they were the only Banū Kūrī spirits summoned. As is true of other spirit families, when an adept of the Banū Kūrī group dances, she dances to and is possessed by several spirits in succession. The host wears a black *kashabiyya* when she or he is possessed by any of these five spirits, beginning with Dakākī, "the crawler" (a.k.a. Mai-Ja-Chikki, "drawer along on the stomach," in the *bori* context), who dances by squirming in a prone position on the ground, gradually advancing toward the *gumbrī*.[16] Once he reaches the *gumbrī*, it is Kūrī's turn to enter. Kūrī (Hausa: "hyena") is known as a spirit that enjoys drinking wine. In the past, his hosts would often take swigs of wine while possessed. At the time of my research, those afflicted by Kūrī would instead make wine part of their sacrifice to him by pouring a bottle of red wine at a four-way crossroads as an offering. In the Songhay context, Kūrī is a Hausa spirit, and the four-way crossroads represents the intersection of social and spirit worlds (Stoller 1989). Kūrī begins his dance on his knees, reaching up into the air with each hand, alternately, as if climbing. After this strenuous episode, he will fall back and request his wooden pestle, which he uses to beat the head and stomach of his host. Next comes Migzū, a brother of Kūrī, who dances in a manner similar to Kūrī's but beats his host with a walking stick rather than a pestle. Following these (without stopping, but with an abrupt change in rhythm) are Kūrī's brother Jamarkay (Jam Maraki, "the white *maraki* tree," in Hausa) and Bābā Magojay (or Ba Maguje in Hausaland).[17] The mutual proximity of these spirits is a consistent feature of the *bori* pantheon in sub-Saharan Africa: Kūrī and Jamarkay are adjacent in *bori* rituals in Katsina (King 1966) and Maradi (Erlmann and Magagi 1989) and cohabit the same spirit house in Kano (Besmer 1983).

I was told that Yā Arnawēt, a rarely performed *nūba*, is situated in this part of the *silsila*. The name refers to a subgroup of spirits called the Arnawēt (lit. "those of Arnī," Arnī being a spirit originally from the *bori* pantheon) but is not usually differentiated from the Banū Kūrī at Dār Bārnū. The only time Bābā Majīd spoke to me of the Arnawēt was in response to a direct question I posed to him. He referred me back to the list of Banū Kūrī spirits he had previously dictated to me and singled out Kūrī, Migzū, Jamarkay, Bābā Magojay, Nikīrī, Sayyed, and Salama as "also" Arnawēt.[18]

Bābā Majīd usually ended the Banū Kūrī *silsila* with Ummī Yenna (a.k.a.

Mai-Inna or Doguwa in Hausaland) and her sisters. Ummī Yenna is Kūrī's wife, and her host sits on the ground, covered by a white cloth. Four women each take one corner of the cloth and beat it up and down in time with the music. When the music stops, the host usually emerges from this speaking as Ummī Yenna, divining the futures of those present. When the consultations are completed, the *silsila* begins again, this time with Ummī Yenna's sisters Māmā Zahra and Adama. Other spirits in this *silsila* include Nikīrī (Kūrī's brother, who hits his host with a club with a hooked end), Salama, and Sayyed. The latter spirit is the youngest of the family and often instead appears at the end of the ceremony to begin the *silsila* for the Sghār spirits. Less frequently appearing *nūba*s, including Kumār Karkajī, Wādā, Yarga Yarga, Danīlya, and Jīgū, are often classified as Banū Kūrī as well. The Brāwnā spirits, whose *nūba*s may be performed as a separate *silsila* or incorporated into the Banū Kūrī *silsila*, include Gindīma, Yakba, Jato, Ubana, Guwaray, Megrū, Tatanī (*tatanī* is Kanuri for "my child"), Baybay, and Sīwa.

BAḤRIYYA (WATER SPIRITS): TRANS-SAHARAN CONTINUITIES

The Baḥriyya are spirits that reside in or around water. This includes not only seas, rivers, and lakes, but also wells, drains, bathtubs, water closets, and the like. Baḥriyya often afflict those whose work involves water, such as fishermen, Turkish bath attendants, and maids. When involved in ritualized possession, a Baḥriyya spirit can be coaxed out of its host only by the *ʿarīfa* sprinkling water on the neck and head of the host. The Baḥriyya are led by Mūlay Brāhīm (Lord Ibrahim), who is also known as Dodo Ibrahim, *dodo* referring, in the Hausa language, to evil spirits in general, but also to "a chief, a European, or anything feared" (Bargery 1934: 262). At Dār Bārnū he is also known as Sārkin Kaʿba (sometimes Sārkin Kaʿbī). He, along with several other Baḥriyya spirits, dances in a swimming motion. His *nūba* follows that of Jawayay (while Ṣālaḥ Warglī, the current yinna of the Dār Bārnū troupe, puts Ummī Yenna at the beginning of the Baḥriyya *silsila*, Bābā Majīd insisted that Jawayay is the first *nūba* of the Baḥriyya), and, if played, the *nūba* of Badam Khiyārū, which serves as an opening to the *silsila*. Mūlay Brāhīm is usually followed by Baḥriyya (the name of a spirit as well as the family), Bakaba, and Sārkin Garī (see chap. 6 for more detail). This group also includes May Saderwa (Mūlay Brāhīm's mother), Sīdī ʿAlī Dīwān (also described as a hunter), Bābā Mūsā (or Mūsā Baḥriyya), Lilla Malīka, Derna, and Badaydū.

Water spirits, whether associated with rainfall, streams, rivers, lakes, or the sea, are ubiquitous in spirit pantheons across West, central, and East Africa. In North Africa, fishermen and other seafarers often make sacrifices to water spirits or Muslim saints with special connections to water such as Sīdī Manṣūr or Sīdī Dāwd.[19] Carelessness with water (e.g., disposing of hot water by pouring it on the ground or down the drain without uttering "bismillāh") is one of the most common ways of inviting affliction by spirits. Although he is part of the White *silsila*, Sīdī Manṣūr, who is known as a protector of those stricken by water-related afflictions, frequently appears just before or after the Baḥriyya *silsila*.

BĒYĒT (ROYALTY): TRANS-SAHARAN TRANSFORMATIONS

The category of Bēyēt (the Beys, or rulers of Ottoman Tunisia) invokes the historical era of Husaynid Tunisia. Although their names are often easily traceable to the *bori* pantheon, their identities and meanings have become distinctly Tunisian. Unlike the members of the Banū Kūrī or the Baḥriyya, several of the Hausa Muslim spirits outlined by Tremearne have been reinterpreted and reclassified into this category, which is an important one at Dār Bārnū. At the time of Tremearne's study in 1914, May Nasra was one of the "Little Spots," so classified due to his penchant for causing smallpox, sore eyes, and rashes. He was also characterized by holding a large spear. Today, May Nasra wears a tarboosh, carries a *lūḥa* (schoolchild's chalkboard), and complains of problems in school. Such a change in identity suggests that *sṭambēlī* is a dynamic practice that adapts to changing social circumstances and individual needs. Here there is a parallel with Sudanese *ṭumbura*: in both traditions, the Ottoman rulers were the main slaveholders but are remembered positively because they fought on behalf of the slaves (in *ṭumbura*) and abolished slavery and supported the free black community (in *sṭambēlī*).

The oral history at Dār Bārnū exhibits a great deal of nostalgia for the late Husaynid Dynasty, which is referred to simply as the "time of the beys" (*waqt il-bēyēt*). It was during this time that slavery was abolished, the black community had a political voice, and *sṭambēlī* was not only tolerated, but even supported by the ruling regime (see chap. 2). This era ended abruptly in 1956, on the eve of Tunisian independence from France. Ever since, Tunisian politics and society have been concerned with connecting the country's aspirations to Western models of developmental modernism while defining its heritage in terms of its Arab-Islamic history, traced to the Middle East. Tunisia's history of interaction with continental Africa—and slavery, for that matter—has been minimized, even erased from dominant narratives of national identity. In stark contrast, according to Bābā Majīd, the beys recognized "that Tunisia is part of Africa."

The Bēyēt *silsila* begins with Maʿllem Sofū, followed by Lawra, Bābā

Ndūzū, May Gājiya, May Ftīla, and Jījī. Most wear a red tarboosh, a marker of Ottoman or Husaynid nobility. Yā Rīma (also known as Yā Rimshī or Sīdī Rīma; a.k.a. Dan Galadima in Hausaland) presides over the assembly seated in a chair; he wears luxurious silken robes and smokes a cigarette from a long holder. His sister May Gājiya sits cross-legged under a yellow *sunjuq*, crying out and stabbing herself with wooden daggers. Irzīqī, Kulayta, Badawrī, and Matango are spirits in this *silsila* that appear less frequently. May Nasra and Gindīma may be classified with the Bēyēt, but their location within the Sghār and Brāwnā families, respectively, are more often emphasized.

The final two *nūba*s of Dār Bārnū *sṭambēlī* ceremonies are those of Miryamū and Nana ʿAysha, two of Ummī Yenna's daughters who are also understood as the first spirits of the Sghār. Nana ʿAysha is associated with treating women's sterility, while Miryamū helps women find suitable husbands. These two spirits in particular are described at Dār Bārnū as exemplifying the closeness and compatibility of Christianity and Islam; I was reminded several times that just as Miryamū (Mary) is a central figure in the former, ʿAysha, one of the Prophet's wives, is an important figure in Islam. ʿArabiyya and Māmā Zahra are also part of this *silsila*, and Sayyed, Sīwa, and May Nasra, as the youngest in their families, are also considered Sghār spirits.

Just before the *nūba* of Miryamū, a large, decorated bowl of sweets is brought in front of the *gumbrī* and covered with a cloth. Miryamu and ʿAysha descend into their host's body in order to bless the sweets, which are distributed to all attendees by members of the group, sometimes being tossed into the audience, where children scramble to gather as many as possible. While the distribution of sweets is a moment that everyone looks forward to and ends the ceremony with a sense of celebration, this closing episode has much deeper symbolic import: by presiding over the sweets and distributing them to all, Miryamu and ʿAysha recreate the generosity of the beys, who would reward the *sṭambēlī* community each holiday with food, gifts, and money.

It is clear from my experience inside the Dār Bārnū community that the historical narrative of *waqt il-bēyēt* is a strategy for implicitly criticizing subsequent Tunisian social changes and political regimes. *Sṭambēlī*'s counterhistories employ a particular reading of the past in order to come to terms with a discomfiting present. The beys were everything that subsequent ruling regimes were not: supportive of the black community not only culturally, but also socially, politically, and economically.

Embodying Histories and Geographies

The embodiment of spirit possession is not only about "becoming" other, but also about evoking and redefining relations with others. The trans-Saharan routes that carried sub-Saharan slaves into North Africa also prompted the crossing of the Sahara by members of the spirit world. The presence of sub-Saharan spirits in the communal houses was not simply a matter of maintaining preexisting human-spirit relationships in a new setting. These spirits, and their ensuing encounter with Muslim saints, helped shape the geocultural encounter of sub-Saharans with Arab Tunisians in terms other than those of slavery and servitude. Spirit possession rituals, then, are about far more than spiritual encounter alone.

In this chapter I have sketched a maximally inclusive paradigm of *sṭambēlī* performance, through which the *sṭambēlī* pantheon is organized and made publicly accessible. The routes from sub-Saharan to North Africa are performed via the musical routes followed in ritual performance. Although it is, in part, the otherness of *sṭambēlī* that makes it appealing to Tunisians and efficacious in treating affliction by sub-Saharan spirits, the structure of the music ritually negotiates that difference by charting geocultural connections between sub-Saharan spirit possession practices and North African Islam. *Sṭambēlī* is a product of, and a commentary on, the historical encounter between sub-Saharan and North Africa. The composition of the *sṭambēlī* pantheon, and how it is understood by *sṭambēlī* practitioners, shows that much of the cultural work of *sṭambēlī* is concerned with making connections between these two Africas rather than setting them apart. It is, however, in the aesthetics of *sṭambēlī* ritual that sub-Saharan-ness is celebrated as providing an aural and visceral space in which these two Africas can converge. It is to these aesthetics that I now turn.

PART II

Musical Aesthetics and Ritual Dynamics

CHAPTER FOUR

Voices of Ritual Authority

MUSICIANS, INSTRUMENTS, AND VOCALITY

The capacity of the *gumbrī* to communicate with the sacred and facilitate the metaphysical encounter between human and spirit worlds is at the ontological foundation of *sṭambēlī*. More specifically, it is the music (*mūsīqā*), defined as the *gumbrī* melody, that *sṭambēlī* musicians and clients alike identify as the active agent in communicating with the members of the *sṭambēlī* pantheon. Its privileged role means that it can be played only by the *yinna*, the master musician and main ritual authority in *sṭambēlī*.[1] He may also be referred to by the honorific *mʿallim* (master), a term used to signify accomplished musicians and other artists. By definition he is the leader of the *sṭambēlī* troupe and mentor to the *ṣunnāʿ* (also referred to as *shqāshiqiyya*), the usually younger musicians who play the *shqāshiq* and constitute the responsorial chorus. At Dār Bārnū, the *yinna* sometimes diagnoses the afflicted, selects proper medicines, and determines the appropriate ritual procedures. In ritual, he structures the ceremony through the selection and ordering of *nūba*s, marking their beginnings and endings, and responds to the sometimes unpredictable behavior of spirits and dancers.

In performance, the *yinna* is flanked on both sides by the *ṣunnāʿ*.[2] While the *yinna* has authority over the *ṣunnāʿ*, there is also an informal hierarchy among the latter. To the immediate right of the *yinna* normally sits the most accomplished and knowledgeable of the *ṣunnāʿ*; he is usually the lead singer, although the *yinna* will often sing lead on several *nūba*s. The rest of the *ṣunnāʿ* respond to the lead lines with unison responses. The *ṣunnāʿ* are also responsible for preparing many of the components of the ritual, such as lighting appropriate incense, retrieving accoutrements for dancers, and sometimes slaughtering sacrificial animals.

The *ṣunnāʿ* receive their musical and ritual training from the *yinna*, who typically nurtures their development over a number of years. At Dār Bārnū, they are expected to refer to the *yinna*, who is usually elder, as *bābā* (father), while *sṭambēlī* musicians who are not regular members of his troupe may instead call him *khālī* (maternal uncle).[3] The *ṣunnāʿ*, in turn, are usually treated as family at Dār Bārnū. Their acquisition of *sṭambēlī* knowledge typically begins with attendance at ceremonies, where they may be relegated to a limited supporting role. Through imitating the *shqāshiq* patterns and responsorial singing of the rest of the troupe, they pick up the aural and embodied knowledge performed by the other musicians. As they become more and more competent, they may be invited to fill in for one of the other *ṣunnāʿ* on occasion, and if they demonstrate some talent and reliability, they become part of a short list from which the *yinna* will select his *ṣunnāʿ* for future ceremonies.

Bābā Majīd grew up listening to his father playing the *gumbrī* with his troupe at Dār Bārnū. As a youngster, he built a small *gumbrī* that he would play every day, often falling asleep at night with it still in his lap. At the time, there were many *yinna*s and other *sṭambēlī* musicians who lived in or frequented Dār Bārnū. Bābā Majīd remembers them as being highly possessive of their ritual knowledge and reluctant to pass it on to him and other novices. He contrasts this reluctance of the "African" elders to teach others with his own desire to impart his knowledge to his *ṣunnāʿ*. He often conveyed his frustration at what he perceived as their unwillingness to take the time to learn properly. "I say, 'Here—take [this knowledge] from me,' but they don't want to learn," he told me. "Every house has its rent," he would also say, referring to the investment of time and effort necessary to acquire the appropriate knowledge.

Since his elders were not forthcoming with their knowledge, Bābā Majīd learned discreetly, paying close attention to the *gumbrī* during the ceremonies that were virtually a part of everyday life at Dār Bārnū. He would sing the melodies to himself until he was free to pick up his *gumbrī* after the ceremony to try to figure them out on the instrument. Frequent *sṭambēlī* activity at Dār Bārnū enabled Bābā Majīd in his younger days to observe different approaches to playing the *gumbrī* and leading *sṭambēlī* rituals. He emphasized that a *yinna*'s musical knowledge is in large part a product of the abilities of his predecessors, acknowledging Muḥammad Yinna, Fanūn Yinna, Dada Yinna, Frej Yinna, Frej Wazīr, and Muḥammad Khadīja as his main influences. "Each one had his own style," he told me. "I combined from all of them." After years of observing the *yinna*s, mimicking their playing, and absorbing their ritual knowledge, Bābā Majīd started correcting some of the other players' playing and was finally invited by the elders to take part in their ceremonies, where he would sing and play *shqāshiq*, until little by little they allowed him to play *gumbrī* in ritual situations.

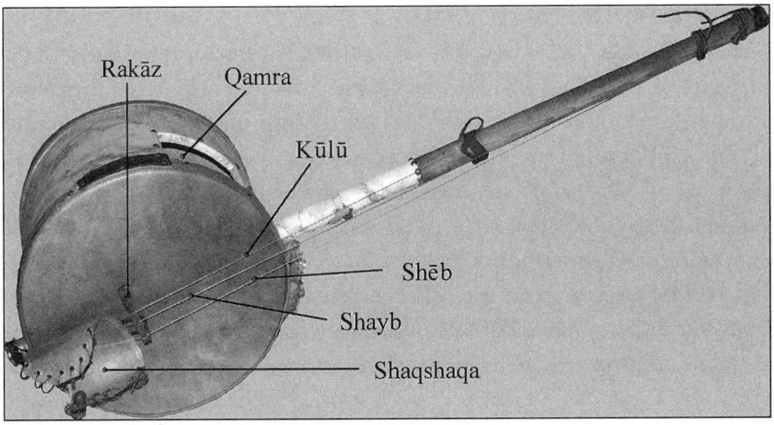

FIGURE 6. Components of the *gumbrī*.

The *Gumbrī*

THE INSTRUMENT

The *gumbrī* is a three-stringed, bass-register plucked lute with a cylindrical body typically fashioned from several plies of wood (fig. 6); *gumbrī*s made from a single piece of wood, carved from a tree trunk, are now rare. For a few years in the mid-twentieth century, round wooden boxes used to import Italian cookies were occasionally used. Tom-toms from Western drum kits are sometimes used to make "modern" (*ʿaṣrī*) *gumbrī*s, though they are not used in ritual situations. A smaller version of the instrument, called *gumbrī dhaʿīf*, was once used for certain ceremonies and street processions but is now relegated to use as a practice instrument.

A goatskin drumhead (*jild*; lit. "skin") is stretched tightly across the body of the *gumbrī*, fastened with glue and small nails. A typical *gumbrī* has a body diameter of about fifteen inches and a depth of twelve; the total length is about forty-four inches. The neck (*yidd*; lit. "arm") fully transpierces the body. A rectangular sound hole (*qamra*; lit. "moon") is carved into the side of the body facing the performer. It is through the *qamra* that the *yinna* can access the items stored inside the body of *gumbrī*, including a number of amulets and charms, spare instrument parts, and any monetary offerings (*rishq*) made to the musicians and put away for safe keeping.[4] The strings (*awtār*; sing. *watr*) are attached to the neck by thin leather straps (*fudha*), which are loosened, moved up or down the neck, and then retightened to tune the instrument. A small wooden bridge (*rakāz*; lit. "support"),[5] with a groove for each string carved into the top, suspends the strings above the drumhead. Just behind the bridge sits a thin, curved metallic resonating plate (*shaqshaqa*; lit. "shaker"), which is pierced by numerous metallic rings, many of which hold metal amulets. It is secured snugly between the center string below and the two other strings above, ensuring that a buzzing sound accompanies every articulation of each string. In between performances, the *rakāz* and *shaqshaqa* are stored inside the body of the *gumbrī*, accessed through the sound hole.

The *gumbrī*'s appearance is highly valued, and a great deal of time and effort is spent by performers personalizing their instruments through decoration. The body is often ornately painted. Cowry shells, which provide a clear visual connection to sub-Saharan Africa, are often conspicuously attached to the body. The drumhead, even though it needs to be replaced at least once each year, may also be decorated, often with paint, henna, or *ḥarqūs* (black body paint used to decorate the hands and feet of brides). Numerous auspicious metallic charms adorn the *shaqshaqa*. These include miniature figures representing fish, the Qurʿān, and the hand of Fāṭima, all of which are traditionally used to bring good luck and ward off the "evil eye."

Similar spiked, long-necked, plucked lutes are found across West Africa, where they take a variety of forms and appellations.[6] Lutes similar to the *gumbrī*, which have cylindrical bodies fully transpierced by the neck of the instrument, are most prominent in the Lake Chad area (Blench 1984: 170), Tunisia's main source of slaves. The *gumbrī*, which today is the only stringed instrument used in *sṭambēlī* in Tunis, was also the main ritual instrument used at Dār Kūfa—the communal house visited by all the other houses—according to the earliest descriptions of *sṭambēlī*, in 1808, where it is described as a sacred instrument, honored by *sṭambēlī* practitioners with votive offerings and sacrifices (Montana 2004a: 181). A large proportion of slaves came from Hausa-speaking areas where similar instruments also abound. While the two-stringed Hausa *gumri* may be etymologically related to the *gumbrī*, the three-stringed *molo* is more similar to the *gumbrī* in morphology and performance technique (see Ames and King 1971: 46–47).[7]

The *gumbrī* is the instrument that "speaks" (*yitkallem*) to the spirits and entices them (*yijbidhum*, lit. "pulls them") into the ceremony. This communicatory function is reflected in the prominence of the metaphor of the voice in describing its components and playing technique. By striking a string, the right hand is said to "speak" (*yaʿṭīk il-klām*, lit. "gives you the words") while the left hand "answers" (*yjāwbik*) by moving to the appropriate place on the neck to press down on the string, determining the pitch of the note. The lowest-pitched string is called *shayb* (old man), since it speaks in a low voice. The next string, tuned a fourth above the *shayb*, is called *shēb* (youngster), for it speaks at a higher pitch. The third string, an octave above the *shayb*, is called *kūlū*, which was described to me as a sub-Saharan term that translates into the Arabic *rdād*, or "the one who answers or replies."[8] The *kūlū* extends about halfway up the neck of the *gumbrī*, much like the upper string of the banjo. Unlike the other strings, the *kūlū* is always played open, without the fingers stopping the string on the neck. It not only provides depth to the *shayb* when the two are played together to produce an octave simultaneity, but also serves as a note in its own right, forming the upper limit of the *gumbrī*'s octave range. The *kūlū* often fills in the space between other notes, providing a dronelike effect that may reinforce a sense of tonicity (see chap. 5).

TIMBRE AND TECHNIQUE

The characteristic sound of the *gumbrī* comes from a layering of three sonic elements: vibration of the strings, reverberations of the skin of the instrument, and the rattling of the resonating metal plate attached to the strings. A distinct buzzing sound produced by the *shaqshaqa* accompanies every strum of a string and each strike of the drumhead. The vibrations of the strings and the drumhead produce a sympathetic resonance that rattles the multitude (between sixteen and twenty-four) of metal rings that pierce this thin metal resonating plate. The intentional superimposition of noise and tone, which is a defining feature of numerous African musics, can take several forms. Cornelia Fales and Stephen McAdams (1994) classify these noise-tone relationships at three levels: fusion (the noise and tone are perceptually inseparable), layering (the noise and tone are mutually distinguishable), and masking (the noise covers up the tone). The *gumbrī* aesthetic corresponds most closely to the "layering" classification, and it is this dynamic that is implied by musicians' discourse. Bābā Majīd often spoke of the "true" sounds of the *gumbrī* in terms of the appropriate balance among the strings, *shaqshaqa*, and drumhead. Unlike the strings and drumhead, however, the *shaqshaqa* is only indirectly controlled by the performer, thus resulting in a "rich . . . aperiodic complexity" (Fales and McAdams 1994: 69). Requisite accents of certain notes, usually accompanied by strikes on the drumhead, increase the volume and lengthen the decay of some sympathetic resonances while maintaining the continuous buzz characteristic of the *gumbrī*'s sound. The synergy between the strings, drumhead, and *shaqshaqa* results in a timbral density at the micro level (individual notes), which in turn contributes to a textural density at the macro level (ensemble performance). The buzzing not only adds a distinctive timbral quality to each articulation, but also sustains the sonic event of the stroke, lengthening the duration of each note, in effect filling in the aural-temporal space between articulations.[9]

Gumbrī technique is characterized by a remarkable economy of motion involving subtle finger techniques, such as hammer-ons, pull-offs, and left-hand plucking of open strings, that give the cyclic melody a flow that would be impossible if the fingers of the strumming hand alone articulated every note. Right-hand technique involves strumming the strings individually (in the case of two strings strummed simultaneously, it will always be the *shayb* and *kūlū* to produce an octave simultaneity) or strumming a string while striking the skin of the instrument. The thumb utilizes both upward and downward motions to strum the *kūlū* and *shayb* strings. The *shēb* is struck by the forefinger, just above the base of the fingernail, in a downward flicking motion. The middle and ring fingers are used to strike the drumhead just below the strings.

The left hand has only two positions on the neck of the *gumbrī*, which further contributes to the economy of motion. In the first position, closest to the end of the neck, the forefinger can stop the *shayb* to produce a minor second. In this position, the middle finger can also stop the *shēb* to produce an interval of a fifth. In the second position, about two to three inches higher up the neck, the middle finger can stop the string to produce a sixth. The *shēb*'s open note (played by either the right hand forefinger or the left hand middle finger) is a fourth above. Thus, there are a total of six pitches utilized (see ex. 1).

In addition to stopping the string against the neck as the right hand strums, left-hand technique also involves hammer-ons, pull-offs, and open-string strums. In the hammer-on, the forefinger (on the *shayb*) or the middle finger (on the *shēb*) presses down on the string immediately after that open string has been strummed by the right hand. The left hand, in effect, takes advantage of the vibrations of the open string struck by the right hand. This technique produces two notes in quick succession: that of the open string strummed by the right hand and the higher note produced by the left finger stopping the string against the neck. In the pull-off, the forefinger (on the *shayb*) or the middle finger (on the *shēb*) plucks the string away from the neck after sounding a note with the finger pressed against the string. The effect is basically the opposite of the hammer: here, the left hand sounds the open string shortly after playing a note further up the neck. The open-string strum of the left hand is similar to the pull-off, but since the left-hand finger is not already pressing against the string, there is less of a lateral plucking motion, and thus, it produces a slightly softer sound.

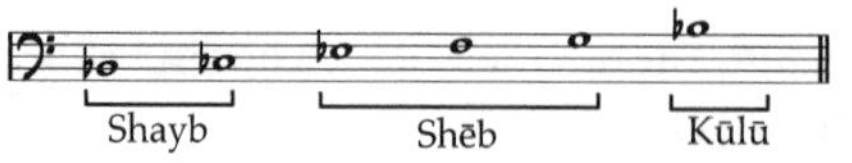

EXAMPLE 1. Pitches of the *gumbrī*

Gumbrī techniques on any given *nūba* typically involve most, if not all, of the following:

1 Up or down strums on the *shayb* and/or *kūlū* (right thumb)
2 Downward strokes on the *shēb* (right index finger)
3 Open-string plucks on the *shēb* (left middle finger)
4 Hammer-ons on the *shayb* (left index finger) or *shēb* (left middle finger)
5 Pull-offs on the *shayb* (left index finger) or *shēb* (left middle finger)
6 Strokes on the drumhead (right middle and ring fingers; usually with simultaneous strumming of a string)

These techniques are not optional or utilized at the players' discretion. Rather, they are fundamental to the *nūba*'s identity. To substitute, for example, a left-hand pull-off with a right-hand strum—which would result in the "same" note, at least in terms of pitch—would be considered incorrect at least, and most likely unacceptable. Although the pitch of the two notes would be identical, the volume, sharpness, and duration of the note produced by the right-hand strum could all differ from those of the left-hand pull-off. Moreover, because the hands or fingers would then be out of position, that substitution would probably jeopardize the proper articulation of any subsequent note(s). By altering note durations and patterns of accenting, such substitutions of technique could therefore alter the sonic contour of the *nūba*. Moreover, by undermining the physical economy built into the *nūba*, they might also make it difficult for the performer to play the cycle over and over without experiencing fatigue sooner than desired. Considering that some *nūba*s may be played for over ten minutes, and most ceremonies involve dozens of *nūba*s, this is not an insignificant matter. To put it another way, the physical pattern of finger and hand motions that provide the conditions for the melody is also a defining feature of that melody.

Bābā Majīd emphasized the interdependence of the parts of the body, taking care to explain that each arm must be positioned correctly in order for the hands to move efficiently, so that the fingers can be positioned correctly. In our discussions about the responsibilities of the *yinna*, and in his criticisms of the impatient *ṣunnāʿ* attempting to become *yinna*s, Bābā stressed the importance of the subtleties of *gumbrī* technique, which should result in a seamless flow of sound. He suggested that inexperienced players strike the skin of the *gumbrī* too hard, interrupting the ideal flow of the melody and masking the "true words" of the *gumbrī*. Sometimes Bābā was more blunt. "The *gumbrī* needs to speak," he once told me in reference to younger players' tendency to smack the skin of the *gumbrī* too hard, "not scream in pain."

John Baily has shown how the ergonomics of playing the two-stringed

Herati *dutar* interface with the modal system of its traditional repertoire. He notes that the melodic features of that repertoire, in conjunction with the morphology of the instrument, produce fewer hand movements in relation to finger movements (Baily 1977: 313). Similarly, the pentatonic mode, the often stepwise motion of the melody, and the ergonomic economy of motion in *gumbrī* technique produce what Baily would call "good gestalts" (Baily 1977: 318), which seem well suited to the repetitions of cyclic music and a large repertoire of tunes based on short pentatonic melodies.

This is especially important because the *nūba* is defined, first and foremost, by the melody played by the *gumbrī*. Without this melody, the words praising the spirit would be inconsequential, since the spirit would not appear without hearing its tune on the *gumbrī*.[10] Lyrics and vocal melodies can, in theory, be altered, though there are rarely any changes more radical than inserting more or less conventional melodic variations or lyrical substitutions that remain consistent with the objective of praising the saint or spirit. The *gumbrī*, in fact, can communicate with the spirits without any vocals or *shqāshiq* accompanying it, as is the case with divination sessions (see chap. 6). A *nūba* performed in a possession ceremony, however, is not considered complete without the *shqāshiq*, and although the *gumbrī* melody alone might attract a spirit to descend, without the *shqāshiq* it is unlikely that the spirit would remain for long, or become placated, since the spirits prefer to dance to the full ensemble. Despite—or perhaps because of—the importance of the *gumbrī* line, it is often the case that it is barely audible for those situated far away from the ritual area, as the overpowering volume of the multiple *shqāshiq* often obscures the intricacies of the *gumbrī* melodies.[11] That being said, I have often been amazed at how clearly Bābā Majīd's *gumbrī* lines could be heard from a variety of vantage points in and around the performance area (*mīdān*), without amplification, despite the high volume and large number of *shqāshiq* players.

The *Shqāshiq*

THE INSTRUMENT

The *shqāshiq* are metal clappers. Each set consists of four identical iron plates, two for each hand (see fig. 11 below). Two circular, convex domes protrude on the outer side of each figure-eight-shaped plate. Leather or string straps attached to the center of each plate fasten the *shqāshiq* to the hands. Each hand holds one plate fastened to the thumb and another to the ring and middle fingers. The basic playing technique produces sound through clashing two plates of the same hand against each other by opening and closing the hands. The result is a loud, metallic *shaqa-shaqa* (right-left, right-left), the inspiration behind its onomatopoetic name. The minimum number of *shqāshiq* players for a performance is two, which means that four pairs of *shqāshiq* are played simultaneously. Ideally, however, there should be at least four performers, two on each side of the *yinna*, while at the annual pilgrimage there may be several more.

Similar metal clappers also exist in sub-Saharan Africa, where, in contrast to the Maghrib (where they are associated exclusively with trance traditions of slaves and their descendants), they are played in a variety of musical contexts. Called *sambani* among the Hausa (Bargery 1934: 894), they, like the *bori* rituals they accompanied, were banned by Islamic authorities during the early Sokoto Empire, only to reemerge later as a women's instrument accompanying Islamic songs (Erlmann 1986). They are known by the same name among the Dagbamba of northern Ghana, where they are used for the dance musics of blacksmiths. Kenneth Gourlay speculates that "proto-clappers" made of wood or bone were brought from sub-Saharan Africa to the Maghrib, where blacksmiths—who were often black Africans in Maghribi society—introduced similar instruments forged from iron. From the Maghrib, he posits, the metal clappers were brought back to sub-Saharan Africa (Erlmann 1986: 14). Viviana Pâques reports that the first *shqāshiq* used in Tunis were made from the shoulder blades of an ostrich (Pâques 1964: 549).

TIMBRE AND TECHNIQUE

Shqāshiq technique capitalizes on the subtle differences in sound produced by combinations of open and closed positions, either by each pair independently, simultaneously, or one pair striking the other. In the case of the latter, further distinctions arise between strikes on the bell and on the lip of the instrument. A louder, more resonant sound is sometimes created by opening the hands as widely as possible after clenching the *shqāshiq* together. The opposite process—clenching them together tightly after opening the hands widely—may be employed when improvising to create a more pronounced sound that can cut through the others. The domes of one pair of *shqāshiq* are often struck against those of the other pair to produce accented articulations. At slower tempos, when one *shqāshiq* articulation may dissipate before the next, one pair of *shqāshiq* may be held so the plates touch slightly while the other pair strikes it with the bell, letting the struck pair sizzle (in a manner somewhat akin to what one might do with a Western high hat) before closing them. This technique contributes to a sense of continuous sonic motion by extending the duration of the sound event and filling in the aural-temporal space between articulations.

This last point is highlighted through a brief consideration of how the *ṣunnāʿ* perceive the difference between the Tunisian *shqāshiq* and their Moroccan counterpart, called *qrāqeb* (also *qrāqesh*, *qarqabū*), a similarly onomatopoetic appellation. Although at first glance they may appear virtually identical, subtle differences in morphology and performance practice differentiate the two. Tunisian *shqāshiq* are generally heavier than the Moroccan *qrāqeb*, and while the *shqāshiq* are fashioned in the shape of the figure eight, the *qrāqeb* might be described as resembling barbells, with a straight bar joining the two domed ends. Each pair of *qrāqeb* is also fastened together by a small metal clasp passing through a small hole drilled at the bottom of each plate. This restricts the movement of each plate away from the one fastened to it, limiting the volume each pair is capable of producing. Tunisian *shqāshiq*, in contrast, are not fastened together, and playing technique is geared toward maximizing reverberation and volume by allowing the plates to vibrate as freely as possible. Awareness of these regional differences has sharpened since some of the Dār Bārnū musicians performed at a festival in Morocco, where they encountered live *gnāwa* music for the first time. In the middle of a *nūba* we were playing during the annual pilgrimage, Belḥassen once turned to me and said, "No, not like the *gnāwa*, like this . . ." and demonstrated, in exaggerated fashion, how the hands need to open as far as possible to pull the plates far apart from each other between each articulation. They must also not be lined up precisely; Bābā Majīd not infrequently told his musicians to hold their *shqāshiq* slightly askew so that air did not become trapped between the plates, which would muffle the sound.

In performance, the positioning of the *shqāshiq* players approximates a semicircle in which they more or less face each other. The loud pulsations of their multiple *shqāshiq* produce layers of oscillating reverberations that intensify as one moves closer to the *mīdān*, where musicians, healers, and especially dancers are enveloped by this confluence of sonic activity. When *sṭambēlī* ceremonies take place inside a client's home or in the courtyard of a *zāwiya* or Dār Bārnū, the surrounding walls add to the saturation of space with sound, enabling all who attend to experience the ever-multiplying, overlapping metallic reverberations.

The *Ṭabla*

The *ṭabla* (pl. *ṭabālī*) is a double-headed barrel drum played with a straight drumstick and one open hand, both on the same side of the instrument. The drummer uses a stick in one hand to strike the drum near the center. These strokes can produce an open sound (by striking and releasing) and a closed sound (by pressing the stick against the drumhead). The other hand dangles over the top of the drum, striking the head near the rim.

The *ṭabla* is used in place of the *gumbrī* during ceremonies that begin before sunset, as the *gumbrī* is mainly reserved for evening and nighttime performance. The *ṭabla* fills the same role as the *gumbrī*: it "speaks" to the spirits; according to Bābā, "Whatever the *gumbrī* says, the *ṭabla* can say." The *ṭabla* rhythms for any *nūba*, in fact, are usually based on the rhythmic patterns of the *gumbrī* melody for the same *nūba*. In most cases, the open-hand strokes of the *ṭabla* fill in the spaces between the stick strokes in a manner analogous to the strumming of the *kūlū* string on the *gumbrī*. Like the *gumbrī*, it is also accompanied by *shqāshiq* and singing. The *ṭabla* also replaces the *gumbrī* during the *kharja*, or street procession, performed during the annual pilgrimage. In this context, it is slung over the shoulder with a leather or fabric strap.

The *ṭabla* is the only *sṭambēlī* instrument in common use that closely resembles those used in other Tunisian musics. It is similar to the Bedouin *ṭbal*, which typically accompanies the *zukra* (double-reed aerophone), and is also used in the *kharajāt* (street processions; sing. *kharja*) of some Sufi orders. The *ṭbal*, however, is played with two sticks. *Sṭambēlī* musicians also distinguish their *ṭabla* from the *ṭbal* in terms of performance practice: the *ṭabla* is played in a *sūdānī* manner that differentiates its aesthetic from that produced by similar drums in non-*sṭambēlī* contexts. Bābā Majīd sometimes derided inexperienced *ṣunnāʿ* for failing to produce such an aesthetic on the *ṭabla*. "You're playing *dūm-tek, dūm-tek*, like a *darbūkka*," I heard him tell one apprentice. "You need to be playing *dauw-shteka, dauw-shteka*, like the *ṭabla*." In this statement, Bābā Majīd was contrasting the vocables *dūm* (low) and *tek* (high), widely used to represent the staccato attacks of the ubiquitous Arabic goblet drum (*darbūkka*), with the *sūdānī* approach to the *ṭabla*, using the sounds *dauw* (low, played with the stick bouncing off the drumhead), *shtek* (high, played with the stick pressed against the head), and *a* (highest, played with an open hand near the rim). By replacing the staccato *dūm* vocable with the legato *dauw*, Bābā was emphasizing that the drumhead needs to be allowed to resonate freely after being struck, which means that the free hand should not be left dangling against the skin, which would mute the articulation. In a similar vein, he replaced the short *tek* of the *darbūkka* with the *shteka* of the *ṭabla* to draw attention to the importance of allowing the stick to bounce back gently against the drumhead after a pressed stroke, as well as the importance of filling in the space between the pressed stroke and the open stroke with an open-hand stroke. Ideal *ṭabla* aesthetics presuppose a constancy of sound produced by proper and consistent technique of the stick hand and open hand. When played together correctly, the *ṭabla* patterns create and maintain a rolling and continually resonating sonic presence.

Other Instruments

The *gumbrī* and *shqāshiq* are necessary components of every *sṭambēlī* ceremony. The *ṭabla* will replace the gumbrī for some presunset rituals, including the street procession of the annual pilgrimage. In the past, a smaller and longer barrel drum called a *dūndūfa* was used in such processions. No longer in use, the *dūndūfa* was most likely replaced by the *ṭabla*, which it closely resembles and is more readily available in Tunis. During the pilgrimage, there is also a percussion ensemble called *debdabū*, after the ceremony of assembly that has been connected to sub-Saharan court music as early as the thirteenth century. In the *debdabū*, the musicians are seated in the same formation as in other *sṭambēlī* ceremonies. The *yinna* plays the *ṭabla*, but not in the manner described earlier. In this context, the *ṭabla* is positioned upright in front of the seated *yinna*, so that the right hand can strike one drumhead while the left hand can strike the other. The drum is played with two sticks, one round and the other flat. The *ṣunnāʿ* do not play their *shqāshiq*; rather, they play their rhythmic cycles on one *gaṣʿa* (a drum resembling an upside-down bowl), two *kurkutūwāt* (sing. *kurkutū*; small kettledrums), and two *bendīr*s (frame drums with snares). The drums of *debdabū* are discussed in further detail in chapter 7, which is devoted to the pilgrimage.

Since many of the communal houses had distinctive *sṭambēlī* styles related to their specific regions of origin in sub-Saharan Africa, other instruments from those areas were also employed. At Dār Bambara, a rectangular lute with no resonating metallic plate was the instrument of choice (Pâques 1964; Bābā Majīd, personal communication). Similar to the Bambara *ngoni*, this instrument is considered in Tunisia to be the gumbrī's smaller "sister," called the *gambara* (the feminine form of *gumbrī*). It is for this reason that members of Dār Bārnū also referred to Dār Bambara by the rhyming appellation "Dār Gambara." Although it was never used in the context of possession ceremonies at Dār Bārnū, the *gambara* was played for entertainment (see chap. 2). It is rarely played any more in Tunis, where Bābā Majīd was one of the last known experts. He believes the *gambara* was played at Dār Bārnū in part through the influence of Algerians who came to the house, drawing attention to the lateral movement of instruments and other influences across the Maghrib. While the cylindrical *gumbrī* has been the lute of choice in Tunisian *sṭambēlī*, and the rectangular *ginbrī* the main instrument in Moroccan *gnāwa*, in Algeria we find both instruments in use.

The *fakrūn* (lit. "turtle") is a plucked lute similar to the *gumbrī* in many ways. It is a spiked lute in which the neck transpierces the entire body, it has a similar bridge supporting three strings that correspond in name and tuning to those of the *gumbrī*, it utilizes leather straps, and it features a goatskin drumhead. Unlike the *gumbrī*, however, the *fakrūn* has a body made from a large tortoise shell, sound holes are cut into the skin covering the body, and the neck rests against the skin. The latter feature suggests a closer relation to West African plucked lutes from Mali, Mauritania, and Senegal, in which the neck sits in a slight indentation above the body and below the skin of the resonator. As the majority of slaves in Tunis came from further east than these areas, it is plausible to speculate that the *fakrūn* was brought to Tunis and played by a relatively small proportion of the sub-Saharan diasporic community originating further west.

The *gūgāy* is a one- or two-stringed spiked fiddle fashioned from a half gourd and played with a bow. Like the *fakrūn*, *gambara*, and *gumbrī*, it features a round neck, leather tuning straps, and a similarly shaped bridge. We have as little documentation of the *gūgāy's* presence in Tunis as we have of the *fakrūn*'s, though Tremearne (1914: 284) noted that while the *gumbrī* was the main *sṭambēlī* instrument, a "violin" was sometimes used in ritual. A photo from Bābā Majīd's collection shows a *gūgāy* player and a drummer, both dressed up in Bū Saʿdiyya regalia (see fig. 7). However, there is a great deal more documentation concerning this instrument and others like it in sub-Saharan Africa, where, as in earlier times in Tunisia, it is mostly associated with spirit possession music. It is strikingly similar to monochord fiddles such as the Songhay *godji* (Stoller 1989), the Zarma *goje* (Surugue 1972) and the Dagomba *gonje* (Nketia 1974). The closest etymological, morphological, and most likely historical, relative of the Tunisian *gūgāy* is the Hausa *goge*, which, like the *molo* lute, was targeted by the Fulani reformers of nineteenth-century Hausaland for its association with *bori* possession practices (Erlmann 1986: 15).[12]

Voice

The *shqāshiq* players are also responsorial singers, who answer in unison the calls sung by either the *yinna* or a lead singer among them. Often, the lead vocals are less audible to those outside the ritual perimeter, as they are competing with the high volume of the *shqāshiq*. The lyrics are considered *duʿāʾ*, or invocations; their purpose is to summon and welcome the spirits and saints. Unlike many Tunisian Sufi saint songs, which are comparatively lengthier hagiographic and historiographical records of saints' acts, the *sṭambēlī* songs are short and mainly invocatory in nature, repeatedly inviting the saint or spirit to join the ceremony, as in the chorus for the *nūba* of Sīdī Marzūg:

Salēm ʿalīh (×3)	Greet him (×3)
Sīdī Marzūg mūl id-dīwān	Sīdī Marzūg, master of the assembly

FIGURE 7. Detail of a postcard depicting musicians playing the *ṭabla* and *gūgāy*, most likely in Touggourt, Algeria (near the Tunisian border), ca. 1920. (Editions Combi, Oran, Algeria, photographer unknown.)

In addition to praising the spirit or saint, the songs often praise God and the Prophet Muḥammad or invoke phrases from the Islamic testimony of faith (*shahāda*), as the *nūba* of Sīdī Bū Ra's el-ʿAjmī shows:

Lē illah illā Alḷah	There is no God but God
W-Muḥammad ir-rasūl	And Muḥammad is the Prophet

In addition to those that are entirely in Arabic, the lyrics to some *nūba*s are a combination of Arabic and Hausa, Kanuri, or Zarma. For instance, the *nūba* for Sīdī Bilāl (Jerma) combines Arabic with Zarma (see chap. 3).

Several *nūba*s for the Bēyēt are almost entirely in Hausa, a language the musicians no longer speak:

> Yay saki rura ya mulaya
> Garu rura ya rura rura (Yā Rīma)

Or

> Magadiyay saman gado
> Jamayay kazarbada Bābā al-haj sufu (Mʿallem Sofū)

Musicians often told me that the words were "not important," since it is the *gumbrī* that speaks to the spirits and lyrics could be altered without compromising the efficacy of the *nūba*. The lesser status of lyrics may also have been a rather practical matter: while several sub-Saharan languages were still spoken in Tunis, it was not uncommon for a singer to introduce a few words or substitute some lyrics for others in his native tongue (Tremearne 1914: 250). The responses, however, are quite standardized and formulaic, since the *ṣunnāʿ* need to sing them in unison. And while there is more room for variation in the calls, these too are drawn from a set of phrases appropriate to each member of the pantheon and must remain faithful to the style and purpose of praise singing. The lyrics, especially in the *nūba*s for the spirits, also preserve many words and phrases in Hausa and Kanuri whose meanings are no longer known. Ironically, in being considered "unimportant," the lyrics are, in fact, defining and iconic features of the *sṭambēlī* tradition, sometimes evoking, literally in the same breath, sub-Saharan Africa and Arabia, in what constitutes, in Martin Stokes's (2007) terms, a musical diasporic cosmopolitanism (see also Kapchan 2007: 185).

Vocal delivery of the words, however, is a more fundamental aesthetic concern than the words themselves. As in sorcerous incantations, it is the sounds of the words themselves, not just the meanings they denote, that embody their power (Stoller 1997). The language of the songs is a mixture of Tunisian Arabic and *ʿajmī* (in the context of language, meaning not only "foreign" and "non-Arabic," but also "incorrect" and "barbarous"), the latter originating in various languages of sub-Saharan Africa but mostly derived from the Hausa and Kanuri languages. The rationale behind this designation mostly lies in the aesthetics of vocal delivery, which is, ideally, *sūdānī* (sub-Saharan). According to Bābā Majīd, "We in Tunis don't have the same pronunciation [*naṭq*] as the sub-Saharans. In Tunis, they pronounce clearly [he demonstrated singing in the Arabic style]. But it is not clear [*mūsh muṣarriḥ*] in sub-Saharan Africa. . . . This is why I told you to take the melody, then build the words however you want" (Bābā Majīd, personal communication).

Bābā Majīd demonstrated often how the timbre of the voice should reflect that of the *gumbrī*. Not clear and staccato, but understated and flowing. While this aesthetic is sometimes described by *sṭambēlī* musicians as "nasal," it is more often referred to as "not clearly enunciated" (*mūsh muṣarriḥ*), a distinction made in contrast to the ideal Arabic aesthetic of delivery, which prizes clear diction (see Danielson 1997: 138–141). A *sūdānī* manner of delivery is, in the context of Tunisia, an indexical marker of otherness and renders all the words, whether Arabic or non-Arabic in origin, *ʿajmī*.

Music, Voice, and Authority

Sūdānī and *ʿajmī* are central concepts in the descriptive and evaluative discourse about instrumental morphology, technique, and timbre, as well as vocal content and delivery, at Dār Bārnū. These are the foundational elements of the musical processes explored further in the following chapter. For our present purposes, I wish to simply highlight the connection between the production of musical sound and the concept of authority—two ideas that converge usefully in the notion of "voice" (Feld and Fox 1994; Tolbert 2001). *Sṭambēlī* vocality—whether in the layered sounds of the *gumbrī*'s "words" or in the praises sung in admixtures of Arabic, Hausa, and Kanuri—both performs *and* disguises ritual knowledge. In the Arab-Islamic context of Tunisia, language and clarity of vocal diction are considered essential to sonic communication with the sacred; recitation of the Qur'ān and the sung poetry of Sufi orders provide the traditional models of voicing spiritual authority. But *sṭambēlī* vocality, with its malleable and multilingual lyrics and ambiguous and understated style of delivery, adheres to a quite different set of assumptions about the relationship between sound and language—so much so, in fact, that the real voice of ritual authority is found not in the human voice but instead in the "words" enunciated by a musical instrument. To the uninitiated, the *sṭambēlī* aesthetic is radically other, even incomprehensible, two conventional shades of the meaning of the term *ʿajmī* in the Arab world. But from within the *sṭambēlī* community, *ʿajmī* is not a derogatory term connoting incorrectness or incomprehensibility; rather, it is deliberate, distinctive, and highly valued, and implies an aesthetic ideal that is different from, but no less valid than, indigenous forms of envoicing the sacred. *ʿAjmī* and *sūdānī*, though definitions of exclusion from without, are from within evidence of connections to aesthetic values prized by powerful spiritual authorities—from the Prophet, Bilāl, and well-known Muslim saints to the sub-Saharan spirits and lesser-known Muslim saints from Bornu—that hold sway with and influence the lives of black and Arab Tunisians alike. By invoking these unseen beings musically, *sṭambēlī* reaffirms its proximity to a local superstructure of belief while simultaneously insisting on its distance from local performance practice and aesthetic conventions. Musical technique, then, encodes into aesthetic form elements of identity that are particularly salient for the *sṭambēlī* community. In the following chapter, I expand on this line of thought to explore the musical processes that capitalize on these foundational aesthetic elements in establishing the transformational dynamic of *sṭambēlī* ritual.

CHAPTER FIVE

Sounding the Spirits

THE RITUAL DYNAMICS OF TEMPORALITY, MODALITY, AND DENSITY

"The efficacy of much ritual," writes Bruce Kapferer, "is founded in its aesthetics." For Kapferer, aesthetic processes in ritual follow their own "dynamic logic" and constitute a "thoroughgoing pragmatic force" that conditions experience and produces meaning (2005b: 129). In *sṭambēlī* that force is overwhelmingly sonic. Musical aesthetics direct the senses into an experience of possibility and transformation, progressively disclosing the structure and content of the *sṭambēlī* pantheon, the power of its members to intervene profoundly in the human realm, and the capacity of "sub-Saharan" and "non-Arab" aesthetics and bodies to mediate these relationships. It does so largely by creating and manipulating multiple, interrelated, and overlapping temporal orders. I find that Gilbert Rouget's thoughts on the temporal aspects of possession musics provide a particularly useful point of departure for this chapter's consideration of the ritual dynamics of musical time. Spirit possession tunes, such as the *nūba*, Rouget writes, "are melodic or rhythmic statements, and consequently temporal forms." He continues: "They are capable of being varied and ornamented. In the course of a ceremony they follow one another and thus form sequences that should be seen as the multiple ways of renewing and developing musical time, which preserves its unity all the while since the pieces following one another belong to the same genre. By thus transforming our awareness of time and space, in different ways, music modifies our 'being-in-the-world'" (Rouget 1986: 122).

The musical relations and transformations Rouget describes are all the more heightened and reinforced through their performance in the context of ritual, which, by virtue of its very apartness from the everyday, directs attention to its own internal mechanisms of performance and aesthetic processes. Another way of looking at the relationship between music and ritual is to view the purpose of ritual as demonstrating and putting on display the efficacy of music and its transformational potential. It is in the ritual dynamics of musical movement—as articulated in and through internal musical structures defined by their capacity for progression and transformation—that *sṭambēlī* communicates both the concrete and the abstract—the techne of healing and the production of an imaginal space of sociospiritual encounter. As Kapferer argues, "Music is not sound or even tone but is made out of sound and intonation *and the dynamic movement of its elements*. Its meaning or the possibility of meaning in experience is *vital in its internal structure*" (Kapferer 1991: 256, my italics). In other words, musical sound is a force whose power is harnessed and revealed by the musicians who produce and organize it. In *sṭambēlī*, gradual and multifaceted transformations in both musical time and sonic density work synergically to create a sense of directed motion. From the timbral and durational qualities of single tones to the nuances of microrhythmic relationships, from the subtle shifts in multistable rhythmic cycles to the structuring of the ritual in its entirety, the *sṭambēlī* musical aesthetic constructs a temporal order based on multiple levels of musico-ritual motion.[1]

Musical technique is crucial to ritual efficacy, as it is the most prominent means of directing the senses into a sense of continual becoming, a transformational dynamic at the heart of the *sṭambēlī* experience. This musical-ritual knowledge is transmitted in embodied ways; musicians rarely address technical or theoretical dimensions of the music explicitly through verbal discourse. However, there is one commonly spoken phrase that highlights a fundamental *sṭambēlī* aesthetic concern. Criticism of a musician's inadequate playing is often expressed by asking the simple question "Where is he going [*wīn māshī*]?" The question alludes to the importance of a sense of directed musical motion; the music must *go* somewhere. It is asked in relation to one of two levels of musical motion: how the musicians "distribute" (*yuqasmū*) the *nūba*s over the course of the ceremony, and how they proceed within each *nūba*, which is the concern of the present chapter. The sense of musical direction may seem to be a counterintuitive concern in the context of a music that is cyclic and highly repetitive. Yet it is precisely this cyclicity and repetition that create the conditions for the music's gradual and subtle development through time.

The *yinna* begins each *nūba* with the *gumbrī* melody, with the *shqāshiq* entering immediately thereafter. The *shqāshiq* players will often recognize the *nūba* from these first few notes and know which rhythm to play. Since there is a loosely prescribed order to the succession of *nūba*s, a knowledgeable *shqāshiq* player will be able to narrow down the possibilities. Some may be able to discern the appropriate rhythm from that of the *gumbrī* melody, while less experienced players may simply follow the lead of the more experienced among them. After a few cycles of the *gumbrī* melody, the vocals enter, with either the *yinna* or the lead singer singing the call and the rest of the group answering with the response. The singing may last for as few as four or five cycles, or up to two or three dozen. In some cases, a second vocal phrase, usually shorter than the first, is sung. Once the vocal section ends, the instruments continue playing their cyclic patterns, and the tempo increases further. If a trancer is present, there is a more marked musical intensification during this section in which the tempo will increase dramatically and the musicians may physically advance toward the trancer, surrounding her with their music.

A single *nūba* typically lasts several minutes, though it can last as little as thirty seconds or as much as a quarter of an hour. The duration of a *nūba* is determined by a constellation of variables that includes the presence or absence of a dancer, the type of trance and its trajectory, the personal preferences and predilections of the *yinna*, and, if in the context of a private healing ceremony, the relationship of the *nūba* to those afflicting the client (see chap. 6). In terms of ritual structural factors affecting duration, a *nūba* for a saint is more likely to be on the longer end of the spectrum than one for a spirit. While there are no melodic or rhythmic distinctions that distinguish *nūba*s for the saints from those for the spirits, there is, generally speaking, stricter adherence to the *silsila* of *nūbas* for the spirits. Since a person in possession trance may not finish a trance (*dūkh*, lit. "faint") until she has been possessed by a succession of spirits in the same family, each constituent *nūba* of a spirit's *silsila* may be relatively short. With the exception of the *nūba*s for the Prophet and Bilāl, which always open the ceremony, the sequence of *nūba*s within the *silsila* of the saints is not as rigidly prescribed as those of the spirits; in fact, a saint may appear at virtually any time during a ceremony. These are usually longer and relatively self-contained, since for some adepts it will be the only *nūba* they dance to, as opposed to a series of shorter *nūba*s for the spirits (the one, however, does not preclude the other; those possessed by spirits often also trance to the *nūba* of at least one saint).

In both cases, a common denominator is a dual sense of progression: at the level of *silsila*, the musical routes taken from one member of the pantheon to the next, and at the level of the *nūba*, a compression of the rhythmic cells characterized by acceleration and an increase in sonic density. The compression of the rhythmic cell is not merely an increase in tempo; it also actualizes a similarly normative transformation in rhythmic contour, as well as highlights the presence of—and ambiguities created by—the accents inherent in each *shqāshiq* pattern. It also concentrates musical sound into progressively smaller and smaller temporal spaces, thus increasing the density of musical sound in time. In the following sections I examine the constitution of the *ṣṭambēlī* rhythmic cell and the temporal transformations that accompany the *nūba*'s musical trajectory.

Rhythmic Elasticity and Offset Accentuation

If ritual temporality, as discussed in chapter 1, is largely concerned with slowing down the chaotic and fractured nature of quotidian experience, and music situates listeners within another world of virtual time (Blacking 1995: 34; Kapferer 2005b), what is the nature of this temporal reorientation, and how is it achieved? How is time organized into periodicities, and how are they calibrated? Although described from within and without as "African," the rhythmic structure and sensibility are not instances of the simultaneous multilinearity and 3:2 polymeter conventionally considered hallmarks of "African rhythm"; the *sṭambēlī* rhythmic framework is not reducible to a series of fast, evenly spaced underlying pulses serving as felt, if not always articulated, basic time units (see Kauffman 1980). And whereas the relationship of binary and ternary metrical structures in many sub-Saharan African contexts is one of simultaneity and copresence (Brandel 1959; Nketia 1974), in *sṭambēlī* the duple-triple ambiguity is of a different order: the rhythms are neither fully binary nor ternary, but can be suggestive of—but not easily reducible to—either one. This is because the *sṭambēlī* temporal system is best understood as a succession of self-referential rhythmic cells containing short, repeated, accented patterns of articulations whose identities are based on their relative spacing from each other, rather than on an underlying series of equidistant pulses.[2] The macrorhythmic and microrhythmic features of these cells transform the temporal flow in ways that create a kinetic sense of forward motion. The looping of these cells throughout a *nūba* creates a temporal flow that is cyclical yet progressive; it capitalizes on the dynamic between repetition and transformation.

It is perhaps most effective to begin explaining this rhythmic system by way of illustration. Listen to the performance of the *nūba* of Sīdī Marzūg on the accompanying compact disc (track 2). Sīdī Marzūg's *nūba* is in the *sūdānī* rhythm, a three-note pattern (here *sūdānī* is the name of the rhythmic pattern, not just a descriptor of a "sub-Saharan" aesthetic). The *nūba* begins at a moderate tempo, with the relative spacing between articulations unequally distributed. But as the *nūba* progresses it undergoes a gradual increase in tempo and compression of the rhythmic cell. As the cells compress, the notes of the cell become increasingly equidistant. The first stages of this tendency are evident in the audio example. At the beginning of the *nūba* the space between the first and second strikes of the *shqāshiq* is 40 percent of the cell. The space between the second and third strikes is 20 percent, and the space between the third strike and first strike of the subsequent cell is 40 percent. By the end of the vocal section, the relative spacing between strikes is evening out, decreasing the ratio to 39:25:36. The full transformation—to cells composed of nearly equidistant articulations—is not realized on this

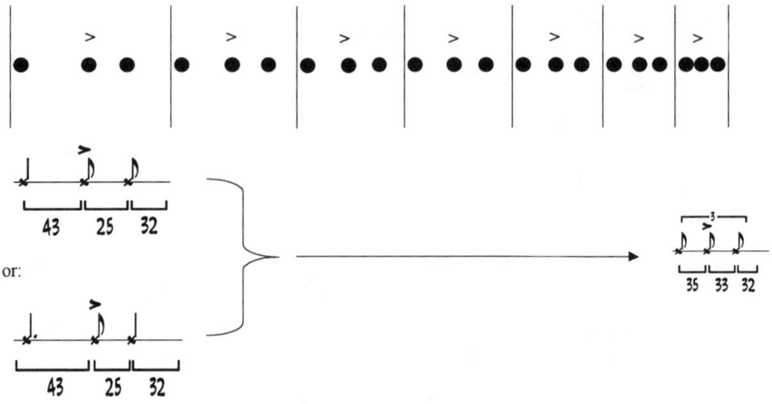

FIGURE 8. Compression of the *sūdānī* rhythmic cell.

recording simply because this performance ends soon after the vocal section, without the pronounced acceleration (and concomitant cell compression) of an instrumental section. In most cases, however, the space between the three notes of the rhythmic pattern will become nearly equidistant.

Microrhythmic analysis of a more complete version of this *nūba* (performed by Bābā Majīd and available at www.stambeli.com) reveals that, at the beginning of the *nūba*, the space between the first and second strikes takes up 43 percent of the cell, while the space between the second and third strikes is 25 percent of the cell; the space between the third strike and the first strike of the following cell constitutes the remaining 32 percent of the cell. By the end of the *nūba*, those percentages have nearly evened out, to 35, 33, and 32, respectively. (Keep in mind that the "control group" for the first cell would be a theoretical exactitude of 50-25-25 [if notated in duple meter] or 50-16.7-33.3 [if notated in triple meter] and would be 33.3-33.3-33.3 for the second cell.) Figure 8 provides a visual representation of the compression of the rhythmic cell and the concomitant evening out of the spacing between articulations.

One issue this example immediately raises concerns representation: these measurements suggest that even the patterns of a single, isolated rhythmic cell resist unequivocal representation in either duple or triple meter, even when allowing for a "swing" feel. (For the sake of illustration, I have provided both alternatives in figures 8, 9, and 10; for the sake of clarity, I have had to choose one or the other in subsequent examples, which are based on the starting patterns of the *nūba*s and which should be understood as following the same logic of compression and transformation I am describing here.) This is largely because the rhythmic cell is not divisible into equidistant

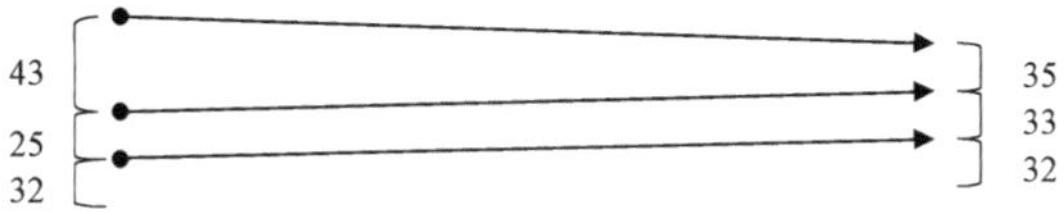

FIGURE 9. Compression of the *sūdānī* rhythmic cell, alternate perspective.

underlying pulses or beats. Rather, it is the relationship between the recurring, accented articulations within the cell, rather than their location relative to an orienting timeline or within a matrix of abstracted regular pulses, that defines the pattern.[3]

In Sīdī Marzūg's *nūba*, as well as in the vast majority of *nūba*s, the sonic events within the cells transition from an asymmetrical pattern toward a symmetrical one. Even though the relative temporal spacing between the notes of the rhythmic cycle changes as the tempo increases, it is still considered the "same" rhythm. Put somewhat differently, the concept of the *sūdānī* rhythm includes, and is defined by, this transformational potential. Visualizing this transformation on another plane provides an additional perspective that conveys the subtle and gradual nature of this process (see fig. 9).

As it decreases the space between articulations, this rhythmic elasticity transforms the contour of the rhythm. But since they occur very gradually, these transitions don't just "switch" the feel; for much of the *nūba* it is somewhere in between those two ends of the metrical spectrum. By naming this rhythm *sūdānī*, *sṭambēlī* musicians are emphasizing its otherness. It is the most prevalent rhythmic pattern in the *sṭambēlī* tradition, and the most ambiguous in terms of perception of the "beat." Its deceptive simplicity creates a number of potential perceptual alignments—binary or ternary feel, accents falling on or off the beat—that are prone to shift as the tempo of the *nūba* increases. The *sūdānī* rhythm, with its structural ambiguities and transformational nature, is iconic of the more broadly conceived *sūdānī sṭambēlī* aesthetic.

A very similar compression of the rhythmic cell occurs in *nūba*s employing the *muthallith* rhythm. Despite a name meaning "triple" (also "triangle"), it is a four-note pattern. None of the musicians I spoke with could explain the reasoning behind the name, and even Bābā Majīd admitted that he was unsure of its origins but proffered that it may have had an arcane and rather prosaic logic that referred to either a historical or ritual situation in which this rhythmic pattern was defined as the "third" one used, an association that it obviously no longer maintains. Microrhythmic analysis of the *muthallith* pattern in a performance of Sīdī Bū Ra's el-ʿAjmī (also at www.stambeli.com), which begins at about one quarter = 82 cells per minute, shows the space between the first and second notes of the cell taking up 30 percent of

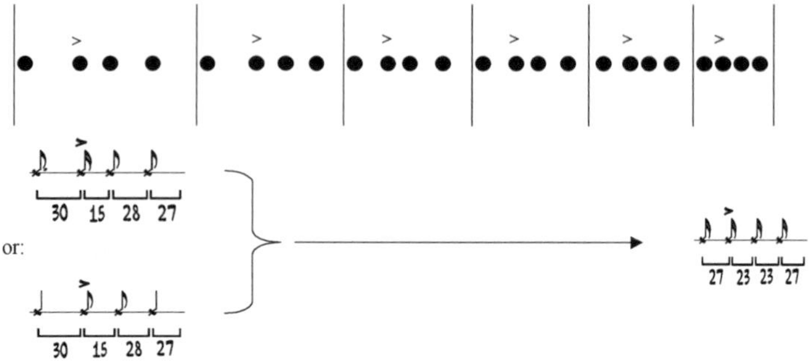

FIGURE 10. Compression of the *muthallith* rhythmic cell.

the cell, and the space between the second and third notes taking up 15 percent (fig. 10). The space between the third and fourth notes is 28, while the space between the fourth note of the cell and the first note of the subsequent cell is 27. (The "control" group here would have a spacing of 37.5-12.5-25-25 if notated in duple meter, or 33.3-16.7-16.7-33.3 if notated in triple meter.) At a much faster tempo, near the end of the *nūba*, the spacing has become symmetrical, resulting in a spacing of 27-23-23-27. Because of the high speed at this point in the *nūba*, the small percentage differences are barely audible, creating a sense of equidistance with a slight "lilt." (In the recorded example on the accompanying compact disc, the pattern transforms from 32-19-22-27 to 27-22-27-24.)

The microrhythmic measurements in figures 8, 9, and 10 are representative of the numerous analyses I conducted at several points in a large sampling of *nūbas*.[4] In every case, the *sūdānī* and *muthallith* rhythmic patterns defied unambiguous classification into duple or triple metrical structures when Western notation was imposed upon them.[5] Because more than 70 percent of *sṭambēlī nūbas* employ either the *sūdānī* or the *muthallith* rhythm, this ambiguity, or indeterminacy, or, better, this otherness is emblematic, in the context of Tunisia, of the alterity of the *sṭambēlī* musical tradition itself.[6]

Only two other rhythms, *saʿdāwī* and *bū saʿdiyya*, are used in *sṭambēlī*, each accounting for about 14 percent of *nūbas*. *Saʿdāwī* is distinctive in that it tends to create a hemiola-style sense of metrical ambiguity in addition to the microrhythmic nuances shared by all *sṭambēlī* rhythmic cell patterns.[7] The *bū saʿdiyya* rhythm is named after the legendary figure Bū Saʿdiyya introduced in chapter 2, and is employed in his *nūba*. This rhythm is also often used for *nūbas* of the few saints who are not members of the *sṭambēlī* pantheon but are played "on demand," such as Sīdī Belḥassen and Sayda Manubiyya (see chap. 3). This rhythm is the least ambiguous of the four and does not typically accelerate as much as the others.

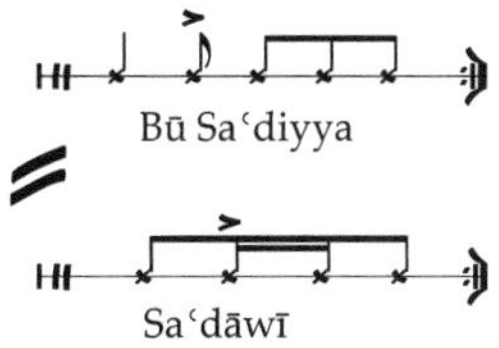

EXAMPLE 2. *Saʿdāwī* and *bū saʿdiyya* rhythms

As the preceding examples indicate, all four rhythmic patterns feature one sonic event that is accentuated more than the others. These accents are always situated after one of the more elongated rhythmic events of the cell, and are inherent, defining features of each *shqāshiq* pattern, produced by the normative sequences of closed (clenched) and open (resonating) articulations and techniques of alternating hands and striking one set of *shqāshiq* against the other.[8] The accents are not produced by the use of more force per se, and are not always much higher in volume than the other notes in the cell. Rather, tone color, temporal placement, and duration, relative to the other notes, contribute greatly to create a sense of accentuation. The physical motionality of performance technique also plays a major role: the accented notes are played with the *shqāshiq* held higher and further from the body than the others. This sense of accentuation is often very subtle at moderate tempos but becomes quite obvious at faster tempos, especially when a "gestalt flip" occurs, shifting the listener's perception of the accent from "off" the beat to "on" the beat (Locke 1998: 22; Friedson 1996: 140–143).[9] These accents are also often emphasized in rhythmic variations interjected by the lead *shqāshiq* player.

This sense of accentuation in the *shqāshiq* cycles is in a dynamic interrelation with those of the *gumbrī* melodic-rhythmic patterns. Strikes on the drumhead of the *gumbrī* accompany and accentuate certain notes of the melody, providing a subtle percussive foundation underlying and inseparable from the melodic pattern. These strikes produce a rhythmic contour in the melody and provide an orienting framework that underscores especially the tonal resolutions of melodic movement. Typically, the rhythms of the *gumbrī* attacks do not occur simultaneously with the regular accents of the *shqāshiq*; rather, they provide a rhythmic counterpoint, resulting in a metrical tension between the *gumbrī* and the *shqāshiq* that only intensifies as the *nūba* increases in tempo. While there is no explicitly articulated sense of a downbeat in musicians' discourse, the main orienting points of reference seem to be those notes of the *gumbrī* melody underscored by strikes on the *gumbrī* drumhead. The dance movements of experienced dancers usually align with these emphasized notes of the cycle, which are offset from those accented by the *shqāshiq*. The *nūba* of Sīdī Bū Ra's el-ʿAjmī (ex. 3 and CD

EXAMPLE 3. Main theme of Sīdī Bū Ra's el-ʿAjmī. *P*, pull-off; *H*, hammer-on; *L*, left-hand strum.

track 3) features a pronounced sense of the beat in the *gumbrī* and vocal lines, provides a good example of the offset nature of the *shqāshiq* accents.

In a few *nūba*s, however, the *gumbrī* and *shqāshiq* accents are partially aligned, which may create a strong sense of accentuation on the beat, especially if the *nūba* begins at a relatively fast tempo and the dancer's movements also correspond to those accents, as in the *nūba* for Kūrī. Despite this powerful sense of pulse, there remains a metrical tension or ambiguity—it may sound like a syncopated binary rather than a straight ternary feel. Listen to Bābā Majīd's solo performance on the accompanying Web site, then compare it to the example performed by the entire troupe (toward the end of CD track 4). Example 4 shows two ways of grouping the notes of Kūrī's *nūba* that roughly convey two possible rhythmic gestalts.

Throughout a *nūba*, there is a sense of in-betweenness or ambiguity that obtains due to the microrhythmic dynamics of the rhythmic cell. Through incessant repetition, these nuances also generate a sense of tension and increasing intensification. Such transformations and inherent ambiguities are made possible by the cyclic nature of the music. This suggests that the experiential force of the rhythmic cycle is not reducible to the process of merely oversaturating the listener with repetition or sensory overload. Rather, a combination of repetition, progression, and transformation, and the tension that obtains between them, is essential to the ritual dynamics that order the aesthetic experience of each individual *nūba*.

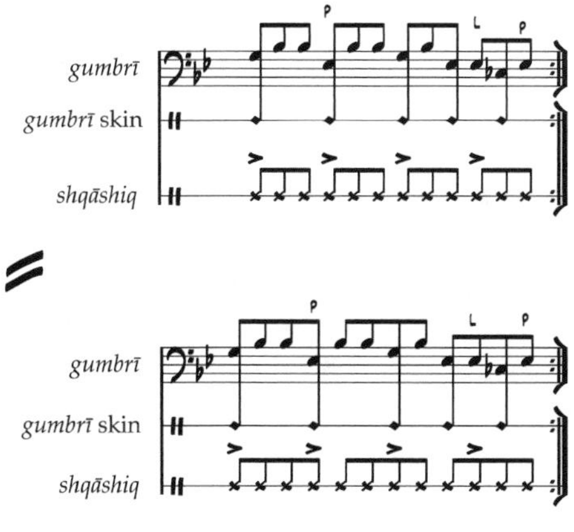

EXAMPLE 4. Two groupings of the Kūrī melody. *P*, pull-off; *H*, hammer-on; *L*, left-hand strum.

Tempo and Acceleration

Each *nūba*, as I have already indicated, undergoes a gradual and deliberate increase in tempo that contributes to the sense of musical movement, temporal transformation, and ritual progression that constitute core dynamics of *sṭambēlī* ritual.[10] In a sampling of forty-seven complete performances (of twenty-two different *nūba*s) by the same troupe in the same year (2001), the tempo increase ranged from as little as 2.5 percent to nearly 60 percent of the starting tempo, with an average increase of about 23 percent. I provide these numbers simply to give the reader a sense of the across-the-board presence of accelerated tempos. It is more important, however, to examine the parameters of the process of acceleration in order to account for how musicians decide tempo changes on any given *nūba*. This is of significant interest because, in spite of the wide range in the degree of acceleration, there is remarkable consistency in the amount of the increase in tempo of any given *nūba* from performance to performance, especially when conditions are similar.

Sṭambēlī musicians must be attuned to each other in order to make the acceleration both unified and fluid. The more I performed with Bābā Majīd's troupe, the more I realized that the degree of acceleration I could expect in any *nūba* we were playing was largely contingent upon two main conditions: whether or not there was a dancer (and, if so, the nature of the trance), and the place of a *nūba* within the *silsila* and its rhythmic pattern in relation to those preceding and following it. Analysis of dozens of field recordings confirms these general tendencies. (While the *nūba*s with the least acceleration tend to be relatively short, there is no hard-and-fast correlation between the length of the *nūba* and the acceleration; of the forty-seven *nūba*s I analyzed, the *nūba* with the least acceleration, as well as the one with the most, were both less than two minutes thirty seconds in duration.)

The recordings of Sīdī Marzūg and Sīdī Bū Ra's el-ʿAjmī provided on the accompanying compact disc demonstrate clearly this dynamic of gradual acceleration. Since they are both stand-alone *nūba*s—that is, each can be performed without a direct segue into another—there is some flexibility in starting and ending speeds. Nevertheless, there is a generally consistent tempo range for each. Video footage of a performance of Sīdī Bū Ra's el-ʿAjmī (found at this book's accompanying Web site) shows the *nūba* beginning at 82 rhythmic cells per minute and ending, four minutes thirty-two seconds later, at a tempo of 112; the other recordings I made of this *nūba* by the same troupe, which involved a dancer, end at speeds of 114–117 rhythmic cells per minute, an increase that is consistent with the tendency to accelerate slightly more in the presence of a recreational dancer. A performance of Sīdī Marzūg (also on the stambeli.com Web site) begins at about 84 cells per minute and ends at 134 cells per minute, a 40.5 percent increase in tempo.

Things get more complicated, however, when *nūba*s are tied together within a *silsila*. Table 3 shows the relative increases in tempo in three performances, each of a tripartite chain of *nūba*s: Ṣlāt in-Nabī, Jerma, and Bū Ḥijba, which are played together in succession without stopping (thus, the ending tempo for Ṣlāt in-Nabī is the same as the starting tempo for Jerma, and the ending tempo for Jerma is the same as the starting tempo for Bū Ḥijba). As the three *nūba*s are in the same rhythm (*muthallith*) and each one segues directly into the subsequent *nūba* with no pause, tempos for the first two *nūba*s must be carefully monitored by the musicians, since too much of an acceleration in one would cause the subsequent *nūba* to begin at too fast a rate. The starting tempo was virtually the same for the first *nūba*, Ṣlāt in-Nabī, each time it was performed (89, 90, and 88 cells per minute), and the ending tempo was also remarkably consistent (115, 112, and 114 cells per minute), resulting in very similar increases in tempo (29.2, 24, and 29.5 percent of the starting tempo). Any greater increase in tempo would compromise Jerma, into which Ṣlāt in-Nabī segues. *Nūba*s with a smaller percentage increase in tempo, such as Jerma, are more often than not elements of a *silsila* in which the following *nūba* is in the same rhythm, in order to ensure that the following *nūba* does not begin too fast. Since its tempo relies on the other two *nūba*s, Jerma undergoes the least acceleration, while Bū Ḥijba may undergo a wider range of tempo increases because it is not tied to any subsequent *nūba*. Thus, the musicians can increase the tempo as much as they like—so long it is musically acceptable—since there will be a pause before the following *nūba*.[11]

Notice that the first and third occurrences of Bū Ḥijba are very similar in their ending tempos (126 and 128 cells per minute, respectively), while the second performance accelerates to a much higher rate of 142 cells per

TABLE 3. Tempo increases in three performances each of Ṣlāt in-Nabī, Jerma, and Bū Ḥijba

Nūba	*Duration (min:sec)*	*Starting tempo*	*Ending tempo*	*Increase (%)*
Performance 1:				
Ṣlāt in-Nabī	3:47	89	115	29.2
Jerma	1:14	115	118	2.5
Bū Ḥijba	1:10	118	126	6.8
Performance 2:				
Ṣlāt in-Nabī	3:50	90	112	24.4
Jerma	1:16	112	120	7.1
Bū Ḥijba	4:01	120	142	18.3
Performance 3:				
Ṣlāt in-Nabī	4:24	88	114	29.5
Jerma	1:47	114	121	6.1
Bū Ḥijba	1:41	121	128	5.7

minute. The reason for this is that the second performance, unlike the first and third, involved a dancer. Whenever there is a dancer, it is more likely that there will be a more marked increase in tempo. How much of an increase often depends on the nature of the dance. A more recreational dance, in which two or more dancers take turns during the early part of a ceremony, will probably have a less dramatic acceleration than a more intense trance dance (see chap. 6).

The *Gumbrī*, Melody, and Modality

Since they are constitutive of the same rhythmic cells as the *shqāshiq*, the *gumbrī* and vocals, it should be said, also adhere to the same logics of rhythmic elasticity and acceleration. However, they also add crucial dimensions to the construction of *sṭambēlī* temporality. *Sṭambēlī* melodic modality is largely pentatonic and features a strong sense of tonicity. Vamps on, and prominent resolutions to, the lowest open string, establish a tonal reference point, which is reinforced by the use of the upper-octave tonic (the open *kūlū* string) as an intermittent drone. Descending melodic patterns, especially at the ends of vocal phrases, also reinforce a strong sense of tonicity. Many *nūbas* feature descending vocal patterns that resolve strongly on the tonic (B♭) at the end of the lyrical line. The compulsion of the flattened second to lead toward the tonic in such phrases further reinforces this sense of tonicity,[12] as do deliberate suspensions of resolution in certain situations (e.g., the *sūga*; see below). But because of the cyclic nature of the *nūba* and the tendency to emphasize intervals of a fourth and a fifth, these suspensions of resolutions, as well as the main structure of s a few *nūba*s with more ambiguous melodies, can generate alternative senses of a tonic. Kūrī, for example, emphasizes the fourth scale degree (E♭) and never reaches the lower tonic (see ex. 4 above). Like the rhythmic cells, *sṭambēlī* tonal structure may also suggest a simultaneous or alternative point of orientation, in this case a sense of tonicity that gravitates toward the fourth above the tonic.

The *gumbrī* provides the main orienting tonal presence for the vocals. It should be emphasized that musicians are more concerned with the relative relationships between notes than with a strict sense of intervallic size; the function, for example, of the second scale degree as leading to the tonic (or deceptively away), or of the fourth scale degree acting as a site of momentary rest, is more important than the precise tuning of the note. Every cycle of every *nūba* of every *silsila* only reinforces the relationships between the six pitches of the *gumbrī* that constitute, for all practical purposes, the only pitches that are performed throughout the entire ceremony. By saturating the ritual gathering with repeated uses of the same pitch material, this music continually asserts its own aesthetic terms by structuring its own referents and possibilities. In other words, rather than constraining the range of aesthetic possibilities, what at first glance might appear to be a highly limited set of pitches, performed in the space of a similarly limited number of rhythmic patterns, may actually expand the horizons of modal experience by focusing attention on a larger sense of aesthetic coherence and the myriad ways in which this musical material can be organized to produce a complete, robust, and unique *nūba* for each of the dozens of members of the *sṭambēlī* pantheon. Repetition, then, is not necessarily redundancy, and complexity or profundity may be constructed out of relative aesthetic economy.

One of the more dramatic ways in which this is achieved in *sṭambēlī* is during the *sūga*, a period of heightened intensification that suspends tonal resolution and in which dancers enter into the most profound level of trance. The *sūga* could be interpreted as a particularly poignant aesthetic method for "entering within life's vital processes and adjusting its dynamics" (Kapferer 2005a: 48), for during the *sūga*, the trancer—like the sense of tonal resolution—is suspended in a profoundly altered state and will return to a normal (i.e., healed) state of being only after the *sūga* has reached its climax and resolved to the tonic. I elucidate this musical-corporeal-spiritual reorientation of the *sūga* in the following section.

The *Sūga*

The sense of "where" the musicians are going may be simultaneously concentrated and suspended through the *sūga*, which is used in *nūba*s in the *muthallith* rhythm. When a dancer is present, the musicians often respond to and

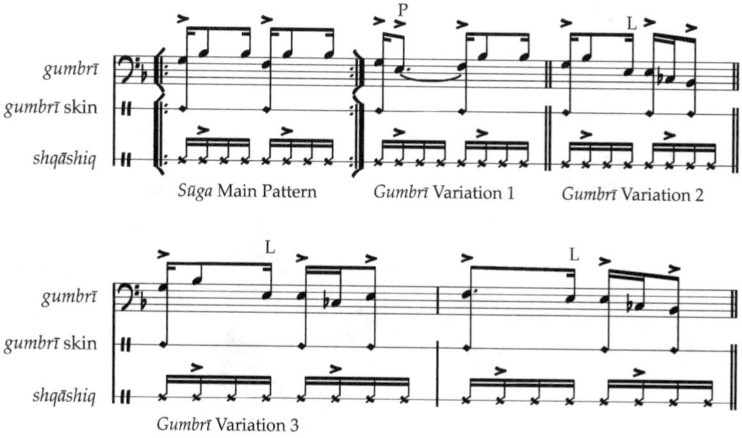

EXAMPLE 5. *Sūga* and variations. *P*, pull-off; *H*, hammer-on; *L*, left-hand strum.

further shape the trance trajectory through a transition to the *sūga*. The *sūga* is marked by a driving (in fact, the term *sūga* is probably derived from the Arabic *ysūq*, "to drive") intensification that involves a further increase in tempo and volume and the suspension of resolution of the *gumbrī* pattern. It is during the *sūga* that a *nūba* reaches its maximum speed and a trance reaches the height of intensity, usually culminating in the desired passing out of the dancer. In the *sūga*, the *gumbrī* plays a sort of holding pattern, alternating between the sixth and the fifth, which are emphasized by corresponding strikes on the drumhead, with the *kūlū* filling in the space between them. This pattern is cycled over and over until it is firmly established, at which time variations may be inserted. A good *sūga* will build tension by occasionally flirting with resolution through variations on the holding pattern. (At high tempos or heard from afar, this holding pattern can sometimes feel as if the *shqāshiq* accents were "on" the beat, which may then be reinforced by a corresponding straight eighth-note feel of the high octave played on the open *kūlū* string.) Variation 1 involves a strongly emphasized pull-off to scale degree four aligned with the *shqāshiq* pattern's accented note (ex. 5). Variation 2 continues descending to the tonic but does so briefly and on a relatively weak beat, making any sense of tonal resolution fleeting. Variation 3 suspends this resolution by inserting a deceptive descent all the way down to the flattened second scale degree (C♭) but ascends back to scale degree 3 (F, the fourth above the tonic) before starting the same descent, this time arriving at the tonic as in variation 2. Before returning to the holding pattern, any of the variations can be inserted singly, repeated two to three times, or combined with one or more other variations.

In more vigorous trances, the *sūga* also involves more focused and en-

FIGURE 11. *Shqāshiq* players moving toward a trancer during the *nūba* of Sīdī Beshīr, 2009. (Photograph by Matthieu Hagene.)

gaged "somatic modes of attention" (Csordas 2002), as the *ṣunnāʿ* will rise to their knees, raise their *shqāshiq* higher, and close in on the dancer (see fig. 11). During the *sūga*, the *shqāshiq* players are also paying attention to each other, as they are now free to alter their rhythms individually by adding certain syncopated patterns against the rhythmic cycle maintained by the others. These are accented patterns played by striking the domes of one pair of *shqāshiq* against the domes of the other pair, or by clenching both pairs together in unison. Variation 1 (see ex. 6) emphasizes the second sixteenth note, just as the *shqāshiq* holding pattern does, while variation 2 plays on the beat in the manner of X-2-3-4 prevalent in West African 4/4 musics (Locke 1998). In example 6, the lead *shqāshiq* player's variations are represented on the top line, while the holding pattern of the rest of the *ṣunnāʿ* is on the bottom line.

The intensification is also marked—and furthered—by the intermittent and overlapping shrill ululations delivered by several women in attendance. The trancer matches the musician's increase in tempo by swinging her head back and forth with correspondingly faster and more vigorous movements; she may now be held from behind to ensure that she does not run into any

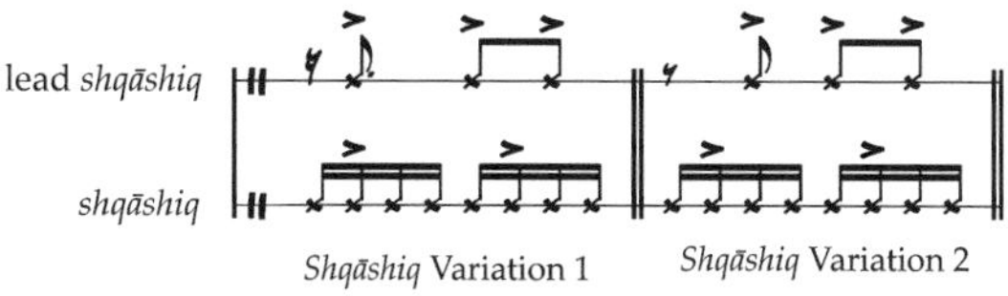

EXAMPLE 6. *Shqāshiq* variations

of the musicians or other participants seated nearby. The musicians will continue to close in, increasing their tempo and volume, until she finally passes out, collapsing onto the floor, indicating that the spirit or saint has let go of her.

Music and Bodily Motion

"Music is in essence movement," writes Gilbert Rouget. "Its origins lie in bodily movements—to sing is to move one's larynx, to drum is to move one's arms, to play the fiddle is to move one's fingers along the stem and a bow across a string—and in return music is an incitement to movement" (Rouget 1986: 121). Phenomenological perspectives have emphasized the need to consider the motional properties of music and trance experiences in addition to their acoustic properties (Friedson 1996). John Blacking's work on the interface between musician and instrument focuses attention on the corporeal source of music, as well as the body's role in shaping the organizational framework of musical production. Senses of musical style, as well as the potential for musical "flow," are inseparable from a musician's physical contact with the musical instrument (Feld 1988; Csikszentmihályi 1990). John Baily refers to the musical instrument as a sort of "transducer" that converts "patterns of body movement into patterns of sound" (1992: 149). He suggests that musical creativity often relies upon mastery of "motor grammars" of an instrument that enables musicians to create new melodies or patterns that are compatible with the stylistic parameters of a musical tradition (Baily 1977: 329). The *sūga* and its variations on the *gumbrī* employ patterns of right- and left-hand movements that are so prevalent throughout the repertoire that they become second nature to the musician. In this case, variation is not about adding notes outside the *gumbrī*'s pentatonic scale, but rather in emphasizing, through selective repetition, certain musical relationships. In the right hand, the main pattern involves the alternation of a downward stroke of the forefinger (on the *shēb*) accompanied by a strike on the drumhead with the middle finger, followed by two downward strokes of the thumb (on the *kūlū*). The left hand moves back and forth between scale degrees 4 and 5 in simultaneity with the downward forefinger strokes and middle finger strikes on the drumhead. In variation 1, there is no significant change in the spatiomotor coordination of alternating movement; the only difference is a lateral pluck of the string as the hand continues its movement between positions. In the other variations, this holding pattern is interrupted briefly to descend to scale degree 2 and 1, but this is done from the first position, which is where the left hand would be anyway (see chap. 4). Some of the *sūga* variations are evident in phrases found in the *nūba* of Sīdī Bū Ra's el-ʿAjmī (ex. 3). The point I am making is that the spatiomotor coordination of the musician is implicated in what is considered idiomatic in *gumbrī* performance.

The motor grammars of the *shqāshiq* are absolutely essential to understand the proper accentuation of the rhythmic patterns they play. On the video examples available online at this book's accompanying Web site, you may have noticed a subtle undulating or rolling motion the *shqāshiq* players make with their hands as they move their instruments in a forward and sometimes almost circular manner. Each revolution corresponds to one cycle of the rhythmic cell, with the accented notes of the pattern occurring at the vertically higher position, farther away from the body than the others, such that they project the sound forward. These motions also ensure that when the domes of the *shqāshiq* are struck together to emphasize that accentuation, both pairs are also positioned farthest from the body.

As we get into the physical motions of the musicians, it is of course essential to note that they move in relation to dancers, which I will touch on now, in order to situate the dancer's movements in this chapter's themes of movement and density, before going into more detail in the following chapter.

Dance and Bodily Motion

The bodily movements of dance in part result from the repeated, gradually intensifying musical movement I have been describing, but also further multiply the layers of repetition, intensification, and directed movement in ritual. There are two main types of dance in *sṭambēlī*: nonpossession trance, which is generated by the saints and is somewhat "abstract," and possession trance, which is made up of the often more "figurative" or "mimetic" dances of the spirits (Rahal 2000; Rouget 1986). The distinction between nonpossession trance and possession trance—the former deals with "taking away" the dancer while the latter concerns a spirit's "entering" the dancer—is an important one that is dealt with further in the following chapter. There is also recreational dance, which, while not considered healing per se, enables a dancer who is not an adept to obtain the *baraka* of the saint. Such dancing usually occurs only near the beginning of the ceremony, and only to the *nūba*s of the saints.

For our present purposes, I draw attention to the dancers' bodily movements because virtually all dance in *sṭambēlī*, whether possession trance or nonpossession trance, involves an aesthetic of repeated, continual, and gradually intensifying movements. Nonpossession trance (*jedba*) involves strenuous and repetitive actions chosen from a small stock repertoire of movements. Possession trance movements are much more variegated, since each spirit has its own specific dance style. Nevertheless, they all involve repeated and intensifying movements, though some do so in more subtle ways than others. These corporeal techniques interface with those of the musicians, putting their bodies in tune with one another. The dancers' bodies are in an active and symbiotic relationship with those of the musicians, and their dance, like the music, is similarly imbued with communicative capacities.[13]

Sonic Density and Musical Motion

My descent into the details of *sṭambēlī* musical production should be understood as part of an attempt to convey the critical importance of the internal dynamics of ritual in accounting for the continued potency of *sṭambēlī* ritual. I have drawn inspiration from Bruce Kapferer's work on ritual dynamics, which takes large steps toward explaining why so many ritualists, in so many contexts, have been seen as obsessed with the "detail and exactitude of their operations" (Kapferer 2005a: 48).[14] A focus on ritual dynamics (aesthetics and somatic modes of attention) sheds new light on statements such as Bābā Majīd's insistence that "*sṭambēlī* is *sṭambēlī*. It is only the people who have changed." While ritual specialists, of course, may find "ideological and instrumental value" in such claims of historical continuity (Kapferer 2005a: 45), it may be true that they are not making this claim about changes in the content and structure of ritual. Undoubtedly such changes do occur, to some extent, over time. These changes, however, may be "less significant than their relatively unchanging constancy through time" (Kapferer 2005a: 45). It may be that the internal dynamics—where meanings are always made anew—are the constants, and that indeed, it is the people, that is, the social and political contexts, that change. There is much evidence that supports the claim of ritual continuity over time, and ritual specialists often display a commitment to maintaining such continuity, as well as maintaining "the disjunction of rite from its embracing context" (Kapferer 2005a: 45). It is precisely this disjunction that suggests that ritual is not reducible to terms external to it, or merely reflective of other realities with which it may or may not share compositional elements.

The musical processes that I have drawn attention to interface with the instrumental design and performance techniques discussed in the previous chapter to expand both sonic density and note duration, thus contributing to a sense of uninterrupted musical motion and a high degree of aural and temporal density. *Shqāshiq* techniques privilege resonating or sizzling sounds over short, crisp articulations, and the more *shqāshiq* players there are in a performance, the more expansive their sonic events. The combination of various finger techniques on the *gumbrī*, such as the *kūlū* drone, strikes on the drumhead, and an economy of motion that enables the hands to move fluidly between only two positions leads to a constant buzzing of the *shaqshaqa* attached to the strings. These aesthetics are further amplified by the cyclic structure of the *nūba* and its normative gradual increase in tempo and concomitant compression of the rhythmic cell. *Sṭambēlī* aesthetics of extending duration militate against experiencing the decay of any note; this becomes even more pronounced as the temporal cell compresses through time. As the music accelerates, the space between notes diminishes and becomes increasingly saturated with overlapping resonances. As these layers of sound build up and collapse onto one another, new perceptual possibilities may arise. At times, prior certainties in the form of temporal references (such as "the beat") may become ambiguities, and new musical relationships may emerge. As Rouget observes, "Since by definition sound is actualized in the unfolding of time, its relations with itself are constantly changing . . . and these changes are integrated, at several levels, into the 'thickness' of time" (1986: 121). This "thickness" of time can be understood not only in terms of the copresence of layers of temporalities, but also in the situational knowledge produced by what has been heard previously and what one expects to hear; music, after, all, is not only a continuous stream of "nows" but also directs our perceptual faculties toward future and past sonic events (Schutz 1964; Kapferer 1991). Going further, this "thickness" of time can also be applied to sonic density: as the *nūba* progresses, its temporal spaces becomes "thicker" or denser with sound as more sonic information is packed into smaller and smaller time units. It lends time a density and "materiality it does not ordinarily have and that is of another order. It indicates that something is happening in the here and now; that time is being occupied by an action being performed, or that a certain state rules over the beings present" (Rouget 1986: 121). The musical aesthetics of movement and density constitute, and are constituted by, the ritual dynamics of progression and transformation. Ritual is about slowing the tempo of lived existence and holding at bay some of life's chaotic nature in order to focus attention on the work of retuning and readjusting the worlds of the ritual gathering (see Kapferer 2005b). I urge the reader to keep these ritual dynamics in mind as we consider the ethnographic material on the body and experience I turn to in the following chapter.

CHAPTER SIX

Trance, Healing, and the Bodily Experience

FROM INDIVIDUAL AFFLICTION TO COLLECTIVE APPEASEMENT

The warm rays of the late afternoon sun, shining into the room through large glass panes on the patio doors, give a slightly bluish hue to the curls of smoke rising from a bowl of burning incense positioned in the middle of the living room floor. As the smoke envelops the live black hen he holds by its feet, Bābā Majīd leads the four *ṣunnāʿ*, who are sitting on long, benchlike cushions positioned against the walls, in reciting the *fātiḥa*. As the short recitation concludes, Bābā Majīd swiftly but gently brushes the hen up and down the arms of the patient, a middle-aged Arab Tunisian woman whom we will call Salīma. Years earlier, Salīma suffered from debilitating bouts of fatigue and dizziness that could not be helped by medical doctors in Tunisia or in France. As her grandmother and other members of her extended family are also afflicted by *sṭambēlī* spirits, her symptoms led her to Dār Bārnū, where she was diagnosed as possessed by Sārkin Gārī, one of the Baḥriyya (Water spirits). Although (or perhaps because) the ensuing sacrifice and possession ceremony succeeded in placating her spirit and relieving her symptoms, she failed to hold the annual possession ceremonies necessary for maintaining positive relations with her afflicting spirit. As do many clients, according to Bābā Majīd, she "forgets about us when she feels fine," and thus, three years have passed since her most recent ceremony. The lapse made her increasingly vulnerable to spirit attack, which culminated in more intense episodes of dizziness and fatigue that forced her to rush home from France to perform this ceremony. Since several years have passed since Salīma's previous *sṭambēlī*, Sārkin Gārī will require an elaborate ritual comparable to a client's first, initiatory ceremony featuring a rite of sacrifice, led by the *ṭabla*, which will be replaced by the *gumbrī* in the main possession ceremony that follows.

As Bābā Majīd leads Salīma back out to the patio, the resounding drumbeats of the *ṭabla* and the metallic clashing of the *shqāshiq* begin to fill the house with Sārkin Gārī's *nūba*. Outside, Bābā Majīd slits the hen's throat and drops it into a large basin of water, which quickly turns red as the fowl struggles briefly before expiring. He does the same with a white hen. After throwing a few handfuls of whole peanuts, still in their shells, into the water, Salīma's adult daughter Amāl wipes some of the bloody water onto her mother's neck and legs.

Small groups of friends and family continue to arrive; about thirty women, ten children, and six men are in attendance. Only two of the men and three of the women are *sṭambēlī* initiates, including Salīma. The patient is then led back into the living room, where the musicians continue to play. Salīma bows in front of the *ṭabla* and commences her dance, alone, in front of the musicians. She bends slightly at the waist, dancing with unceasing side-to-side movements coordinated with repeated swaying of the arms. Her movements quicken as the tempo of the *nūba* increases. A woman puts a green banner over her shoulders and then ties a green and black striped banner around her waist. As the tempo continues to increase, Salima clasps her hands behind her back and deepens her forward bends on each beat. Shrill ululations pierce the air intermittently, and multiply as the music of the *nūba* and the patient's dance movements intensify.

* * *

For *sṭambēlī* clients, the body is the locus of affliction and appeasement, as well as the site of learning about affliction and appeasement. Initial signs of spirit affliction most often include painful or disorienting physiological signs such as paralysis, lethargy, tremors, scratches, bruising, or fainting. Affliction involves a transgression of bodily boundaries and the disruption of balance in one's lived experience. Placating the afflicting spirit is likewise an embodied process. Through enticing the spirit to possess the host, the human-spirit relationship is transformed from one of an unwelcome, aggressive, and even violent affliction of the body to one of an invited and expected accommodation of the spirit within the proper ritual space and time. During *sṭambēlī* rituals, the client's body acts and is acted upon: blood from the sacrificial animal(s) is wiped on the client's extremities; the body is draped in banners or covered in cloaks of proper type and color; the spirit's preferred variety of incense is inhaled; meals made from the sacrificed animal(s) are ingested; and, most dramatic and obvious, the body is penetrated by the spirit (or taken away by the saint) and compelled to trance. The trancing body is also the focus of the musicking bodies of the musicians, who physically surround the trancer and project their music toward the host and her spirit. These interactions also engage the other members of the ritual gathering, who participate in the ceremony in varying degrees but all of whom experience the same aural conditions for the patient's transformation. Music communicates with the spirits while it communicates to humans its communication with the spirits. This metaphysics of musical triangulation between musician, spirit, and listener is affirmed viscerally and collectively; all members of the ritual gathering are situated within the same framework of sonic experience that mediates their relationships. They not only witness the patient's transformation from afflicted to healed, but also experience the conditions for the patient's transformation, conditions that are ultimately musical and, moreover, are inseparable from the history of encounters between sub-Saharan and North Africas.

The *Sṭambēlī* Healing Process

In response to the question "What is *sṭambēlī*?" Bābā Majīd, as well as many other musicians and participants, replied that it was a "cure" (*dwā*'; lit. "medicine," "remedy"). He also maintained that neither he nor his music have the capacity for healing; rather, it is in the hands of the saints and spirits who populate the *sṭambēlī* pantheon. He describes his role as facilitating the healing process by identifying the afflicting spirit, guiding the patient through the appropriate ritual offerings, and, finally, enticing the spirit through music to descend into the body of the patient in order to dance. His role is sometimes misconstrued by potential clients seeking his help. He recounts the story of a woman who believed that he could cure her of her fainting spells simply by playing music, and without consulting the spirits: "What does she want me to do? She says, 'I don't want to faint.' What can I do? Did I tell [her] to faint? Should I tell her when I leave the café, 'Now, don't faint!' What do they think, that I preside over [the spirits]? There are many who come to me and say, 'I want [to be cured of] this or that.' I can't do anything for that" (Bābā Majīd, personal communication).

One consultation I witnessed recently involved a woman who was waking each morning with deep scratches running down both of her legs. Earlier that month, she had come to Dār Bārnū, where Bābā Majīd had started the *sṭambēlī* healing process by giving her a mixture of sub-Saharan medicines targeting the Banū Kūrī. Her condition had improved, suggesting that Bābā's initial diagnosis had been accurate. When she ran out of medicine, she came back asking for more. Baya ran the consultation and became frustrated as the woman insisted that all she needed was more medicine, not any sacrifices or rituals. Baya tried to explain to the client her obligation to compensate for her transgression, whatever that may have been, by mobilizing, as is common in *sṭambēlī*, an analogy between the structures of power dictating accountability in civil society and those governing human-spirit relations: "Listen, when you get a ticket for parking your car illegally, you have to pay the ticket to set things right. You have to pay for your actions. You have angered the spirits, and you have to set things right with them. You must make sacrifices to them. You must make offerings" (Baya, consultation, November 2, 2006).

In *sṭambēlī*, music is a catalyst for healing. Its ritual role is to attract the spirits to manifest themselves through ritualized possession of a host. Once a spirit has taken hold of a host, the music continues to be played for the enjoyment of the spirit, who will be pleased by this rare opportunity to experience the human world and will ordinarily leave the host in peace for the remainder of the year. This is considered a successful cure. Since the objective is to coax the spirit back into the host's body, this process is not exorcism, but rather the reverse—what some scholars, following French anthropologist Luc de Heusch, call "adorcism" (see Boddy 1994: 423). Trance dance constitutes a recurring offering to the spirit. A *sṭambēlī* ceremony, it must be emphasized, does not result in a permanent cure. Rather, it provides a means of managing the relationship between an afflicted human and a sometimes pernicious spirit or saint. Like those of the Sudanese *zār*, such relationships, which typically last the remainder of the host's life, will ideally stabilize over time, transforming from "an uneasy truce" to a relatively "positive symbiosis" (Boddy 1989: 11).

Initial symptoms of spirit affliction may include partial paralysis, convulsions, syncope, tremors, blindness, deafness, muteness, and other uncharacteristic behavior. These are boundary transgressions that compromise the victim's corporeal integrity, control, and wholeness. In the Dār Bārnū *sṭambēlī* tradition, they are evidence that the client has become "shattered" or "broken" (*yukassir*). Such an individual is most often described as either "inhabited" or "struck" by the spirits (cf. Crapanzano 1973: 152–156). They may also say that the spirits are "dressed" in the client (*yilbisū-hā*), meaning that the spirit is inside the client, using her body as "clothing." In one sense, the three terms could be interpreted as different points on a spectrum of relationships: being "struck" referring to single instances of spirit attack, being the spirit's "clothing" evoking a more embodied, but potentially temporary relationship, and being "inhabited" suggesting a more permanent and continuous relationship between host and spirit. I have found, however, that all three terms may be used to refer to a single client, suggesting that they are somewhat interchangeable linguistic strategies to describe but also to conceptualize and gain access to a relationship in which a human's sense of wholeness or integrity has been violated by unseen beings, causing abnormal behavior and sickness. Moreover, the distinction between the three is of negligible practical importance: as long as the affliction has been diagnosed as the work of a member of the *sṭambēlī* pantheon, the same healing process begins.

TABLE 4. The *sṭambēlī* ritual process

	Possession	*Participation*	*Major Elements*
Consultation	Maybe; if so, not induced	Individual	Recitation of Qur'ān; special medicines; various ritual acts at home
Divination	Ritually induced	Individual	Sacrifice; *gumbrī* music
Sacrifice	Ritually induced	Collective	Sacrifice; trance ceremony led by *ṭabla*
Trance ceremony	Ritually induced	Collective	Sacrifice; trance ceremony led by gumbrī

This process is one of incremental transformations. The progression of a patient from illness to wellness consists of several stages, each one bringing the patient and *sṭambēlī* practitioners closer to appeasing the afflicting spirit (table 4). Each step has its own internal structures, symbols, and procedures. The first step is to identify the particular spirit at work. After experiencing an "illness episode" (Kleinman 1980), and typically after visiting doctors who are unable to identify the cause of the problem, a potential client arriving at Dār Bārnū will engage in a consultation with an *ʿarīfa*. If there is sufficient reason to believe a member of the *sṭambēlī* pantheon is causing the problem or may be able to help, the patient may be given certain medications and instructed to perform rites at home. Later, a rite of divination is performed to determine which spirit or saint is involved, after which the client makes a down payment on the *sṭambēlī* ceremony. These preceremony rituals are followed by two collective rituals: the sacrificial rite and the rite of celebration or affirmation.

Diagnosis and Divination

Sacred sounds, and the spirit's response to these sounds, are at the heart of the *sṭambēlī* diagnostic and divination process. During the initial consultation, the patient may be read the Prophet's prayer (*ṣlāt in-nabī*, not to be confused with the *nūba* of the same name) or a verse from the Qur'ān. The client's response to this may determine whether the afflicting spirit is a "believing" spirit or a *kufr* (nonbeliever). In the latter case, the consultation will end with suggesting other more appropriate healing practices, since *sṭambēlī* is unable to help those possessed by an unbelieving spirit. Such a spirit cannot withstand the performance of any Muslim verse or prayer, nor can it tolerate the sound of the *gumbrī*.

I learned this firsthand at Dār Bārnū during one of my daily training sessions on the *gumbrī*. During this session, a woman arrived at the house for diagnosis. I stopped playing as Baya called Bābā Majīd out of the room to join the consultation. As he left the room, he signaled to me to resume playing. Before I continued, however, I took the opportunity to indulge in the sweet mint tea and baklava that Baya had dotingly left for me. It also enabled me to rest my sore fingers, which ached from hours of playing that day. A few minutes later I picked up the *gumbrī* and started to play. As soon as I strummed the strings, the patient shrieked and ran out of the house. Immediately thereafter, Baya entered the room. "Neji," she said excitedly, "you just chased away a *kufr*!" She told me that as Bābā Majīd instructed the possessing spirit to recite the Prophet's prayer, the patient winced and turned away. Then she heard the *gumbrī*, which scared her right out of the house. *Sṭambēlī* spirits, I was told, enjoy prayers and are attracted to the *gumbrī*. Bābā Majīd suggested that this patient, who was Jewish and possibly possessed by a Jewish spirit, be taken to the shrine of Sīdī Ḥmad it-Tijānī, where a Tijāniyya Sufi group performs the *dhikr*. This should work, I was told, because the *dhikr* focuses only on God (repeating the names of God), and Jewish spirits worship the same God. Bābā Majīd later explained to her that not all cases of spirit possession fell within the domain of *sṭambēlī*, because there are different types of spirits, each of which responds to a particular healing tradition. He told her, "Coffee, tea, and soda are all drinks, but they are all different. It is the same with the spirits."

If, however, it is suspected that *sṭambēlī* spirits are at work, the consultation continues with a detailed discussion with the patient (and often members of the patient's family) of her symptoms, when they started, and their context. These answers, as well as the patient's physical state (which often manifests itself by this time in trembling, a vacant stare, or some form of dissociation), contribute to making an initial diagnosis. Based on this initial consultation, the patient may be given special medicines (usually from sub-Saharan Africa) and may be directed to perform certain ritual activities. These usually include burning incense at home.

If, for instance, one of the main symptoms is paralysis of the legs, if the patient has come into contact with a dead body, or if there is reason to believe black magic is involved, healers may suspect the spirit is one of the Banū Kūrī, as they are associated with these scenarios. The Dār Bārnū healers will then give the patient *jāwī ākḥal* (lit. "black Java," a dark-colored incense favored by the Banū Kūrī), which the patient must burn before she goes to bed for a specified number of nights. She must carry the incense into each room of the house, making sure not to say "bismillāh" (in the name of God) before lighting it or entering any of the rooms with it (uttering "bismillāh" protects one from the *jnūn* and would thus offend *sṭambēlī* spirits, who are emphatically not *jnūn*). The patient must also take a specified amount of money, dip it into water seven times, and then wrap it in a black cloth. She may be told to sleep with the cloth under her pillow at night and to try to remember her dreams so that she can describe them to the *ʿarīfa* at the divinatory rite. It is often the case that after this stage of the ritual process the patient is showing signs of improvement, which suggests that the spirit is responding to the offerings. Lack of improvement, on the other hand, does not necessarily indicate lack of success. Rather, it may suggest that the spirit is demanding more offerings.

After diagnosis, the patient undergoes a divinatory rite to identify the specific spirit afflicting the patient. The patient is taken to the *ʿarīfa*, who first lights incense to attract the spirits. The patient is seated on the ground, and a sacrificial animal (a dove, chicken, or goat) is circled around the patient. The animal is then slaughtered, and the spirits are called upon musically to descend in order to be identified. To this end, the *yinna* performs the *silsila*s of *nūba*s until one provokes a significant reaction in the patient. This can consist of trembling, shaking, fainting, or convulsive behaviour, as well as, more rarely, dance. In any case, the patient ideally emerges "all better," at least for the time being, and the offending (and offended) spirit has been successfully identified. Soon thereafter, arrangements for the *sṭambēlī* ceremony are sealed through the payment of the *ʿarbūn* (cash advance) to the *yinna* by the patient or her family. At the ceremony, the musicians will entice the spirit to descend into the ritual and dance through the patient's body until it is placated. This will defend the patient against further affliction until the ceremony is repeated the following year.

Diagnoses relating to the spirits are not to be taken lightly. A false diagnosis, whether it acknowledges the work of the spirits or not, could lead to further problems and, I was told, even death. There are stories that circulate in the community about the sometimes tragic results of ignoring a diagnosis. Bābā Majīd once saw a patient whom he diagnosed as not possessed and refused to hold a *sṭambēlī* for her. The patient, however, sought out other *sṭambēlī* troupes, one of which was unwilling to refuse potential income and therefore agreed to hold a *sṭambēlī* for her. The spirits were invoked and descended into the ritual but, since they had not chosen her as a host, became upset. The patient's death a week later only reinforced Bābā Majīd's already strong reputation. During my time at Dār Bārnū, a small number of patients seeking diagnosis became disappointed when told that their problems were not caused by spirits, or at least not *sṭambēlī* spirits. This speaks to what appears to be an emergent type of cultural capital, perhaps bolstered by recent public sphere recognition of the tradition, mediated by the discourses and practices of the world music market (see chap. 8).

Sacrifice

Animal sacrifice is an essential component of all *sṭambēlī* rituals. Each spirit and saint has its own particular sacrifice, usually a rooster, hen, dove, sheep, or goat or combination thereof. The number of sacrifices, as well as the color of the animals, is specific to the desires of each spirit or saint. It is slaughtered according to Islamic custom, butchered on the spot, and cooked for the meal that is also part of every *sṭambēlī*. The sacrificial animal is a commodity.[1] It is one of the more expensive components of the *sṭambēlī* ritual process. Sacrifice is often depicted in anthropological studies as emphasizing one of three stages: presacrifice manipulation of the animal, the act of killing the animal, and the consumption of the animal. The *sṭambēlī* sacrifice is more concerned with the last. It is not ceremoniously decorated beforehand, as in the Sudanese *zār* described by Janice Boddy (1989), nor do any participants imbibe the freshly flowing blood, as René Brunel (1926) and Vincent Crapanzano (1973) have shown for the ʿAissāwa and Ḥamadsha in Morocco, although both of these acts were probably performed in the *sṭambēlī* context in the past. Indeed, the act of wiping the sacrificial blood on the patient's body may have replaced the act of drinking sacrificial blood, which is prohibited in Islam.

Animal sacrifice not only opens up the channels of communication between human and spirit realms; it is also an act of communication in and of itself. In the Maghrib, animal sacrifice is part of the dynamics of exchange that often govern relations between Muslims and the divine or supernatural. Offerings to God may take the form of daily prayers, making the hajj, or fasting during Ramadan, as well as more material gifts, such as animal sacrifices at holidays. These are in exchange for avoiding God's anger or for reward in the afterlife. A more visceral and immediate relationship obtains between many North Africans and Muslim saints. These relationships are often understood as bonds of obligation (*ḥaqq*) that follow certain rules of deference and reciprocity (Eickelman 1976). Ascertaining the demands of a saint or spirit, however, is not always straightforward. Spoken communication of the spirit through the vessel of a human host does not constitute a major element of the spirit-host relationship or a normative component of every adept's ritualized trance, as it appears to do in Malagasy *tromba* (Lambek 1981) and Sudanese *zār* (Boddy 1989), where spirits will make their demands known publicly by requesting certain kinds of offerings or a particular type of ritual. Rather, a *sṭambēlī* spirit may speak to patients individually through an *ʿarīfa*, interpreted by another *ʿarīfa* or an assistant called *kashaka*, at a specified moment in the ceremony.

The Ceremonies

Unlike non-*sṭambēlī* possession ceremonies in Tunis, which take place at public shrines, the private home is the most popular setting for holding a *sṭambēlī*. Through *sṭambēlī*, sub-Saharans began to enter the homes of Tunisians not as slaves or servants, but as invited ritual specialists who would be paid for their services. In addition, the local Tunisian would enter the sonic ritual world of the sub-Saharan community. By the time the ceremony was held in a private home, the patient would have already gone to one of the communal houses for consultation, diagnosis, and divination. She would have been given certain sub-Saharan herbal medications and/or a set of rituals to perform at home. After showing signs of improvement, she would return to the communal house to arrange for a *sṭambēlī* ceremony by negotiating and paying the cash deposit and setting a date for the ceremony, a major ritual and social event designed to appease the afflicting spirit through music, trance dance, and sacrifices. Once diagnosed and initiated into the *sṭambēlī* network, the patient would be expected to hold a *sṭambēlī* every year in order to maintain positive relations with the spirits. Now, as in the past, this arrangement results in enduring social relationships between balck and Arab Tunisians.

A private *sṭambēlī* ceremony requires a considerable outlay of money. In addition to the fee (300TD for Bābā Majīd; 200TD when the ceremony is led by one of his apprentices), which is split among the musicians and the *ʿarīfa*, the host must provide meals and refreshments for all participants, and purchase the appropriate sacrificial animals. It is often the case that new clothing is purchased for the event, which is considered an important social occasion. Poorer initiates could save some money through negotiation, or by holding the *sṭambēlī* at a communal house or a *zāwiya*, and "sharing" the *sṭambēlī* with other initiates. With the decline of the communal houses, the *zāwiya* has become a popular alternative, especially as more and more Tunisians live in large apartment complexes and wish to maintain their privacy.

Sṭambēlī Dance and Trance

Trance is the culmination of the *sṭambēlī* healing process. In addition to animal sacrifices, the patient is expected to offer her body to her afflicting spirit or saint in order to (re)establish positive relations. There is no explicit taxonomy of trance states; the verb *yashṭaḥ* is used to refer to any dancing that occurs in a *sṭambēlī* ceremony. While this term is also used, at Dār Bārnū, to refer to some forms of non-*sṭambēlī* dancing, verbs derived from the more common Arabic term for dancing, *raqṣ*, are not used in the *sṭambēlī* context. The term *yashṭaḥ* derives from the Arabic root that means to "roam" or "stray" and may also connote "escapade" and "excess" (Wehr 1994: 550). Yet this is not an aimless endeavor of excess. The trajectory of trance, with its repetition, acceleration, and intensification, is based on a gestural economy of motion that is highly codified and largely predictable, giving rise to a tension between deliberate action and loss of control. One of the ironies of trance—and by extension the *sṭambēlī* healing process—is that in order to regain control of the self one must be willing and trained to give up that control. As Deborah Kapchan points out in the context of Moroccan *gnāwa*, trance is characterized by a simultaneity of presence and absence, a "volitional invocation of the nonvolitional body" (2007: 63). Embodiment here is impossible without the simultaneity of disembodiment; the paradox of control and the loss thereof is also the tension between self and other.

There is another set of tensions at play in the concept of *sṭambēlī* dance: that between liberation and suffering. A dance whose purpose is to heal the body cannot be separated from the pain that body has endured. The perception of healing is recognition of affliction, pain, disorder, and lack of control. Dance, moreover, which is typically associated with feelings of joy and a certain freedom of expression, is also here associated with the obligation to perform, an act of disciplining of the body. This "dual potential" of dance (Bauman 1995: 39) has been noted in Greece by by Loring Danforth in his study of the Anasteria ritual dance in Greece, where he notes that the initial dance of suffering, an obligatory and punishing act, transforms gradually, as the adept transforms her relationship with Saint Constantine, into a dance of release and happiness (Danforth 1989).

There are nuances and gradations to the *sṭambēlī* trance experience. These can be grouped into three overlapping types of dance, each associated with different relations between human and spirit worlds: recreational dance, nonpossession trance, or *jedba*, and possession trance.

RECREATIONAL DANCE

Early in the ceremony, and only during the *nūba*s for the Whites, there may be recreational dancing. The vocabulary to describe it frames it in terms of simply "having fun" (*yaʿmilū jāw*; lit. "creating atmosphere" or "creating ambiance"). This typically involves several individuals dancing at the same time, but not as a choreographed collective. Rather, each person dances however he or she likes, usually by stepping side to side and bending forward slightly at the waist. This pattern often constitutes the early stage of a dance that will lead to *jedba* trance, and, indeed, it is not unusual for one or two dancers to gradually enter into *jedba*. In such cases, the other dancers will move back to make room for the emerging trancer to make her way to the center of the *mīdān* to finish her trance. Even for those who do not enter into trance, benefits are derived in the form of the *baraka* of the saint whose *nūba* is being performed.

Although recreational dance is absent from scholarly typologies of *sṭambēlī* dance, and often dismissed by musicians as simply "having fun" (as opposed to the real "work" [*khidma*] of facilitating trance), I include it here because it nevertheless constitutes an important space for noninitiates to enter into the visceral world of *sṭambēlī*. It is an inclusive, nonthreatening point of entry that is, at one level, similar to the traditional dance experiences at weddings or other celebrations. Indeed, musicians will often encourage members of the gathering to come up to dance in the early stages of the ceremony. If recreational dancing does lead to trance, it is considered a sign that the dancer has been chosen by the saint and may have to become an initiate in order to procure the protection of the saint. For the dancers who surround her but do not fall into trance, this proximity provides an intimate and experiential sense of the power of *sṭambēlī* music to mediate between the human and spirit realms.

JEDBA

The second type of dance, *jedba*, occurs mainly to the *nūba*s for the Whites. It is a nonpossession trance, for the human-spirit dynamics are understood as the saint's "taking away" the dancer from her body (as opposed to "entering" the hosts body, as is the case in possession trance, described below). The term *jedba* connotes a strong, often irresistable, sense of being enticed or lured toward the saint. It conforms to what Gilbert Rouget calls "abstract" (1986: 114) trance dance, as it does not involve figurative or mimetic dance movements. Rather, it consists of forceful, repetitive movements involving either bending back and forth at the waist or, on all fours, swinging the head to and fro. These movements are also found in other trance traditions in Tunisia associated with the veneration of saints, performed in ceremonies generally referred to as *ḥaḍra* (lit. "presence"). The Arabic *wajd*—which is also used in Sufi contexts—is sometimes used to describe this type of trance. The relationship between saint and dancer is understood as one in which the saint, through trance, "takes the dancer away" (*yuhiz-hā*; sometimes *wajd yuhiz-hā*—"trance takes her away"). Before the onset of trance, dancers may sense the presence of the saint, and when the *nūba* begins, they may "feel it in their blood," as an overwhelming and irresistable urge to dance suddenly takes over.

POSSESSION

Possession trance, in contrast, is caused by the spirits, that is, the Blacks. The mechanism is one by which the spirit is understood to "enter" the body of the dancing host. Unlike the saints, each spirit has its own unique figurative or mimetic dance movements. There are as many dance movements as there are spirits. Some are relatively taciturn: Yā Rīma, the leader of the Bēyēt spirits, will dress in fine robes and a red fez, sit in a chair, and calmly survey the proceedings. Others partake in more lively somatic movements, such as the writhing and swimming motions of some of the Baḥriyya spirits (see fig. 12). Still others can be violent, such as some members of the Banū Kūrī known for beating their hosts with clubs. For the most part, however, they engage in series of repetitive motions and end up situated in front of the *gumbrī*. Typically, both possession and *jedba* trance involve a single dancer situated directly in front of the musicians. Both types of trance also end with the passing out of the dancer (*dūkh*). In some instances, two or three trancers affected by the same spirit or saint may enter into trance, but each must then be dealt with separately.

* * *

After the sacrifice of the hens and the application of their blood to her body (described in this chapter's introduction), Salīma dances alone for the entire nine-and-a-half-minute duration of the *nūba* of Sārkin Gārī. The proximity of the dancer's body to those of the musicians and their instruments is remarkable: after bowing in front of the *ṭabla*, she continues dancing with her head bowed down almost vertically above the drum and between the *shqāshiq* on either side. She is enveloped in a pocket of sound. Her feet hit the floor in time with the *ṭabla* beats, which closely precede the accented articulations of the *shqāshiq*. The aesthetics of temporal progression are made clear: this *nūba* began at a tempo of 94 cells per minute and ended at 156, nearly a 66 percent increase in tempo that results in very little sense that any note dissipates before the subsequent note arrives.

As more women arrive and begin to congregate around Salīma, the musicians begin the *nūba* of Sīdī Frej. They sing: "Lē illah ilā Allah frej yā walī Allah" (There is no God but God, Frej, O friend of God) and then a shorter refrain, "Yā aḥbāb Allah" (O beloved of God). The first offering of money is made to the musicians: Amāl takes a five-dinar note[2] and waves it over the head of Salīma, in effect making a contribution to the musicians, as an offering to the saint, in the name of the dancer. In contrast to the *nūba* of Sārkin Gārī, to which only Salīma dances, numerous women may, and do, dance to Sīdī Frej (and subsequent *nūbas*). Many of the women partake in

FIGURE 12. Dancers possessed by Baḥriyya spirits, 2009. (Photograph by Matthieu Hagene.)

some light dancing (not trance or possession), but Salīma remains dancing in front of them, nearest to the musicians. The musicians increase the tempo gradually over the course of the *nūba*, and after a dozen or so repeats of the lyrics, play instrumentally. The *nūba* ends after three and a half minutes with two loud beats of the *ṭabla*, stick held high to signal to the *ṣunnāʿ* the end of the *nūba*.

Salīma is still standing, swaying liminally. She appears coherent and self-aware: as Bābā Majīd approaches her, she tells him, "I haven't fainted yet." "I know, I know," replies Bābā Majīd, as he guides her into a sitting position on the floor. Salīma's spirit is still inside her body. She will have to dance again later, as Sārkin Gārī is not yet satisfied with the trance experience. This was to be expected, since the spirits prefer to be summoned after sunset, when the *gumbrī* will be calling on more and more members of the pantheon to descend. Had he been satisfied with the dance and the sacrifice, he would have caused Salīma to faint (*dūkh*) at the end of the dance as he departed her body willingly. The process of driving the spirit out of the body requires what resembles a chiropractic manipulation of certain body parts. First, Bābā Majīd pulls Salīma's arms backward behind her. He then pushes down on her shoulders from behind her. Then he moves in front of her, and, like a chiropractor, pulls her right arm behind her, as if cracking her back. He then repeats the procedure using her left arm. He turns her head to the right, and then to the left, both times resulting in audible "cracking" sounds from the vertebrae. Finally, he pulls both of her arms forward, jerking them together and then apart repeatedly until they fall loosely to her sides.

The music resumes with the *nūba* of Sīdī ʿAbd el-Qādir, which meets with a chorus of ululations from the women in the room. There is a palpable sense of excitement, and several women move up to the *mīdān* to dance. Light, communal dancing ensues. More money is waved over the heads of various dancers and thrown in front of the *ṭabla*. After the *nūba* settles into a brisk tempo, the musicians transition to the *sūga*, the repeated musical formula of high intensity (see chap. 5). The *sūga* is marked by a driving, regular onbeat rhythm on the *ṭabla* that matches and replaces the accented notes of the *gumbrī* when that instrument plays a *sūga*; in fact, the left-hand articulations of the *ṭabla*, which fill in the space between those regular, accented downbeats, line up exactly with the notes of the *kūlū* that are played in between the accented notes in a *gumbrī*-led *sūga*. The *shqāshiq* continue the *muthallith* pattern but have more latitude to play a variety of syncopated variations. The *sūga* is also physically marked by each of the *ṣunnāʿ* rising from their seats on the floor and onto one or two knees. This brings them closer together, raises their instruments vertically higher, and creates a more concentrated pocket of sound at the front of the *mīdān*. The noticeable increase in intensity is usually acknowledged with *zaghrāt* (ululations) from the women. It is during this first *sūga* that the first trance begins.

In the midst of the group of dancers, a young woman with a green *sunjuq* wrapped around her waist begins to dance more and more intensely, bending further at the waist and closing her eyes. The musicians instantly recognize the signs of an imminent trance, and one of the *ṣunnāʿ* calls out "ṣalī ʿalīh rāk tirba'!" (lit. "Pray to him and be blessed"), the euphemistic call for the women in attendance to ululate. Shrill ululations pierce the air as other dancers make way while others usher this dancer to the front of the *mīdān*. As the trancer swings her head frenetically from side to side in time with the music, another woman takes notice and rushes over to her, removes the elastic band from the dancer's hair, allowing her dark, shoulder-length hair to swing freely, punctuating each contraction of her dancing body, and grabs her from behind to ensure she does not run into a wall or any of the other musicians and dancers. For the next several minutes, she keeps her arms wrapped around the dancer's waist as she dances by bending forward and backward, repeatedly, gradually increasing in intensity until she finally faints, falling backward into the ready arms of the *ʿarīfa* and Amāl, who guide her body gently to the floor. Bābā Majīd reminds the women to cense the dancer's legs, and the musicians rest for a few minutes to allow her to recover. This *ṭabla*-led portion of the ceremony returns to the *nūba* for Sārkin Gārī, then musically invokes two more of the Shaikhs—Sīdī Marzūg and Sīdī Saʿd—to which several more women dance and trance. The ceremony concludes with *nūba*s for Mūlay Brāhīm—the head of the Baḥriyya spirits—and, once again, Sārkin Gārī.

The sacrifice trance ceremony first focused exclusively on the patient and her afflicting spirit but soon became more inclusive, as the musicians transitioned from the spirits (Sārkin Gārī) to the saints (Sīdī Frej and Sīdī ʿAbd el-Qādir) in the second and third *nūba*s. In just these three *nūba*s we witnessed recreational dance, *jedba* (nonpossession trance), and possession trance overlapping in two different ways. First, an individual's recreational dance turned into *jedba* trance. Second, there were moments characterized by a simultaneity of dance and trance performed by different individuals to the same *nūba*.

In the midst of *sṭambēlī* ritual performance, the musicians' attention is manifestly focused on the dancer's body and the development of the trance. Yet inseparable from that focus on the individual is an awareness of the identity of the spirit, who is the subject of the sung lyrics and musically targeted by his own distinct melody. This awareness includes knowledge of where the spirit is situated in the ritual order in relation to others who appeared earlier and those who may be summoned later. As the main goal of the rite of sacrifice is to placate Sārkin Gārī, his *nūba* occupies a prominent place in the route followed by the musicians. It is the only *nūba* that is repeated in this ritual episode; it is performed first, fourth, and last (see table 5). His spirit

TABLE 5. *Nūba*s played during the sacrifice ceremony

	Spirit	*Saint*	*Dance type (number of dancers)*
Time ↓	Sārkin Gārī		Possession trance (1)
		Sīdī Frej	Recreational dance (3); jedba trance (1)
		Sīdī ʿAbd el-Qādir	Recreational dance (5); jedba trance (1)
	Sārkin Gārī		Possession trance (1); recreational dance behind Salīma (3); jedba trance (1)
		Sīdī Marzūg	Recreational dance (2)
		Sīdī Sa'd	Recreational dance (5)
	Mūlay Brāhīm		None
	Sārkin Gārī		Recreational dance (7); possession trance (1)

family, the Baḥriyya, is the only spirit family invoked in this section, and the Shaikhs, the most powerful of the *sṭambēlī* saints, are the only saints called upon. Schematically, the *nūba*s performed during today's ritual of sacrifice could be organized as in table 5.

The sacrifice ceremony is more concerned with praising and placating the afflicting spirit than it is with demonstrating adherence to hierarchy, or, rather, it privileges the afflicting spirit while acknowledging its place within the pantheon's hierarchy. The sacrifice also serves as a prelude to the evening ceremony, which is not only more elaborate, but also adds to and amplifies the messages communicated.

The Ritual of Celebration

The ritual of celebration, which is led by the *gumbrī* rather than the *ṭabla*, follows a logic of musical progression decidedly different from but related to that of the ritual of sacrifice. It also amplifies and expands the scope of referents and meanings communicated and experienced by the musicians, dancers, and other members of the ritual gathering. Once the communal meal is finished and the sun has set, Bābā Majīd tunes his *gumbrī*, then holds it above the incense, which is then passed in front of each of the *ṣunnāʿ* so that they can likewise cense their *shqāshiq*. They recite the *fātiḥa*, which, as it ends, meets, surprisingly, with virtual silence. The lead *shqāshiq* player mockingly utters "badadadadadada," mimicking the *zaghrāt*, in order to remind the women that the *zaghrāt* are not only appropriate, but expected, at that time. The women respond with a loud series of ululations. For a moment the *zaghrāt*, though seemingly peripheral to the larger ritual acts of the ceremony, are highlighted for the important role they play. Some of the women laugh or blush, appearing to be suddenly aware of their role in contributing to the tone of the ceremony.[3]

In beginning the ceremony, Bābā Majīd's options for *nūba*s are relatively limited, as the *gumbrī* part of the ceremony always begins with the same three *nūba*s: Ṣlāt in-Nabī, Jerma, and Bū Ḥijba. A few more dancers arrive, now dressed in their finest traditional Tunisian clothing. Several *nūba*s for the Shaikhs ensue: Sīdī Marzūg, Sīdī Frej, Sīdī ʿAbd el-Qādir, Sīdī ʿAbd es-Salēm, and Sīdī Saʿd. Some women partake in recreational dances, but Amāl becomes deeply entranced by both Sīdī ʿAbd el-Qādir and Sīdī ʿAbd es-Salēm.

The musicians return to the spirits with the *nūba* of Mūlay Brāhīm, to which an older woman wearing a red and green banner begins to dance. After Mūlay Brāhīm, she becomes possessed by Nana ʿAysha, one of the Bēyēt (Royalty) and Sghār (Children) spirits. The possession by Nana ʿAysha constitutes the ceremony's only verbal communication between spirit and human. As her *nūba* ends, Nana ʿAysha is immediately surrounded by a flock of young women who wish to have their futures told. Some wish to know if they will marry soon, others seek advice on solving personal or family problems. This is a highlight of the ceremony for many and demonstrates that *sṭambēlī* is not for the benefit of the afflicted only. The following ritual, the *gaṣʿa* Sīdī ʿAbd el-Qādir (Sīdī ʿAbd el-Qādir's Bowl), is also aimed at the wider congregation, especially single women of marital age.

SĪDĪ ʿABD EL-QĀDIR'S BOWL

All the lights in the room have been turned off, and there is an air of anticipation. The musicians begin the *nūba* of Sīdī ʿAbd el-Qādir as one of the *ṣunnāʿ* walks into the *mīdān*, balancing an enormous bowl of couscous on top of his head. He is followed in procession by members of the ritual gathering, each holding a lighted candle. This ritual is especially for unmarried women; only single women and *sṭambēlī* initiates carry candles, but everyone takes part in the slowly moving procession, which, lighted only by the flicker of candles, circumambulates the *mīdān* seven times. As the procession ends, the lights are turned on. The musicians break into the *sūga*, and many members of the congregation, some still with candles, begin to dance. *Nūba*s for Sīdī Bū Ra's el-ʿAjmī and Sīdī ʿAmr precede the communal recitation of the *fātiḥa*. At this time, an older man kneels down in front of the bowl and eats from it directly, without using any hands. He then does the same in front of a bowl of water, drinking from it without the use of his hands. One of the *ṣunnāʿ* sprinkles water on the head of this kneeling adept, which is a sign of placating a Baḥriyya spirit. All initiates, including Salīma, Amāl, two men, and one boy, must eat from the bowl in this manner. Tremearne (1914: 466) notes that in Nigeria, this is understood to confer upon initiates the ability to throw themselves on the ground without getting hurt. He also suggests that it may be in imitation of the sacrificial animal. What is significant here, I believe, is not so much the abstract associations of these bodily acts, but the fact that they constitute for initiates new ways of using and experiencing the body. The gestures of bodily posturing—whether in this act of consumption or in the movements of trance—are patterns of behavior that not only represent, but also enact performatively the initate's definition of self involving affiliation with the *sṭambēlī* community. Bowing before the musicians, being drawn ineluctably toward the *gumbrī*, prostrating oneself on the floor, and eating without using one's hands are bodily positionings and manipulations that make physical certain relationships between self and other, which in turn draw attention to the codes, conventions, and, indeed, ontologies of *sṭambēlī*.

The performance of *gaṣʿa* Sīdī ʿAbd el-Qādir is considered a highlight of the *sṭambēlī* ceremony. This special rite is an acknowledgment of his special status in *sṭambēlī*. Having initiates eat and drink from his bowl, without using their hands, marks this off as a particularly esoteric point in the ritual and only reinforces the perception of his potency. Remarkably, however, this rite is, in another way, the most easily understood and recognized by ordinary Tunisians. The most common reason for a visit to a saint's shrine in North Africa is to ask for a saint's intercession in issues of marriage and fertility. A young Tunisian woman of any class would not find it unusual to be brought by an older relative to a saint's shrine in order to make an offering to the saint in hopes of help in finding a good husband (though some might find it old fashioned or superstitious). To obtain this blessing, the woman would ordinarily purchase a candle and light it over the saint's tomb. The performance of Sīdī ʿAbd el-Qādir's Bowl speaks to the members of the congregation in very local terms and serves as a bridge connecting *sṭambēlī* to wider local practices of saint veneration.

FINAL OFFERINGS

The trance ceremony resumes as one of the *ṣunnāʿ* asks loudly, "Who hasn't danced yet?" Bābā Majīd echoes this, with "Who's left?" The musicians play the *nūba* of Sīdī Frej, followed by that of Sīdī ʿAbd es-Salēm. The *fātiḥa* is recited once again as Bābā Majīd uncovers another *gaṣʿa*, this one filled with *mlukhīya*, the dark-sauced dish that is eaten at Dār Bārnū *sṭambēlī* ceremonies to satisfy the requirement that "something black" be eaten. This meal will be eaten by everyone in attendance, not only initiates.

After this pause in the ceremony, the final sacrifice begins. Bābā Majīd enters with another hen, this time white, and Salīma is seated in the middle of the *mīdān* and covered in a white and black cloth. Bābā Majīd swings the hen by the feet in the four cardinal directions. He then circles it over a seated Salīma seven times and up and down each arm. He then places it on her head, where it sits, virtually motionless, provoking a chorus of ululations. The obeisance of the hen demonstrates that the spirit is placated, satisfied with the dancing and the sacrifices that have been offered. Bābā Majīd removes the hen from the top of her head, gets Salīma to stand, and swings it between her feet. He then leads everyone in reciting the *fātiḥa*. Two of the *ṣunnāʿ* then leave the room with the hen, taking it to be slaughtered, along with the black goat, on the patio.

Although Sārkin Gārī has indicated his acceptance of Salīma's offerings of blood and body, the ritual does not end there. Two additional families of spirits—the Banū Kūrī and the Bēyēt—must be addressed through music and dance before the ritual can end appropriately. Although the aim of the ceremony was to placate Salīma's afflicting spirit, these other spirits, not part of Sārkin Gārī's Baḥriyya family of spirits, must be invoked, affirming the earlier point that individual ritual healing is about much more than an individual's ailment. The Banū Kūrī are invoked simply with Kūrī's *nūba* before the Bēyēt, or Royalty spirits, are called upon to descend, possessing Amāl, who is dressed in appropriately regal gold and red attire along with conspicuous amounts of jewelry.

Two large bowls filled with copious amounts of sweets are censed and set in front of the musicians as they begin the *nūba*s for Miryamu and Nana ʿAysha. As we near the end of the ceremony, Nana ʿAysha possesses Amāl, who lurches forward, grabs the larger bowl of sweets, raises it above her and places it on top of her head, where she balances it as she dances. As the *nūba* ends, the bowl is placed back on the ground, Nana ʿAysha takes leave of Amāl, and the musicians recite the *fātiḥa*. The candy and nuts are generously distributed to all. The bags of sweets each of us will bring home, in addition to providing tasty treats, will bring good luck (they are considered blessed by the saints and spirits), will serve as reminders of the ritual, and for those with this ritual knowledge, will evoke the generosity of the time of the beys.

Ritual Aesthetics and Bodily Empathy

In many ways, this performance resonates with many other rituals in the Islamic world in which women embrace the opportunity for self-expression, leadership, and even social critique. A common theme in the scholarship is that these women's religious rituals, which emphasize emotion, physicality, and embodiment, must be understood in relation to more text-based rituals of the male sphere. In Sudan, Janice Boddy demonstrates how women are responsible for the practices (such as *zār*) that ensure the continuity of the internal social life of the village, whereas men are responsible for those that extend beyond the village (Boddy 1989). Within the *zār* context, the spirits may, through the vehicle of the woman's body, criticize certain men or demand from them offerings that the men are socially compelled to give.

In Turkey, Nancy Tapper and Richard Tapper show how the *mevlûd* ritual (based on a text recounting the Prophet's birthday) has parallel but differing manifestations in male and female spheres (Tapper and Tapper 1987). The women's *mevlûd* is much more elaborate, more dramatic, and longer than that of the men. It focuses on the chapter of the text that deals specifically with the birth of Muḥammad, which the women mark by the distribution of sweets, repositioning and covering of their bodies, and physical contact, stroking each other's backs in imitation of Emine, the Prophet's mother.

When they reach the passage in the text that describes the greeting of the newborn, the women move around the room and greet each other with intense eye contact and emotion. Indeed, these rituals, which often bring many of the women to tears, are highly emotional in comparison to the shorter, men's versions. They allow women the rare opportunity for self-expression and leadership outside the household, enabling them to strengthen ties among houses in the social network.

In the context of urban Tunisia the parallel existences of men's and women's rituals is particularly acute in the rituals at the shrine of Sīdī Belḥassen esh-Shādihlī, where an exclusively male ritual involves the *hizb* (a religious chant that incorporates verses of the Qur'ān and praises of God) and the *dhikr* (the repetitive chanting of the name of God), which is performed with increasing intensity and is accompanied by the regulated swaying of the body. What is significant for the present discussion is that in an adjacent room is a gathering of women who, sealed off visually from the men, take part in the same ritual but become possessed by *jnūn*. The chants performed by the men order the women's ritual experience, but the women respond by dancing and becoming possessed. The men create the sonic context for the separate, fully female gathering.

Sṭambēlī, like these other rituals, offers women a space for self-expression, leadership, therapy, and entertainment. It is also provides a means for cementing social ties and for coping with structural exclusion. What is interesting in the *sṭambēlī* context, however, is that *sṭambēlī* ceremonies are by no means exclusive, separate, female contexts. They are not understood to be the "female" counterpart to any specifically "male" ritual. While women do constitute the majority of patients, there are also many men who participate in each type of *sṭambēlī* dance. More obviously, the musicians are all male, as are some of the *ʿarīfa*s.

By placating Sārkin Gārī through blood sacrifice and possession dance, this ceremony transformed Salīma from a passive victim still vulnerable to spirit attack to an active participant in a functional and balanced relationship with her afflicting spirit. While this constitutes a demonstrably effective and profoundly meaningful transition, I wish to suggest that this was but one effect of the ritual, as the possessed body conveys meanings beyond its immediate, physical symptoms and actions. In witnessing the patient's possession, other attendees also witness and socialize her affliction. Some adepts in attendance will also benefit from trance, thus reaffirming their relations with the saints or spirits; uninitiated novices may experience their first trance, marking their introduction into the embodied world of *sṭambēlī*; others may merely enjoy the music, the spectacle, the food, and the socializing.

Sṭambēlī aesthetics of timbre, texture, and continuous and directed motion saturate the ritual space. Through these aesthetics, musicking, trancing, listening, and gazing bodies interface experientially and share in the production of meaning. To put it another way, it is in the aesthetics of ritual that feeling and sensation are married to cognition and meaning (Kapferer and Hobart 2005: 13). The numerous observing, listening, and sensing bodies that do not experience trance nevertheless experience the aesthetic conditions for the patient's trance experience; they witness and perceive the force of *sṭambēlī*'s distinctive aesthetics. This is the capacity for musical aesthetics to create an experiential ritual empathy described by Robert Desjarlais as "one body mak[ing] sense of another" (1992: 183). John Blacking also referred to such states as "fellow-feeling," "bodily resonance," or "bodily empathy" (see Sager 2006). Transcendence, for Blacking, is not just about the individual, but is eminently social, based on a "mutual tuning-in relationship." By simply attending a ceremony, all members of the ritual gathering experience the aesthetics of *sṭambēlī* and thus also experience the patient's potential for navigating the terrain between afflicted and healed, and between self and other.

PART III

Movements and Trajectories

CHAPTER SEVEN

Pilgrimage and Place

LOCAL PERFORMANCES, TRANSNATIONAL IMAGINARIES

On a dusty side road in a tranquil agricultural region northwest of Tunis, four musicians stand outside the entrance to the *zāwiya* of Sīdī Frej, a black Muslim saint and former slave who lived in the region over two centuries ago. They recite the *fātiḥa* together as Bābā Majīd holds a chicken in the billows of incense smoke, then slaughters the animal above the *ṭabla* drums, making sure to let some of its blood trickle onto the instruments. As the first ritual act of the three-day annual pilgrimage (*ziyāra*, lit. "visit") to the shrine, the blessing of the instruments highlights the agency and centrality of music to the events that unfold over the three-day pilgrimage. Soon after the *ṭabla* players sling their drums over their shoulders and the *shqāshiq* players fasten their instruments to their hands, the *kharja* (street procession, lit. "departure") begins, the resounding drumbeats of the *ṭabla* and the loud metallic pulses of the *shqāshiq* publicly announcing the commencement of the pilgrimage. With its drumming, flag-waving, and air of celebration, this loud and colorful street procession is not dissimilar to the well-known public processions of Tunisian Sufi orders such as the ʿĪsāwiyya. To the local observer, however, it is immediately identifiable as other by its unusual instrumentation, foreign musical aesthetics, obscure lyrics, and predominance of black bodies as musicians and in other ritually privileged roles. Other aspects of the pilgrimage, such as certain "black" or sub-Saharan victuals, an elaborate decor featuring spears, swords, and the mask of Bū Saʿdiyya, and the arrival of spirits from south of the Sahara Desert all serve as reminders that the pilgrimage is a ritual that developed at the interstices of local religious practices and possession traditions from sub-Saharan Africa carried to North Africa by forcibly displaced slaves.

During the *kharja*, the four musicians, five flag bearers, one person carrying the bowl of incense, and about a dozen other pilgrims march down the road toward the entrance of the *zāwiya*, where the shrine's caretaker stands holding in place a wooden flagpole to which Sīdī Frej's red and green banner is attached. The five flags in the procession represent the five saints who are first to be invoked musically; in order of appearance, they are Sīdī ʿAbd el-Qādir, Sīdī ʿAbd es-Salēm, Sīdī Bū Ra's el-ʿAjmī, Sīdī Frej, and Sīdī Saʿd. In the *nūba*s for the first three of these saints, the rhythms of the *ṭabla* and *shqāshiq* guide the pilgrims toward the entrance of the *zāwiya*, where participants form a single line in order to perform the *ḥalqa* (circle), a series of five counterclockwise circumambulations. After the last of these, the flag bearers exit the circle in order to return the flags to their places inside the shrine, where Bābā Majīd is preparing a communal drink called *dindrī* by mixing together sorghum, soured milk, water, and sugar in a large bowl situated atop Sīdī Frej's tomb.

Outside, as the musicians begin the *nūba* of Sīdī Frej, a woman lurches forward into the middle of the circle and begins to trance. The woman, who is sometimes described as *bint sīdī frej* (lit. "daughter of Sīdī Frej"), is "taken away" into trance by Sīdī Frej whenever the musicians play his *nūba* in her presence. The trancer, who bobs up and down to the music by bending forward and back at the waist, is led by the musicians inside the *zāwiya* and into the room housing Sīdī Frej's tomb. The musicians surround the tomb, quickly filling the tiny room with a barrage of sound and sweat as she trances in the entryway, with the caretaker pulling her back from time to time to ensure that her trance, which steadily increases in force, does not result in injury to her head from hitting the tomb. Soon the trance reaches its climax, and the trancer passes out, indicating that Sīdī Frej is pleased with the offering. The communal recitation of the *fātiḥa* marks the end of the *kharja*. The *dindrī* is then distributed to all in small metal mugs passed around the courtyard.

As I sought repose, with the rest of the *ṣunnāʿ*, on some of the white plastic rental chairs situated at the perimeter of the courtyard, a child came over to us with one of the mugs and asked what kind of beverage it was. One of the musicians replied, "Just drink it. It's [sub-Saharan] African, and blessed by Sīdī Frej." This concise statement highlighted the simultaneity and interdependence of the porosity of the body (in this case, the act of ingestion), local religious sensibilities, and the transnational imagination that would constitute a recurring theme throughout the remainder of the pilgrimage: by imbibing in the *dindrī*, we partake in something explicitly linked to "Africa"—however distant and vaguely defined—while simultaneously fulfilling a religious objective that is well known to any Tunisian, namely, to receive a saint's *baraka*.

There is a second *kharja* on the final day of the pilgrimage. Unlike the first, this *kharja* focuses on the spirits rather than the saints and has a trajectory that leads away from the shrine toward a water well located at the far northern perimeter of the *zāwiya* property before returning to Sīdī Frej's tomb. The procession, which by this time has swelled to several dozen pilgrims, marches to the water well, where the musicians perform the *silsila* for the Baḥriyya spirits, who possess an *ʿarīfa* to trance. When the *silsila* ends, the communal recitation of the *fātiḥa* marks the end of the outward route of the *kharja* and the beginning of the return journey to the *zāwiya*. A short *silsila* for the Banū Kūrī is played as the procession marches back down the road to a shaded spot near the *zāwiya*, where everyone pauses to witness the sacrifice of two black goats. One of the *ṭabla* players notices a woman falling into trance as soon as the throat of the first goat is slit and changes his rhythm to the *nūba* of Sīdī Frej. As the rest of the *ṣunnāʿ*, transfixed on the sacrifice, miss his cues, he walks over to them, hits them on the arms with his drumstick to get their attention, and points to the trancing woman. They immediately switch to the *nūba* of Sīdī Frej, surrounding the trancer until she falls backward into the arms of several women, who escort her back inside the *zāwiya*. The remaining pilgrims perform a much larger *ḥalqa* in front of the *zāwiya* doors, then enter the shrine. Like the first *kharja*, this one ends at the tomb of Sīdī Frej.

The two street processions of the *ziyāra* demonstrate vividly the differentiation between the saints and the spirits as well as their ritually aesthetic and embodied compatibility. The first, performed on the opening day of the *ziyāra*, is dedicated to the saints, involves nonpossession trance (*jedba*), and moves toward the *zāwiya*, highlighting moments of arrival at the entrance of the *zāwiya* and at the tomb of Sīdī Frej. The second *kharja*, in contrast, is undertaken on the final day, is focused on the spirits, involves possession trance, and moves away from the *zāwiya* to a sacred water well on the outer edge of the wall enclosing the cemetery and the rest of the *zāwiya* compound. These movements reflect the pilgrimage's trajectory from the saints to the spirits as well as the gradual increase in ritual densities that accompany that transition. Yet at no time are the saints and spirits mutually exclusive; even at the end of the pilgrimage, when the spirits are the focal point, *nūba*s for saints, especially Sīdī Frej, may be inserted into the ritual with no sense of disruption.

The journeys of pilgrimage, of the *kharja*, and of trance are physical acts as well as acts of the imagination; the routes that carried the first *sṭambēlī* practitioners and spirits across the Sahara continue to signify in the Tunisian imagination. These geographies are utterly transnational; they signify trans-Saharan connections that existed before and beyond the borders of the nation-state. If we understand ritual music as having the power "to structure ritual time—to create a 'virtual' time which creates a sense of shared experience and . . . collapse[s] the temporal boundaries between the past, present and future" (Harris and Norton 2002: 2), we might add that it also creates a virtual space in which the multiple *geographies* of migration are recreated and reworked. The musical routes of the pilgrimage guide participants along these journeys of the imagination; the *silsila* is about connections and routes, not categories or stations. The *sṭambēlī* pilgrimage cannot be understood outside musical structures (i.e., the *nūba*, *silsila*, and internal dynamics of progression) and ontologies (i.e., the capacity of the *gumbrī* and *ṭabla* to communicate with the spirit world). While this chapter extends to the Maghrib perspectives from south of the Sahara on the veneration of saints as a plural, border-crossing practice (Gibb 1999) and spirits as signifying and shaping social histories and identities (Lambek 1998; Stoller 1995), it is equally concerned with the centrality of sound to establishing presence, to rendering places meaningful and actively sensed (Feld and Basso 1996). The pilgrimage to a saint's shrine, the largest and most emblematic collective ritual associated with the veneration of saints in Tunisia, provides an inclusive space for *sṭambēlī*'s pantheon of saints and spirits to arrive, interact, and signify. It is through the aesthetics of music and the embodiment of trance that this is made possible, and it is during the annual *ziyāra* that these geocultural histories are performed in their most comprehensive form and are made most publicly accessible.

Pilgrimage and Place

By holding an annual *ziyāra*, *sṭambēlī* interfaces with a widespread and familiar practice in Tunisian society. This sacred journey to a sacred space makes the *sṭambēlī ziyāra* immediately comprehensible in terms of common practices associated with the veneration of saints in Tunisia. The distinctive yet simple architecture of the *zāwiya*, characterized by whitewashed walls and a domed roof, is ubiquitous throughout the North African landscape. Each shrine is built in honor of a Muslim saint (*walī*), who is understood as having a special *baraka* from God. Some saints and their teachings became the locus of Sufi orders. Far more prevalent, however, are saints whose followers are not organized into formal religious organizations, and are rather the object of veneration by supplicants seeking the saint's intercession with God on their behalf. Colonial-era scholars of Maghribi Islam constructed an influential distinction between "serious" saints, who were often religious scholars and the subjects of hagiographies, and "folk" saints, who are the subjects of local legend and veneration through the so-called cult of saints that characterizes Islam in the region (Dermenghem 1954). The dichotomy is also presented in the Francophone literature in terms of Sufi saints and *marabouts*, the latter having roots in the Arabic *mrābiṭ* ("tied [to God]"). The hard and fast distinction between the two categories, however, can obscure as much as it reveals. Not only is there a wide spectrum of beliefs and practices within each category, but the distinction can blur, for example, when "serious" Sufi saints, such as Sīdī ʿAbd es-Salēm, are invoked through "folk" traditions such as *sṭambēlī* not for their religious teachings, but for their spiritual potency demonstrated through the embodiment of trance.

While the Tunisian state of the Husaynid era promoted the veneration of saints in part to integrate its minorities into the institutions of Tunisian society (and thus discipline them and keep them under surveillance), the postindependence nation-state has proven much more suspicious of Sufi orders and saint veneration traditions. Despite (or, perhaps, because of) their ubiquity in Tunisian society, the practices associated with the *zāwiya* have generated a great deal of anxiety among many self-consciously modernist intellectuals, the Muslim religious elite (*ʿulamā*ʾ), colonizers fearing organized opposition, and nationalists concerned with constructing a unified, modernized nation. There is some evidence that colonial powers in North Africa identified the *ziyāra* as a potential forum for generating resistance; French authorities in Algeria, for instance, tried to limit and even prohibit these visits (Clancy-Smith 1990: 206). Similarly, postcolonial nationalist elites were just as suspicious of such activities, which performed allegiances to authorities other than those of the nation-state. In the 1950s, Habib Bourguiba pursued a targeted offensive against the institution of the *zāwiya*, closing, reappropriating, or destroying numerous shrines. Sīdī Saʿd's *zāwiya* was closed down in 1958, not to reopen again until 1966, when renewed interest in Tunisian folklore and American jazz precipitated documentation efforts and performances sponsored by government offices responsible for culture, media, and tourism (see chap. 8). The transformation of shrines communicated clearly the state's perception of the incompatibility of Sufism and the veneration of saints with the government's agenda of modernization and development. While the shrine to Sīdī Aḥmed et-Tijānī was razed to further develop the city's medina to promote tourism, the shrine to Sīdī Riaḥī was taken over by the state and turned into an office for the National Women's Union, and one of the city's two shrines to Sayda Manubiyya was transformed into a local Neo-Dustūr Party headquarters (Ferchiou 1991: 193). Accounts from the 1960s reported that through such efforts, the nationalist regime had already "successfully decimated" the Sufi orders of the Tunis region (Brown 1964). Nevertheless, while the state has exerted a great deal of control over the country's mosques (all imams are employed by the state, and it is rumored that the secret police attend all mosque activities), it was never able to eradicate the entrenched traditions of the *zāwiya*. With their resistance to state suppression, both Sufism and the veneration of saints remain, in many ways, beyond the nation-state. *Sṭambēlī*, as a relatively organized ritual institution that invokes saints, features elements of both but moves beyond the nation-state in other, more specific ways.

By evoking its own historical movements and senses of place, the *sṭambēlī* pilgrimage maps its geographies of encounter, and through a roughly predetermined trajectory of tunes associated with various groups of saints and spirits, music organizes aesthetically and temporally the ritual appearance and presentation of these movements. The capacity for music to signify in the collective imagination is especially powerful in the context of pilgrimage. In the context of the New Europe, Philip V. Bohlman argues that the music of pilgrimage "charts landscapes different from those bounded by the politics of nationalism . . . whose disharmonies they audibly reconfigure into a future they do not yet know" (1996: 427–428). Whereas Bohlman's pilgrims physically chart paths across the New Europe, *sṭambēlī* pilgrims do not physically cross the borders of the nation-state. Rather, it is in the historical imagination that alternative geographies—that is, geographies that acknowledge, indeed celebrate, the sub-Saharan connection to Tunisia—are performed.

The pilgrimage also navigates and reworks social boundaries. Saints' shrines in the Maghrib have been considered important sites for providing women with therapy and social support (Mernissi 1977). *Sṭambēlī* ceremonies are not gender segregated like most Sufi rituals in Tunisia, such as the Shādhiliyya ceremony described in the previous chapter. Unlike the Sufi orders, where the clerical and ritual positions of power are held by men alone, in *sṭambēlī*, women, as well as some (often effeminate) men, have privileged roles as healers with esoteric ritual knowledge. Women, both black and Arab, also constitute the majority—but by no means all—of the clients who have the special status of serving as conduits for spirit possession. They represent a variety of socioeconomic levels, although a large proportion comes from the lower and lower-middle strata. It is also worth noting that the pilgrimage is a family event in which children constitute a significant minority and acquire knowledge of and from the event through watching, listening, tasting, smelling, and, to a limited extent, dancing during some of the afternoon ceremonies. The musicians, whose performances structure the entirety of the *ziyāra* and entice the saints and spirits to descend, are all male and are typically—but again, not exclusively—black Tunisians. *Sṭambēlī* ceremonies, then, not only mediate between the human and spirit worlds; they also cross boundaries of gender, class, age, and ethnicity. Although identified with a specific minority, *sṭambēlī* nevertheless provides a space of remarkable spiritual and social inclusion. If place, as Edward Casey argues, is the site of collecting and recollecting the experiences, histories, and trajectories of persons and things, then part of the power of the *zāwiya* resides in its capacity to "gather . . . these lives and things, each with its own space and time, into one arena of common engagement" (1996: 26). It is through music that these multiple geocultural and temporal signifiers are produced, providing a vivid example of how music "evokes and organises collective memories and present experiences of place with an intensity, power and simplicity unmatched by any other social activity" (Stokes 1994: 3).

Victor Turner (1973) has argued that pilgrimage constitutes a movement between center and periphery in which everyday social structures are suspended as pilgrims share a common goal and enter into *communitas*. In the context of Maghribi Islam, Dale Eickelman argues instead that social inequities implicit in everyday life remain intact during the *ziyāra* to the shrine of Sīdī Muḥammed Sherqī in Morocco (1976: 175). Elements of both of these contrasting perspectives are relevant here. Participants experience the *sūdānī* aesthetics of the *sṭambēlī* pilgrimage in multiple ways. For the musicians of the Dār Bārnū troupe, they seem to evoke their pride of place within a genealogy of ritual musicians descended from slaves and other sub-Saharans and reinforce their Barnāwī lineage through their privileged connection to Sīdī Frej, an indication of "closeness" (*qaraba*) that sustains ritual authority. For many trancers, they signify the physically, and often socially, taxing experience of affliction by spirits with sub-Saharan identities, as well as the protection from spirit attack they can acquire by offering their bodies to these spirits through possession trance. For the diverse membership of the audience, ranging from individuals who are lifelong members of the *sṭambēlī* network to neophytes accompanying friends, they may support the common Tunisian sentiment that blacks have a particular power to intervene in matters of the spirit world. For some visitors, these aesthetics even appear to constitute annoyances that must be withstood in order to partake in the socializing and to consume the delicious, blessed (and free) meals served throughout the event. Moreover, unlike other Tunisian pilgrimages, and many religious pilgrimages outside North Africa, the *ziyāra* does not have music structured to facilitate collective participation. Rather, the music, as well as most trances, is performed by specialists who have acquired privileged knowledge and skills. The only collective performance is in the recitation of the *fātiḥa*, which is recited in unison (though not by all attendees and often under the breath) to mark the beginning and ending of each major ritual episode.

This specialized nature of musical participation sets *sṭambēlī* apart from other pilgrimage traditions in Tunisia, where the most common performances involve singing songs whose lyrics are known to most if not all pilgrims and rhythmic accompaniment on multiple *bendīr*s. Singing, and to some extent, drumming, in these contexts is more communal, performed by specialists and nonspecialists alike. Just as important, the songs often focus on the saint whose shrine is the site of pilgrimage, and perhaps a few other saints associated with major Sufi orders.

Sṭambēlī, in contrast, is far more inclusive in its recognition and praise of the dozens of saints and spirits who populate its pantheon. As the identities of the saints and spirits are inextricably linked to their movements between sub-Saharan and North Africas, this inclusivity creates an alternative historiography that emphasizes the connection between the two regions. However, it is also more exclusive, as ritual knowledge is in the hands of specialists; the music is a privileged repertoire. It is a demonstration of the potency and longevity of this sub-Saharan system of knowledge, and the mastery over this knowledge by specialists connected to the historical movement of displaced sub-Saharans across the Sahara Desert. Nevertheless, in the rituals of the *sṭambēlī ziyāra*, all pilgrims—musicians, trancers, and the audience—are situated within the same imaginal space saturated by the sonic, visual, and olfactory aesthetics of *sṭambēlī*.

Sīdī Frej

Little biographical information is known about Sīdī Frej. The oral history at Dār Bārnū attests that he was from the Bornu region of sub-Saharan Africa and came to Tunis via the trans-Saharan slave trade routes. Like many North African saints, while he was alive, Sīdī Frej was a mendicant, known for his lack of desire for worldly goods. In one legend, he is remembered as turning dates to stone when some harvesters tried to deceive him. While this act of transformation is considered miraculous, the story is also recited for its message against selfishness. According to Bābā Majīd,

> Sīdī Frej was *ʿajmī*, Barnāwī. He would always sit under the tree. He came from Africa. And stayed here. He never asked for food or drink or anything. He was known by everyone and lived in La Marsa. He was a holy man [*rājil ṣāliḥ*].[1] . . . Once, some men came by with donkeys carrying dates. And he was sitting there [under the tree]. He asked them to "give me a little of what you have." They replied, "What do we have? We have only stones." Sīdī Frej said, "Okay, then, give me some stones." When they went to their donkeys, they found that the dates had turned into stones! They returned to him. "What's the matter?" he said. "I asked for stones, so give me some stones." (Personal communication, 2001)

Sīdī Frej's *baraka* was reaffirmed after his death, when he interceded with his followers who were trying to build a shrine to house his tomb: "Everyone in Sūkra knew him. When he died, they built a small shrine for him. The next day, they found it destroyed. They built another, and it was destroyed; each time this would happen. It was too small. Sīdī Frej wanted a larger one. So they built a large shrine. Many Africans came and lived there [in Sūkra]. They would visit him; he was their saint. They would visit him, and perform their rituals there" (Bābā Majīd, personal communication, 2001).

The bright blue metal doors of the *zāwiya* stand out against the weathered and dusty whitewashed outside walls. The doors lead to an open courtyard, which provides access to Sīdī Frej's burial chamber, four small guest rooms for visitors, a kitchen, an outhouse, and the modest accommodations of the caretaker. The *zāwiya* is surrounded on two sides by a small graveyard. It is a modest and relatively remote compound; Tunisians with no ties to the neighborhood or to *sṭambēlī* may not even know of its existence, let alone its location (as attendees who rely on taxis to get to the *zāwiya* inevitably discover).

While the shrine is firmly rooted in the local, at the same time, pilgrims are situated within and rerouted, via the transnational imagination, through a wider landscape of human and spirit movements between North Africa, Arabia, and sub-Saharan Africa. The day before the *ziyāra*, the interior of the *zāwiya* is decorated elaborately with sub-Saharan and Islamic paraphernalia, temporarily transforming the shrine into a distinctively *sṭambēlī* setting for the next three days. Swords, daggers, and spears dangle against the backdrop of brightly colored rugs depicting Mecca and nature scenes hanging on the walls. A plaque of the ninety-nine names of God is prominently displayed below the *kuruna* (Tunisian Arabic for "crown," from the French *couronne*), a bright red cloth mantle situated above the *yinna*. Equally prominent is the colorful, cowry-shell-laced costume of Bū Saʿdiyya (see chap. 2). The multiple referents of the visual decor transform the interior courtyard of the *zāwiya* into a site in which the African presence in Tunisia is reinforced and legitimized through its integration within the fabric of Tunisian religious practice, while its distinctiveness remains intact.

The Pilgrimage: An Overview

The *ziyāra* is held in early July, and, like most *ziyāra*s in Tunisia, it takes place from Wednesday to Friday. Each of the three days of the *ziyāra* features ceremonies of trance and possession, as well as the *debdabū* call to assembly (see table 6). The first and last days are the most ritually active, as they also include a street procession, animal sacrifices, and other ritual episodes. Over the course of the three days, the presence of the saints and spirits gradually intensifies as the musicians perform a wider variety of *nūba*s, to which a larger number of initiates dance. The size of the congregation grows steadily

TABLE 6. The order of major ritual episodes during the *ziyāra*

Day 1 (Wednesday)	*Day 2 (Thursday)*	*Day 3 (Friday)*
Blessing of instruments		Afternoon *sṭambēlī*
Kharja (to the shrine and tomb)		*Kharja* (out of shrine and to the well) and sacrifice
Afternoon *sṭambēlī*	Afternoon *sṭambēlī*	Afternoon *sṭambēlī*
Debdabū	*Debdabū*	*Debdabū*
	Candle ceremony	Mufti's blessing
Nighttime *sṭambēlī*	Nighttime *sṭambēlī*	Nighttime *sṭambēlī*

during the course of the event, with nearly two hundred musicians, healers, and adepts, as well as their families and friends, in attendance at Friday night's ceremony.

The musicians of the Dār Bārnū troupe, the clients they treat, other members of the extended Dār Bārnū household, and a handful of other members of the *sṭambēlī* community who have moved away from the area but return each year for the pilgrimage compose the core group of participants who are present for the entire three days. As more and more pilgrims arrive, the pilgrimage is transformed gradually from a situation of relative intimacy to one of broader inclusion, albeit still restricted socially. While initiates will dance to placate their spirits and to receive the added protection of Sīdī Frej, noninitiates may come to socialize, to obtain the *baraka* of Sīdī Frej, or to enjoy the dramatic performances. More generally, holding the pilgrimage serves to protect its attendees from spirit affliction, as it seeks to please Sīdī Frej and the saints and spirits who visit his sacred site.

Table 6 shows the order of ritual events for the three days of the pilgrimage. Although some of "the same" rituals are performed on each of the three days, I am convinced that they are not entirely identical. Rather, meanings accrue or change because the musical choices, the participants, the audience and other factors are distinctive to each occurrence. The musico-spiritual trajectory of the pilgrimage is one in which the presence of the spirits gradually intensifies over the three days. While there is a "frontloading" of saints during the first day, by the third evening, the spirits are in full force. At no time, however, are they mutually exclusive.

Call to Assembly: The *Debdabū* Percussion Ensemble

During the pilgrimage, the *debdabū* percussion ensemble also aurally connects pilgrims to sub-Saharan Africa. *Debdabū* refers to the ceremony of assembly and the music of its percussion ensemble, which features the *ṭabla*, two small kettledrums, two handheld frame drums, and a metal drum resembling an overturned bowl. The word *debdabū* was used to refer to a sub-Saharan kettledrum as early as the eleventh century (Erlmann 1986: 10) but may also be related to the Arabic term *dabdaba*, defined as "the sound of footsteps," derived from the verb "to tread" or "to tap" (Wehr 1994: 312). Every evening during the pilgrimage, the *debdabū* is performed as a prelude to the nighttime possession ceremony, calling the members of the community to congregate for the evening's communal meal and *gumbrī* ceremony that follows. It is also often described as honoring Sīdī ʿAbd el-Qādir in particular. The *debdabū*'s origins can be traced to the royal court music of Mali, described as early as the thirteenth century in Ibn Battuta's famous *Rihla* (Travels). In Mali, it announced the arrival of the king. In the *sṭambēlī* context, it also heralds the arrival of those in power, but here those in power take the form of saints and spirits.

As is the *gumbrī* ceremony, the *debdabū* is performed by musicians sitting in a semicircle around the *mīdān*. The instrumentation, however, is entirely different. Leading the ceremony, and replacing the *gumbrī*, is the *ṭabla*. Unlike the *ṭabla* that leads the *kharja*, however, the *ṭabla* in the context of the *debdabū* is played with two sticks, one on each drumhead. The *shqāshiq* are not played and are replaced by three percussion instruments: the *kurkutū*, the *gaṣʿa*, and the *bendīr*. The *kurkutū* is played with two thin sticks made of tree branches. The drum is held between the feet so that it remains slightly tilted, allowing air to escape out of the barrel of the drum. Veit Erlmann contends that *kurkutū* is an antiquated term that was replaced by *naqqarāt*. In the Tunisian context, however, the term *kurkutū* is still used in *sṭambēlī* and is distinct from the *naqqarāt*, which, although physically analogous to the *kurkutuwāt*, are used mainly in Arab-Andalusian classical music. The *gaṣʿa* is a drum played with two thick sticks striking the metal body of the instrument. Apart from the *ṭabla* (whose performance technique marks it as *sūdānī*), the *bendīr* is the only instance of a local "Arab" instrument's being used in *sṭambēlī*.

Unlike the *ṭabla* rhythms of the *kharja*, which correspond to the rhythms of the *gumbrī*, the *debdabū* repertoire is unique. The driving, cyclic patterns played on the *kurkutū* and *gaṣʿa*, however, correspond to the *shqāshiq* patterns characteristic of *sṭambēlī* performance. The *bendīr* plays the same core pattern as the *ṭabla*, although the latter often improvises on the pattern. The *debdabū* repertoire is much more limited than those of the *gumbrī* and the *ṭabla*; it includes only the *nūba*s for Sīdī Frej, Sīdī Saʿd, Sīdī ʿAbd es-Salēm, and Sīdī ʿAbd el-Qādir. As there is no singing, and none of the *nūba*s are announced, noninitiates (and many initiates, as well) will not know that these *nūba*s are for these particular saints. At first, some of this ceremony consists

EXAMPLE 7. *Debdabū* cycle

of Bābā Majīd instructing all but the most seasoned performers in how to play their instruments. Especially problematic are the *kurkutū* parts, which, with their high-pitched tones, should stand out above the others (a common difficulty among the *sunnāʿ*, who otherwise do not play drums with sticks, is maintaining the lilting R-L-R/R-L-R *sūdānī* pattern, which involves two right-hand strokes in succession to maintain a regular, if slight, accent on the left-hand stroke).

If *sṭambēlī* is a privileged and esoteric system of knowledge, the *debdabū* is a particularly rarefied subset of that system. As the repertoire and instruments are brought out only three days per year, it is especially difficult for the less experienced *ṣunnāʿ*. When they find their groove, however, the *debdabū* is also a showcase for Bābā Majīd, the last of the elders, to demonstrate the dance patterns that evoke a rich history of trans-Saharan cultural exchange. The music of *debdabū* signifies sub-Saharan Africa and is relatively other even for some of the musicians. However, it is performed in honor of Sīdī ʿAbd el-Qādir, whose origins are widely known to be in Baghdad and who is recognized across the Islamic world. In the *debdabū*, ritual connects two distinct worlds: distinctively sub-Saharan music not only welcomes, but also pleases the most widely venerated saint in the Muslim world.

(En)Trances

The afternoon trance ceremonies that precede the *debdabū*, and the nighttime ones that follow it, constitute the major focal points and longest ritual episodes of each day of the pilgrimage. While each of these six ceremonies follows the logic of hierarchy and succession inherent in the *silsila*s, each one is also situated within a broader trajectory such that the earlier ceremonies feature mainly the saints while the later ceremonies focus almost exclusively on the spirits. One of the implications of this progression is that it leads to a macrolevel increase in musical and spiritual density; that is, since the *nūba*s for the spirits are generally shorter and tied to others in their *silsila*s, there are more *nūba*s performed and thus more spiritual entities embodied within comparable periods of time. At the same time, the microlevel dynamics of each individual *nūba* also generate increases in sonic and temporal density. This is most evident in the longer, individual *nūba*s for the saints, to which a greater number of pilgrims may dance (since possession by the spirits is, for the most part, limited to initiates). (Interestingly, the most inclusive parts of the ceremonies—the *nūba*s for the saints—become fewer and fewer as the congregation grows; by the final ceremony on Friday evening, only the spirits arrive.) This inclusivity can present opportunities as well as challenges, as performances of two "on-demand" *nūba*s, those of Sīdī Belḥassen and Sayda Manubiyya, attest.

After the male *ʿarīfa* finished his possession by Sīdī ʿAbd es-Salēm (see this book's introduction), we continued playing the *silsila* of the Shaikhs with the *nūba* of Sīdī Saʿd. Despite a large crowd, there were no dancers for the *nūba* at this time, so we ended the piece after only about three minutes, after which Bābā Majīd immediately started the *nūba* for Sīdī Belḥassen. This *nūba* was the deliberate result of "introducing to the *gumbrī*" the Tunisian Sufi praise song in honor of Sīdī Belḥassen esh-Shādhilī and keeping intact its catchy, well-known melody and lyrics. Although nobody danced to the *nūba* this time, it was familiar to the entire gathering, many of whom sang along or clapped their hands—two participatory acts that rarely occur in the context of a *sṭambēlī* ceremony. As we played the *bū saʿdiyya* rhythm, which, with its strong sense of downbeat, is the least metrically ambiguous *sṭambēlī* rhythmic pattern (see chap. 5), I also noticed that despite the ever-present tendency to accelerate, the *nūba* increased only slightly in tempo relative to others we had been playing. This is partly a product of the rhythm itself, which with its lilting triplet-feel and high number of articulations per rhythmic cell (with five, it is the highest) can be played comfortably only at a moderate tempo.

Like that of Sīdī Belḥassen, Sayda Manubiyya's *nūba* is also in the *bū saʿdiyya* rhythm and maintains melodic and lyrical features of the praise song that comes from a local non-*sṭambēlī* tradition. A performance of this *nūba* during the 2002 pilgrimage, however, demonstrates such inclusivity can have its drawbacks. During the second day of the pilgrimage, Bābā Majīd noticed the presence of an elderly woman he knew to be an adept of Sayda Manubiyya, so he made sure to play the *nūba* for her. As the troupe began the *nūba*, the woman walked to the center of the *mīdān*, where an *ʿarīfa* draped a blue and white banner over her head and shoulders. As she began to dance, calmly, with her head down, under the cloak of the banner, another woman in attendance, unknown to the members of the Dār Bārnū household (and who had sat alone and refused all offers of food or drink the previous day), shrieked and started jerking convulsively as she made her way through the audience and into the *mīdān*. This woman proceeded to rip the banner off the dancer before attempting, with partial success, to tear the carpets, swords, and spears from the walls behind the musicians, shrieking all the while. With astonishing agility and speed, the elderly Bābā Majīd jumped up from his seated position and confronted the possessed woman, yelling, "Stop it! Stop! This one [i.e., this spirit] works for Satan, not the *ṣālḥīn*! Go! Go away from here!" He chased her out the door of the *zāwiya*, and she never returned. After the commotion had settled down, he started the *nūba* once more, providing Sayda Manubiyya's adept with a successful trance dance.

Saints who are part of the *sṭambēlī* pantheon, even if they have popular praise songs from non-*sṭambēlī* veneration traditions, will have distinct *sṭambēlī nūba*s with unique melodies, rhythms, and lyrics, though the latter may have points of overlap. The praise song for Sīdī Manṣūr, for example, traditionally performed by a chorus of men accompanied by traditional percussion (*bendīr*, *darbūkka*, and *ṭār*) and the *gaṣba* (traditional reed flute), is perhaps the most widely recognizable song for a Tunisian saint in the country. Its melody and lyrics have made their way from Sīdī Manṣūr's local *zāwiya* in the coastal city of Sfax to a national listenership via broadcast of the En-naghem company's 45 rpm recording of Mohammed Jerrari, then to the pan-Arab satellite music television stations and beyond, popularized by Tunisian singer Saber el-Robaei's 1990s pop version, soon thereafter incorporated into the electronica of Paris-based Tunisian singer Amina, and gaining a foothold in the world music market in 2001 with Moroccan-Spanish singer Hakim's version, featuring lyrics in Arabic and Spanish, released on Epic Records and distributed by Sony. The catchy refrain welcomes and praises the saint and invokes the ritual visitation of pilgrimage:

Allah Allah yā bābā	God, God, O Father
W-salēm ʿalīk yā bābā	Greetings, O Father
Sīdī Manṣūr yā bābā	Sīdī Manṣūr, O Father
W-njīk nzūr yā bābā	I am coming to visit you, O Father

The song's rhythm is a folk dance pattern called *fezzānī* (referring to the neighboring Libyan region of Fezzan), which is so widespread and popular in Tunisian music that it seems to produce almost intuitive bodily movement in any Tunisian listener. The *sṭambēlī* version of this song, in contrast, is distinctive in its melodic and rhythmic modes; it is in the emblematic *sṭambēlī* rhythm *sūdānī*, and its melody is based on *sṭambēlī*'s characteristic pentatonicism. The lyrics, however, share some phrases. The refrain, sung by the *ṣunnāʿ*, is a short and simple welcome to the saint:

Yā bābā salēm ʿalīh	O Father, greetings to him
Yā bābā mūl id-dīwān	O Father, master of the assembly

This last line is repeated over and over during the second vocal section of the *nūba*. The lead singer has more freedom to improvise phrases in his call; in the Dār Bārnū tradition they are often chosen from the following phrases, which can be altered by repeating, omitting, or substituting words:

Mūl id-dīwān	Master of the assembly
Yā bābā	O Father
Sīdī Manṣūr	Sīdī Manṣūr
Shamāʿ w-bkhūr	Candles and incense
Nimshī nzūr	I am going to visit [the shrine]

Sīdī Manṣūr is mostly known as the patron saint of the *sṭambēlī* community in the city of Sfax. Like the Baḥriyya spirits, he is believed to have the capacity to help humans when their affliction involves water—from babies who cannot produce tears to adults who had been struck by a spirit after forgetting to utter "bismillāh" before pouring a pot of hot water on the ground. In fact, his *nūba* often precedes or follows the *silsila* of the Baḥriyya, providing a smooth and seamless transition between the saints and spirits. Sometimes an individual who is possessed by the Baḥriyya will enter the *mīdān* to trance to Sīdī Manṣūr's *nūba*, in which case the performance will be relatively short and will transition into the Baḥriyya *silsila*. Yet the same *nūba* may last much longer and have a more pronounced intensification for a patient not afflicted by the Baḥriyya who trances to Sīdī Manṣūr's *nūba* when it is played during the White rather than the Black *silsila*.

Possessions

THE BAḤRIYYA

The first spirits to arrive in full force are the Baḥriyya. On the second night of the pilgrimage in 2005, we played this *silsila* twice, first for a new initiate who had become increasingly affected by her afflicting spirit during the previous two days, and then for a young male *ʿarīfa* who was more adept at successfully "working" the spirits. A brief comparison of the two performances is illuminating. The woman's *silsila* consisted of only two *nūba*s, but each was relatively long to accommodate her frenetic trance, which began as soon as we started the *nūba* for Mūlay Brāhīm, the head of the Baḥriyya spirit family. We had sung only one or two of the *nūba*'s short vocal cycles before she collapsed onto the floor in the audience. It took five attendees—all well versed in *sṭambēlī*—to carry her into the *mīdān*, where she lay sprawled on the ground. They covered her with the blue and white cloth favored by the Baḥriyya, and as soon as one of the *ṣunnāʿ* sprinkled some water onto her neck, she began convulsing and lurched forward toward the *gumbrī*. Possession by the Baḥriyya can be relatively violent, I was told, because they are out of their natural element (water) when they descend to possess a human. She gradually rose to her knees and her arms made erratic swimming motions as we continued to sing our short refrain, simply "Mūlay Brāhīm" or sometimes "ḥabīb Allah" (beloved of God) to overlap repeatedly with Bābā Majīd's varied sung calls, which included phrases such as "yā rijāl Allah" (O spirits [lit. "men"] of God), "yā rijāl il-baḥr" (O spirits [lit. "men"] of the sea), and "ʿAlī Bakaba," the last of which is a reference to the deceased *ʿarīfa* of the same name who led Dār Bakaba (see chap. 2), as well as to another Baḥriyya spirit named Bakaba. The strong sense of downbeat and tonicity in this *nūba* is remarkable. The *gumbrī*'s regular soundings of the open low string are underscored by simultaneous strikes on the *gumbrī*'s drumhead, producing a strong sense of "beat," while the *shqāshiq*'s *muthallith* pattern, which accents the second note of each rhythmic cell, counterattacks after the beat.

Two attendants prevented the trancer from running into the musicians by situating themselves behind her and holding the ends of the blue and white cloth wrapped around her waist. Bābā Majīd led us seamlessly into the next *nūba*, for the spirit himself named Baḥriyya, whose *muthallith* rhythm allowed us to transition without stopping. After several verses singing "yā baḥriyya rijāl il-baḥr" (O Baḥriyya, spirits [lit. "men"] of the sea), our increase in tempo became more marked, and we *shqāshiq* players raised our instruments higher in the air and closer to the trancer, who swung her head back and forth frenetically while situated in a kneeling position in front of the *gumbrī*. The lead *shqāshiq* player introduced accented syncopations over our pulsations, which resonated even more as we took care to keep the clappers as open as possible to allow the plates to reverberate. Several minutes into the *nūba*, and about a minute after we reached maximum tempo and volume, the dancer passed out onto her back, a shrill chorus of women's ululations taking over the aural space vacated by the musicians when we stopped the music upon her collapse.

After this trancer recovered, we played the *nūba* of Sīdī Manṣūr, which, as I have indicated, is highly appropriate in the context of the Baḥriyya *silsila*. In this case, it transitioned us (though technically speaking, no "transition" is really necessary) back to the saints, for *nūba*s to Sīdī ʿAmr, Sīdī Frej, and Sīdī ʿAbd es-Salēm, who entranced a male in his early twenties, an elder female *ʿarīfa*, and a younger male *ʿarīfa*.

The younger male *ʿarīfa*'s dance to the Baḥriyya spirits was more complete, with five members of the spirit family descending. His dances were more controlled, showing a level of mastery of the spirits. Yet there was also a point at which Bābā Majīd—despite being seated and continuing to play the *gumbrī* flawlessly—instructed him in a particular dance movement involving the shaking of the shoulders. Although this *ʿarīfa* was competent to diagnose patients afflicted by any of the *sṭambēlī* spirit families, his expertise, due to his personal history of affliction, was with the Bēyēt. As more Baḥriyya spirits needed to be appeased that night (since the earlier trance involved only two of them), and no other qualified *ʿarīfas* happened to be present at the moment, the responsibility—and opportunity—fell to this *ʿarīfa*.

We began as the *silsila* ideally should, with Jawayay, singing "yā jawayay bori baymana" while playing a slow, enchanting *saʿdāwī* rhythm.[2] After a few minutes, Bābā Majīd changed his *gumbrī* melody and rhythm, which we all recognized as the *nūba* for Mūlay Brāhīm. We changed our rhythmic pattern accordingly (to *muthallith*) as he immediately began to sing. What was remarkable to me was how he transitioned with such ease from a *nūba* in one rhythm to another *nūba* in a different rhythm without skipping a beat. In fact, he facilitated our change of rhythm by expanding the melody of Mūlay Brāhīm to fit within two or three cycles of Jawayay's rhythmic pattern such that our accented note (remember, the accented *shqāshiq* note is usually the second in the cell) remained lined up perfectly, but with the new melody. All we had to do was alter the spacing between our articulations, since both *saʿdāwī* and *muthallith* rhythmic patterns have four notes per cell.

At this time, the *ʿarīfa*, whose waist was wrapped with a red and white banner representing the Bēyēt, put a banner of yellow and blue over his shoulders and rose to dance. Bābā Majīd immediately nodded approvingly of his dance movements, which suggested to me that he was unsure of the quality of performance. It also, however, focused my attention more closely on the dancer, which revealed to me for the first time that the dance steps for Mūlay Brāhīm incorporate both the accented notes of the *gumbrī* "on" the beat and the accented second note of the *shqāshiq*'s rhythmic cell. The dancer steps with the full weight of his body on the beat in time with the *gumbrī* accent, then shifts some, but not all, of his weight onto his other foot with the following step by bringing it closer to the planted foot. The non-planted foot then moves back where it started to become the new planted foot, followed by the previously planted foot. The dance cycle takes two rhythmic cells to complete: R L - - / L R - -. The following *nūba*, for the spirit named Baḥriyya, begins with the same general dance movement and pattern but spaces the steps more evenly and widely, thus taking four rhythmic cells to complete: R - - - / L - - - / L - - - / R - - -. The slowly but steadily increasing tempo compensates in part for the widely spaced steps. Unlike Mūlay Brāhīm's alternating arm movements, those of Baḥriyya consist of unison swimminglike motions stretched forward with each bend of the waist. From time to time during this *nūba*, all of these dance movements are temporarily replaced by gestures involving standing in place, the body bent forward toward the *gumbrī*, rocking on the heels in unison, and shaking the shoulders quickly from side to side with hands on hips. This *nūba* has the potential to reach a very fast tempo, but as soon as Bābā Majīd was content that the *ʿarīfa* had mastered this dance (he nodded approvingly), we transitioned to the next *nūba*, that of Bakaba. This time, Bābā Majīd stopped playing the melody, just vamping on an open string for a few beats, which the more experienced *ṣunnāʿ* recognized as a cue to switch, without stopping, to the *sūdānī* rhythm of the following *nūba*. We spent less than a minute playing Bakaba, which involves familiar dance steps R -- / L -- / L -- / R -- with the feet but is accompanied by swings of the arms together on each strong footstep: both down and to the left with the strong step of the left, then both down to the right with the strong step of the right foot. Again, these movements coincide with the "onbeats" of the *gumbrī*, which are in metrical tension with the accented "offbeat" of the *shqāshiq* pattern. With a strong pluck of the open low string, Bābā Majīd signaled to us another transition. By the time he plucked the string again, we had started the *saʿdāwī* rhythm, retroactively treating his open-string pluck as the first note of the rhythmic cell in order to have our accents fall in the right place in relation to those of the *gumbrī*. Thus, we began the *nūba* for Sārkin Gārī, who dances slowly, from side to side, with hands behind the back. After less than a minute, the *ʿarīfa* bowed in front of Bābā Majīd to signal the end of his dance, and as soon as we stopped playing, Bābā Majīd led everyone in reciting the *fātiḥa*. The second night's possession ceremony was over. We had witnessed, and, as musicians, contributed to, two different modes of experiencing the spirits: an afflicted neophyte's frenetic possession and a more experienced healer's learning to "work" the same spirits.

THE BANŪ KŪRĪ

The year that Khemīsī died was a particularly traumatic one for Emna, who had to redouble her trance efforts and sacrifices to bring her relationship with her afflicting spirits back into balance. On the second day of the pilgrimage, Kūrī made his presence known by paralyzing both of Emna's legs, recalling the extended episode of paralysis he had caused her after she had grieved over Khemīsī's body. Those of us familiar with her affliction knew that she would not experience signs of improvement until, as her mother put it, "the blood of a black goat flow[ed]," referring to Kūrī's preferred animal sacrifice, an offering that had been made earlier that day during the *kharja*. At the height of the third night's possession ceremony, her possession began not with the Banū Kūrī *silsila*, but with the *nūba* of Sīdī ʿAbd es-Salēm (see

TABLE 7. Musical routes through the *sṭambēlī* pantheon on day 3 of the 2001 *ziyāra*

Ceremony	*Saint*	*Spirit*
Afternoon *sṭambēlī*:	Ṣlāt in-Nabī	
	Jerma	
	Sīdī Ṣālaḥ Bū Ḥijba	
	Sīdī Frej	
	Sīdī Bū Ra's el-ʿAjmī	
	Sīdī ʿAbd es-Salēm	
	Sīdī Marzūg	
	Sīdī ʿĀmr	
Debdabū:	Sīdī ʿAbd el-Qādir	
	Sīdī Saʿd	
	Sīdī Frej	
	Sīdī ʿAbd es-Salēm	
Nighttime *sṭambēlī*:	Sīdī ʿAbd es-Salēm	
		Dakākī
		Kūrī
		Migzū
		Jamarkay
		Bābā Magojay
		Ummī Yenna
		Māmā Zahra
		Adama
	Sīdī ʿAbd el-Qādir	
	Sīdī Manṣūr	
		Jawayay
		Bakaba
		Dakākī
		Kūrī
		Jamarkay
		Bābā Magojay
		Mūlay Brāhīm
		Baḥriyya
		Sārkin Gārī
		Miryamu
		Nana ʿAysha

table 7), which "pulled her" into the *mīdān*, where she joined two other women who were already in trance. Sīdī ʿAbd es-Salēm is one of the only members of the pantheon who can engender both *jedba* and possession trance. This third night of the *ziyāra*, he chose to take possession of Emna. Recognizing the signs of the saint's impending presence as Emna stood tall, swaying from side to side, an *ʿarīfa* pulled a loose, white *kashabiyya* over Emna's body while one of the *ṣunnāʿ* ran to one of the guest rooms, returning

with a stalk of hay he lit before placing it in Emna's right hand. She moved from side to side in time with the music, her right hand holding the burning stalk, her left hand behind her back. As the *nūba* intensified, her movements become more pronounced, and she held the burning stalk to her left arm, which was now stretched out in front of her. She returned the stalk before stopping the music in order to lead the congregation, her palms faced up, in reciting the *fātiḥa*, which was followed by her passing out and falling straight onto her back. Her mother rushed to her side and called for the black *kashabiyya* which Emna would need to wear for the Banū Kūrī to possess her. There was some confusion, as there were now three bodies in the *mīdān* in need of attention. One of the trancers was finished for the night, since Sīdī ʿAbd es-Salēm was her only *nūba*. But Emna still needed to become possessed by the Banū Kūrī, and the third trancer needed to become entranced by Sīdī ʿAbd el-Qādir. A choice needed to be made in how to proceed. Now that Sīdī ʿAbd es-Salēm had taken his leave, there were two possible routes to take: either move on to the Banū Kūrī for Emna or continue with the Shaikhs for the other trancer to trance to Sīdī ʿAbd el-Qādir. The *ʿarīfa* assessed the two and, with Bābā Majīd, decided to move on to the Banū Kūrī. The other trancer would have to wait, and as soon as the *nūba* for Dakākī began, she surprised us by shrieking and fleeing the *mīdān*, apparently disoriented and suddenly aware that she was in front of all these people.

As Dakākī seized Emna, she writhed on the ground, slithering up to the *gumbrī*. She was so close, in fact, that her father, Bābā Majīd, was able to reach out to put a reassuring hand on her shoulder as the *nūba* ended and he waited for the black *kashabiyya* to be put on her. She rose to a kneeling position as the group began the *nūba* for Kūrī, who danced by repeatedly flinging his hosts' arms up in the air over her head, one after the other, in time with the music.

There was no relief for Emna as Kūrī exited her body. Like other *sṭambēlī* spirits, he will not be placated until other members of his family have shared the privilege of experiencing the human world through music and dance. Without stopping, the musicians invoked a succession of spirits, each with its own musical preferences and dance movements. Emna's possession, which lasted the better part of an hour, continued with Kūrī's brothers Migzū and Jamarkay and with Bābā Magojay, who, like Kūrī, is associated with drinking. Ritual assistants replaced the black *kashabiyya* with a large white cloth as Kūrī's wife Ummī Yenna descended, followed by her sisters Māmā Zahra and Adama, each of whom danced in a sitting position, completely covered by the cloth. When the music and dancing stopped, Adama remained in Emna's body and was quickly surrounded by a throng of young women. Speaking through Emna, Adama foretold futures, provided advice on personal matters, and informed individuals of the well-being of the soul of deceased friends or family members. At the end of the consultations, Emna passed out, signaling that the possessing entities had taken leave of her and were satisfied with her offerings of body and blood. She was then escorted into a nearby room to recover from this physically and emotionally taxing encounter with the spirits, and the second trancer was ushered back into the *mīdān* for the *nūba* of Sīdī ʿAbd el-Qādir.

THE BĒYĒT

The more figurative trance dances of the Banū Kūrī, as well as the more abstract dances of the Shaikhs, gave way to the more mimetic performances of the Bēyēt. The *ʿarīfa* returned and was seated, cross-legged, in front of the *gumbrī*. He pulled at the insides of his cheeks with his fingers, screaming as we played the *nūba* of May Gājiya. He was handed large, wooden daggers that had been censed and proceeded to stab his midsection forcefully. After about two minutes, we paused as his yellow banner was replaced by a red and white one and a fez was placed atop his head. He remained in the cross-legged position as we began the *nūba* of Yā Rīma, the ruler and judge, singing "kakayma ḥabūbāna" and "ayaya ray ayay Bābā." Once we transitioned to the instrumental section, he rose slowly, bowing to the musicians and then dancing to our accelerating pace with one arm extended, his banner draped over his arm, turning slowly. A chair was brought out for him to sit in, facing the *gumbrī*. A cigarette in a long holder was lit and handed to him. In the chair, with his fez still on, he occasionally puffed the cigarette and turned slowly from side to side to survey his surroundings. As we began a second *nūba* for Yā Rīma, we were singing words I did not know or understand; Belḥassen leaned toward me to help me hear his vocals. While the lyrics were all in Hausa and aesthetics were *sūdānī*, the *ʿarīfa*'s clothing and paraphernalia clearly signified visually the beys of Tunisian national history. Through this integration of the national and the other, the past and the distant had been recovered and received for all to see not only that they lived on into the present, but that they were also inseparable from each other.

The pilgrimage ended with the last of the Bēyēt (and also Sghār) spirits, namely, Miryamu and Nana ʿAysha. We sang "Ina Miryamu, ina Miryamu, ina Miryamu, dawarkiyya" and "Gayda Nana ʿAysha, gayda Nana ʿAysha, may tambarī." (Bābā Majīd told me that *tambari* is a *sūdānī* word that here describes Nana ʿAysha as "pure.") They distributed the sweets that all pilgrims would take home with them as a reminder of the event and as a physical means of ingesting the blessing of the saints that results from the profound offerings made over the course of the three days.

Ritual Aesthetics and the Transnational Imagination

Music does not merely accompany the *sṭambēlī* pilgrimage; rather, this is a ritual that is largely about music. Indeed, the very first ritual act of the pilgrimage is the blessing of the musical instruments. It is the music that performs and attests to the histories of displacements and emplacements of the *sṭambēlī* community, and it is the music that dictates the development of each ritual event. The music not only attracts the saints and spirits, but also confirms their embodied presence through trance. Throughout numerous trance and possession ceremonies as well as public street processions of the pilgrimage, the power of music to transform self and other is continually performed, experienced, and witnessed.

It would be much easier for me to make my argument that the music of pilgrimage records a history of trans-Saharan movement and displacement if, for instance, the sung texts were narratives of such movements.[3] But they are not. Indeed, the sung texts are considered relatively "unimportant," in that they can be changed without altering the identity, function, and efficacy of the song. They are formulaic invocations that serve to welcome the members of the pantheon, to praise them, in *ʿajmī* and Arabic, yet they are almost always incomprehensible to the audience. Yet it is this incomprehensibility, this otherness, that is so important. This nonnarrative singing, rather than erasing a history, performs that history, not by recounting it per se, but by continuing to perform in a recognizably nonindigenous tradition. The sung texts record this history of displacement, then, because they are performances of a system of knowledge from sub-Saharan Africa. Similarly, the music itself records and performs that history, a history of border crossing. The music is recognizably different; it adheres to rules and privileges aesthetics alien to those of indigenous or Arabic musics. Historicity, therefore, is not so much narrated as it is embodied and performed in ritual.

The ritual knowledge needed to produce these histories and aesthetics, as part of a larger ritual economy concerned with the circulation of affect, is not evenly distributed. Trancers often have deep knowledge of a small portion of the pantheon. The most extensive knowledge is in the hands of the musicians, who must perform for all trancers and their various saints and spirits. The audience members usually have basic knowledge, at least that the spirits are from sub-Saharan Africa; many of the saints they recognize as local or regional. They will also know that the aesthetics of *sṭambēlī* are palpably other; they are not common components of the Tunisian public sphere. Let me emphasize that this discussion is not about African "survivals," but rather the importance of the idea of "Africa" for participants. For them, Africa provided the source materials that were transformed, mixed, and developed in a specific situation of displacement and interaction with others from many regions of Africa.

The pilgrimage, then, highlights the inseparability of local histories and transnational geographies in *sṭambēlī*. Virtually absent from dominant historical narratives, *sṭambēlī* ritually recollects the histories of encounter experienced by displaced Africans. While its rituals evoke other places and other times that resonate powerfully for certain groups of sub-Saharan slaves and their descendants, *sṭambēlī* is nevertheless defined more by inclusion than exclusion, by openness rather than boundedness. Although the ritual space is populated by black and Arab, male and female, young and old bodies, this inclusiveness is not limited to social identities. *Sṭambēlī* provides a framework, a performative space, for local, pan-Islamic, and "African" worlds to interact; compatibility, not divergence, is the watchword. As the multiple and successive *nūba*s and trances of the *ziyāra* indicate, *sṭambēlī* bodies interact as effectively with sub-Saharan spirits as with Maghribi and pan-Islamic saints, all of whom are attracted, and respond equally, to the distinctive aesthetics of *sṭambēlī*.

CHAPTER EIGHT

Sṭambēlī on Stage

(RE)PRESENTATIONS, MUSICAL COSMOPOLITANISM, AND THE PUBLIC SPHERE

Thus far, I have concentrated on *sṭambēlī* aesthetics and meanings in their ritual contexts, as ceremonies at Dār Bārnū, at the homes of clients, and at *zāwiya*s constitute the vast majority of *sṭambēlī* performances. When speaking about the *sṭambēlī* tradition and their ritual work (*khidma*), musicians are referring to such events. There are, however, performance opportunities that take *sṭambēlī* out of its ritual context. The musicians at Dār Bārnū refer to such nonritual performances as *khidma sūrī*, which can be translated as either "French work" or "foreign work."[1] This phrase does not necessarily mean that the musicians are hired by foreigners (in fact, most *khidma sūrī* is performed for Tunisian organizers and audiences). Rather, it is a context-based designation that at Dār Bārnū is used to refer to any nonritual *sṭambēlī* performance, usually for the sole purpose of entertainment, such as performances at hotels, festivals, and concerts. By using the phrase *khidma sūrī*, *sṭambēlī* musicians are immediately distantiating nonritual performance from a normative, ritually defined *sṭambēlī* tradition. Moreover, it highlights the fact that these performances are for patrons and audiences outside (and "foreign" to) the *sṭambēlī* community who have their own idiosyncratic desires, definitions, and expectations of *sṭambēlī* performance.

The musicians at Dār Bārnū emphasize that in some ways, *khidma sūrī* is "easier" than ritual work. It is less taxing physically, as nonritual performances rarely last longer than thirty minutes. It is also less demanding musically, as they always select some "light" (*khafīf*) *nūba*s to play. Moreover, the stakes are not as high in *khidma sūrī* as they are in ritual, as the primary goal is not to heal humans and please spirits. While nonritual performances also expand *sṭambēlī*'s visibility and potential clientele, they also provide new challenges. The most immediate and problematic aspect for *sṭambēlī* musicians is that, unlike ritual performances, *khidma sūrī* involves terms of engagement that are out of the musicians' hands. The musicians are keenly aware of the differences in expectations and will often debate what they think the organizers want. I have heard the Dār Bārnū musicians engage in surprisingly lengthy discussions about clothing, for instance, as they believe that stage performances require everyone in the troupe to wear matching attire in order to look like a "professional" troupe—an issue of little or no concern in ritual situations. Sometimes they are told of (or infer) a desire for spectacular difference and will accordingly plan to perform the costumed dance of Bū Saʿdiyya. At other times they are hired based on the recognition of a certain aesthetic compatibility that adds *sṭambēlī* sounds to other musics. The *sṭambēlī* sounds in such cases may be foregrounded, as in traditional popular praise singer Hedi Dounia's latest album (which utilizes the *gumbrī* in lieu of a bass guitar), or may be relegated to a virtually inaudible background presence, as in the accompaniment to Hedi Habbouba's performance for the gala spectacle for the opening ceremonies of the Mediterranean Games in 2001. Most often, it is simply inclusion in one of the ubiquitous festivals of "national" culture, such that *sṭambēlī* musicians are made to parade down the street (or, even more awkwardly, around the inside of a horse ring), along with Sufi orchestras, school bands, and acrobats, each stopping at a viewing stage for the viewing pleasure of government officials.

Embedded in the folklorization practices of the state is an underlying discourse of modernity, which, shaped by the ideologies of nationalism, continues to present "folk" traditions in opposition to "modern" practices. There is a widely held assumption outside the *sṭambēlī* network that in order for the tradition to survive, it must be removed from its ritual context and "modernized." In 2001, a few weeks before the annual Tunis jazz festival was to take place, I was interviewed on Tunisian radio about jazz in American culture. While I expected the discussion to turn, at some point, to my research activities on *sṭambēlī*, I was caught off guard when the interviewer asked if I thought *sṭambēlī* could ever become "modern" and develop into a "great" musical tradition like American jazz. I remember the question more clearly than I do my response, which I recall was a rather awkward and long-winded attempt to avoid offending my host while also maintaining that it was perhaps inappropriate to demand a ritual tradition to "develop," become secular, and entertain us when it already had aesthetic and therapeutic value to members of the ritual community. While the expectation that *sṭambēlī* needed to be "improved" belied what I believe to be the interviewer's genuine desire for *sṭambēlī* to become more widely appreciated by Tunisians, a force pulling in the other direction, fueled by the world music market and its burgeoning desire for the "authentically" spiritual, especially African, music, insists that the tradition remain unmediated, unfiltered, and unchanged for consumption by the public.

These two apparently opposing attitudes reflect differing but related fantasies mobilized in part by the discourses circulated by the transnational flows of the world music market. An examination of these attitudes and discourses must take into consideration the historical, sociopolitical, and economic conditions that inform and inflect their realization. Pointing out the difficulties involved in accounting for these transnational musical flows through theories of globalization, Martin Stokes finds a more nuanced and situational approach in the concept of "musical cosmopolitanisms," which enables us to view globalization

> less as a single system, increasingly beyond our conceptual reach and out of our control, and more as a set of projects with cultural and institutional specificity, projects that construct, refer to, dream and fantasize of, in very diverse ways, a "world" as their zone of operation . . . invit[ing] us to think about how people in specific places and at specific times have embraced the music of others, and how, in doing so, they have enabled music styles and musical ideas, musicians and musical instruments to circulate (globally) in particular ways. The shift of emphasis is significant, and, in my view, highly productive. Most importantly, it restores human agencies and creativities to the scene of analysis, and allows us to think of music as a process in the making of "worlds," rather than a passive reaction to global "systems." (Stokes 2007: 5–6)

Cosmopolitanism, Stokes reminds us, embodies a tension between a supposedly benign aspect of post-Enlightenment discourse and less neutral "acts of acquisitive consumption, and the control of others" (Stokes 2007: 10; see also Turino 2000). The cultural encounters facilitated by increasing access to previously "exotic" or foreign musics raises immediate questions about how, by whom, and for whom traditions are to be presented and defined (Stokes 2007). Additionally, the various participants in such musical presentations approach the projects with various and sometimes competing objectives and assumptions. Recent scholarship on the circulation of "trance" musics outside their ritual contexts reveals the tensions and contradictions that result from the various motivations, negotiations, and implications of staging sacred music and trance ceremonies, whether by national folklore troupes established to keep cultural identity within officially sanctioned narratives of national history (Hagedorn 2001), by concert promoters and festival organizers capitalizing on the celebration of difference by staging "authentic" performances merely relocated onto the concert stage (Shannon 2003), or by world music producers and musicians attempting to transcend that difference through "cross-cultural" collaborations or appropriations (Kapchan 2007). But since meanings for each individual listener cannot be dictated once the performance has begun, the results of any of these dynamics are always unstable, as each of the three studies just mentioned have shown.

The various cultural projects involving musical cosmopolitanism in Tunisia have been in an unsteady relationship with the ideology of cultural nationalism. As Thomas Turino (2000) has deftly shown in the context of Zimbabwe, the relationship between musical cosmopolitanism and nationalism is not reducible to a simple binary mutual antagonism, since it has been the cosmopolitan worldview of (often Western-educated) Tunisian officials and elites that has provided many of the tools and motivations for nationalist, anticosmopolitan cultural policies (Stokes 2007). The construction of a "modern" "national" musical tradition called *ma'lūf* asserted a national cultural identity to combat, in part, the encroachment of popular Egyptian musical styles onto Tunisian turf. But the same elites who bemoaned the popularity of Egyptian music in Tunisia looked to Western notation, orchestration, and other components of European concert culture to shore up *ma'lūf* against "corrupting" foreign influences (see Davis 1997). Efforts to document and stage the nation's "folk" traditions are similarly steeped in the uneasy and complex relationship between cosmopolitanism and nationalism. Not only do they constitute sites in which the "diasporic cosmopolitanism" of *sṭambēlī* (Stokes 2007: 9) enters into ambiguous relationships with nationalist projects, but they also interface with the agendas of various culture brokers as well as the forces of the market.

Since independence in 1956, there have been two historical moments in which *sṭambēlī* has received brief but relatively intense bouts of public attention in the form of well-publicized performance events and documentation efforts. The first of these, which took place in 1966, involved a documentary film, a set of studio recordings of traditional *sṭambēlī*, a traditional public performance, and two concerts of "*sṭambēlī*-jazz." An unrelated but uncannily parallel set of events between 1998 and 2001 also involved a documentary film, a sound recording, a traditional public performance, and collaborative concert performances. Although they occurred three decades apart, there are other remarkable similarities between the two sets of events, such as a spate of press articles that sought to explain *sṭambēlī* in terms of foreign traditions such as Moroccan *gnāwa* or Haitian vodou, with which the readership was ostensibly more familiar; the shifting yet vital role of Tunisian authorities and French culture brokers; and a shared concern for *sṭambēlī*'s future "development." Nevertheless, different component projects were initiated by individuals and institutions with different agendas, and engaged in different ways with the ideas and dominant discourses, such as nationalism, modernization, and globalization, that characterized their historical moments.

What I am interested in is what these projects produced and put into circulation, and what new kinds of relationships they allowed to be forged and imagined. Although I consider some audio recordings and films in this chapter, I am mainly concerned with live performances. Until recently, ethnomusicological scholarship has dealt mainly with the "world music" phenomenon in terms of the circulation of mass-mediated commodities, namely, the recorded artifact (see, e.g., Feld 1994, 2000; Hesmondhalgh 2000; Taylor 1997), and examined their uses and abuses in terms that, by extension, also constituted a critique of neoliberal globalization discourse (Stokes 2004). In this discussion I hope to contribute to a growing concern with the performative and institutional contexts in which "world music" circulates, such as national and international tours, festivals, collaborative concerts, and state-sanctioned "folklore" (Bohlman 1997; Hagedorn 2001; Kapchan 2007; Shannon 2003; Stokes 1997). While it is all too easy to slip into cynicism when considering the staging and secular consumption of ritual traditions, I also consider the potential of such shows, and their concomitant discourses of world music, to create constructive spaces for musical, cultural, and social interaction.

Exhibit A: *Sṭambēlī*, Jazz, and the Modern (1966)

Nonritual performances at the Ottoman court during the eighteenth and nineteenth centuries contributed to *sṭambēlī*'s development and incorporation into Tunisian society. During the time of the French protectorate (1881–1956), *sṭambēlī* continued to be performed at the court, which the French kept intact, at least symbolically, in their strategy of indirect colonization. Tunisian independence in 1956 constituted a watershed moment in redefining what it meant to be a musicking or trancing *sṭambēlī* body in Tunisian society as *sṭambēlī* confronted other systems of knowledge and power expressed in the overlapping discourses of nationalism, modernization, and, later, globalization. While they added fodder to certain prejudices against *sṭambēlī*, these discourses also generated new spaces for the performance of *sṭambēlī* in nonritual contexts.

Tunisian nationalism, as espoused by Habib Bourguiba and his Neo-Dustūr Party, envisioned a unified and modernized Tunisia and demonstrated little tolerance for public religious expression, traditional musical and healing practices associated with saints, and activities—such as speaking Berber—that drew attention to ethnic or linguistic difference. The resultant governmental prohibitions, such as the mass closure of shrines, were largely unsuccessful in eradicating *sṭambēlī*, which already relied on other performance contexts, such as the communal houses of the *dār* system and the private home. While the *zāwiya* of Sīdī Saʿd—given to the black community in the early eighteenth century by the ruling Husaynid regime—was shut down in 1958 by the country's first independent government, this had little impact on the Dār Bārnū tradition, since its adherents considered the smaller pilgrimages to Sīdī Frej, which were allowed to continue, to be more important. At Dār Bārnū, Bourguiba's anti-*zāwiya* measures were understood to be part of a broader nationalist politics in which large gatherings of any sort were viewed with suspicion and thus suppressed. When the *zāwiya*s were closed, Bābā Majīd told me, "we would work on our own, going to people's houses." When I asked him whether he felt at risk, considering the regime's stance on Sufism and veneration of the saints, he said, "It was the Islamists that caused problems for Bourguiba. He was afraid of their demonstrations. He didn't like people to gather. It wasn't *sṭambēlī* he didn't like. He was just afraid of the Islamists, and the pamphlets [they distributed]" (personal communication, 2001).[2]

Sṭambēlī's removal from public space, however, would soon be tempered by other forces at work to open up some space, albeit briefly, for *sṭambēlī* to reemerge in the public sphere. These include the state's documentation and folklorization efforts, the impact of the music and attitudes of visiting jazz musicians, and the controversial efforts of a visiting French sociology professor. When the government reopened the *zāwiya* of Sīdī Saʿd in February 1966, it did so in part to facilitate the documentation and performance projects of three state organizations: (1) the Ministry of Cultural Affairs' plans to film a documentary on *sṭambēlī* (*Tunisie: Terre d'Afrique*, directed by Hamadi Essid) to be presented at the following year's Festival d'Art Nègre in Dakar; (2) the Société Tunisienne de Diffusion's recording of two albums of "traditional *sṭambēlī*"; and (3) the Société Hôtelière et Touristique Tunisienne's concert series of "*sṭambēlī*-jazz" featuring the King Pins, an experimental jazz group from the West Indies, and the Ibn El Jazz Quartet, both of which would be collaborating with *sṭambēlī* musicians from Tunis (Lapassade and Ventura 1966). Each of these three projects represents a slightly different slant on the politics of cultural representation. The first two sought to document "traditional" *sṭambēlī*, while the third presented it as potentially compatible with "modern" musics such as jazz.

These measures did not represent an about-face in Tunisian policy against traditional practices associated with the *zāwiya*, but rather resulted from opportunities produced by a convergence of actions and ideas influenced in part by the spread of the ideology of modernization as well as the growing tourist industry, which relied on travelers' expectation of experiencing the exotic. As Abderrahman Ayoub (2000) argues, postcolonial states in North Africa have forcibly discouraged the study of minorities, but not their music, which is good merchandise for tourism. *Sṭambēlī* became a cultural commodity, something with exchange value. This commodity took two forms: first, as folklore to be documented and set on stage for tourist consumption, and second, as a musical object that could be modernized by interacting with progressive musical traditions, namely, jazz. These two processes, however, are two sides of the same modernist coin: in both examples, *sṭambēlī* is reinterpreted as a primitive art form, whether preserved as such through recording or integrated as an aesthetic sonic object—like any other—into other musics.

On February 18, 1966, the Tunisian daily newspaper *La Presse* featured a series of short articles on *sṭambēlī* and the reopening of the *zāwiya* of Sīdī Saʿd after nearly a decade of state-enforced closure. Under the general heading "The African Gods Are Gathering Today at Sīdī Saʿd," the articles, written by Flavio Ventura and French sociologist and visiting professor Georges Lapassade (with help from two of his Tunisian sociology students) attempted to introduce readers to the world of *sṭambēlī*. Headlines such as "Un vaudou tunisien" and "Le *sṭambēlī* et le jazz ont la même origine: Les rythmes d'Afrique Noire" highlight the assumed otherness of *sṭambēlī* to the readership, which was ostensibly more familiar with jazz and even Haitian vodou than with *sṭambēlī*. These headlines speak to the ways in which *sṭambēlī* was represented and understood in Tunisian society at a historical moment in which American jazz signified the epitome of African diasporic musical evolution. By the same token, American jazz is reinterpreted as "music of the slaves," legitimizing *sṭambēlī* by associating it with jazz and suggesting *sṭambēlī*'s potential to "evolve" in a similar manner. Despite the compromises evident in the news coverage of *sṭambēlī*, it is remarkable in its breadth of scope, from the documentary efforts of the government to the possible integration of *sṭambēlī* and jazz, from the ceremonies of the *zīyara* to the presence of *sṭambēlī* in the works of French writers, and from the role of the *ʿarīfa* to an interview with Bābā Brīka, an elderly man who, according to the interview headline, "knew slavery . . . and *sṭambēlī*" (Lapassade and Ventura 1966). Lapassade, who went on to study Moroccan *gnāwa* and other African diasporic possession traditions, was appalled by the racism he found rampant in Tunisia. His sociology classes at the University of Tunis began to attract black students, whom he encouraged to examine issues of race. After they introduced him to *sṭambēlī*, he worked on behalf of *sṭambēlī* troupes to get them more visibility through festival, radio, and television appearances. His self-described managerial activities, as well as his teaching and research in Tunisia, however, were short lived, as his university contract was revoked for reasons he believed were related to his frank and public discussions of the taboo subject of race (Lapassade 1998).

The state's renewed interest in *sṭambēlī* in the 1960s did not go uninterrogated by *sṭambēlī* practitioners. The *sṭambēlī* of Dār Bārnū had much to lose when the nationalist regime took over. For those at Dār Bārnū, the "era of the beys" overlapped with the "era of [French] colonization," during which *sṭambēlī* thrived. In Dār Bārnū's oral histories, the beys as well as the French colonizers treated sub-Saharans in Tunis with respect. On several occasions I was told that both ruling regimes trusted Tunisians of sub-Saharan descent more than they trusted local Arab Tunisians, citing as evidence the exclusive employment of Tunisian blacks as sentries and door guards (*bawāba*).[3] The French ruled indirectly through the beys, the same beys that abolished slavery, employed sub-Saharans, gave them a political voice, built for them a *zāwiya*, and invited them to perform at the court during holidays. With independence from France came the removal of *sṭambēlī* from public spaces and the end of a beneficial relationship with the state. At Dār Bārnū, this transitional moment marked the end of an era and the advent of new dilemmas concerning the ambiguities of the folklore projects of the state. Bābā Majīd, for example, was one of the *sṭambēlī* musicians who performed on the records made by Radiodiffusion-télévision tunisienne (RTT), Tunisia's state-run broadcasting organization. Pleased with the result, the RTT planned a staged performance to air on television. When Bābā Majīd arrived for the taping, he found that the stage setting had been painted like a jungle, and the organizers were insisting that all the musicians wear "African" outfits provided for them. Bābā Majīd told me he and other musicians felt insulted and refused to wear the "African" outfits. "I'm Tunisian," he told me. "My mother was Tunisian. I was born in Tunisia. Why should I wear 'African' clothes? I don't wear that kind of clothing. This [pointing to his *gumbrī*], this is African. But I am Tunisian." The jungle and the African outfits were not just stereotypes, but were active acts of othering, displacing *sṭambēlī* and its practitioners outside the realm of the acceptably "Tunisian." Bābā Majīd bemoaned the tokenism he felt also motivated invitations he received from the government to perform for visiting sub-Saharan heads of state. With typical wryness, he told me, "They forget about us until the president of Senegal visits. Then Tunisia is 'African'?"[4]

Interlude: Moroccan Trance Musics and the Transnational Imaginary

The work of the transnational imagination in relation to North African trance traditions is better documented in the case of Morocco, which, because of its broad impact—in Morocco, the global music market, and, as we shall see, Tunisia—warrants a brief excursus. In 1967, the year following the Lapassade-brokered *sṭambēlī* projects of the Tunisian state, African

American musician Randy Weston attended his first *līla* (*gnāwa* trance ceremony; lit. "night") in Morocco, marking a moment of musical and spiritual epiphany (Kapchan 2007) that inaugurated decades of involvement with the *gnāwa* that inspired his own compositions (most notably, "Blue Moses") and resulted in numerous recordings and tours with *gnāwa* musicians. In an interview with Deborah Kapchan, he recalls the moment: "It was one of the most incredible musical experiences of my life. I had an experience really African. I heard the string instrument out front. Like having an orchestra and having a string bass as the leader. And I heard the black church, the blues, and jazz. I really realized that we're just the little leaves of the branch of mother Africa" (in Kapchan 2007: 189).

While earlier jazz references to Africa, from Eubie Blake's "Sounds of Africa" (1899) to Duke Ellington's "Liberian Suite" (1947), set influential precedents, the idea of the African motherland as a cultural source (and political cause) for African Americans intensified greatly in the context of civil rights America of the 1950s and 1960s, particularly in the prominent jazz recordings by John Coltrane (*Africa Brass*, 1961), Art Blakey (*Ritual*, 1957), and Max Roach (*Freedom Noew Suite*, 1960) and Weston's own 1960 album *Uhuru Africa* (lit. "Freedom Africa" in Kiswahili) (Monson 2007; Kapchan 2007; see also Weinstein 1993).[5] Looking to North African trance rituals for one's musico-spiritual roots, however, was not an interpretive move monopolized by musicians of African descent or performers of African American music. In 1968, the year after Weston's *gnāwa* epiphany, Brian Jones, guitarist and founding member of the Rolling Stones, was taken to the Moroccan village of Jajouka by beat generation painter and writer Brion Gysin to hear their traditional *ghayṭa* (double-reed pipes) and *ṭbal* (double-headed barrel drum) music. The Jajoukans are of Arab origin and live in a village at the foot of the Rif Mountains in Morocco. The first village musicians were, according to legend, trained by a local Sufi saint, who introduced Islam into the region in the ninth century (though most Western portrayals of the Jajoukans ignore this part of their history). In return for their musical services, the saint promised the musicians that they and their descendants would always be able to live by means of music alone. A decade before Brian Jones's arrival, Gysin had opened up a café in Tangier to showcase the music of the master musicians, about which he said, "That's the music I want to hear for the rest of my life" (Schuyler 2000: 150). Many other figures in Western counterculture art movements, including writers Timothy Leary, William Burroughs, and Paul Bowles and rock superstars Jimi Hendrix, Jimmy Page, and Robert Plant, found for themselves an exotic utopia in the lifestyle and music of the Jajoukans, who allegedly smoked copious amounts of marijuana. In the writings of Gysin and Burroughs, the Jajoukans' Islamic rituals are reinterpreted as ancient musico-sexual fertility rites of the Greek god Pan.[6] Timothy Leary described the master musicians of Jajouka as a four-thousand-year-old rock band, and William Boroughs enticed Jones and others who encountered the music to "listen with your whole body, let the music penetrate you and move you, and you will connect with the oldest music on earth." They believed they had uncovered the source, not just of their music, but of the ethos of 1960s popular culture excesses—the sex, drugs, and rock 'n' roll trifecta—and the myth of a group of ancient pagan hippies discovered by the Rolling Stones continues (see Fuson 1996). The notoriety has been welcomed by many Jajoukans, though it has led to some new, often antagonistic, dynamics fueled in part by economic opportunity. Now, after several successful albums and world tours, the Master Musicians of Jajouka consider Jones to be part of their spiritual ancestry. In fact, his glossy public relations photo from 1968 now hangs on the wall of their shrine next to that of the king of Morocco, and the Master Musicians have reimagined their genealogy to include not only the Rolling Stones, but also Jimi Hendrix and members of Led Zeppelin, just as American jazz musicians populate the genealogy of Dār Gnāwa in Morocco (Schuyler 2000; Kapchan 2002, 2007).

At the same time, Moroccan music culture was undergoing radical internal transformation, as a wave of socially "aware" popular groups such as Nāss al-Ghīwān and Jīl Jīlāla emerged onto the national scene. Like their European counterparts, many Moroccans also found an attractive counterculture in the traditions of certain religious brotherhoods. Combining Sufi and *gnāwa* aesthetics with sharply politicized lyrics, Nāss al-Ghīwān played a major role in transforming *shaʿbī* (popular) music from a fixture of local cafés into a national social institution marked as much by its social agenda and reverence for indigenous spiritual musicality as by its affinity for the imagery and production values of Western rock groups. These groups were part of a larger artistic and intellectual movement of the 1960s that drew its inspiration from local culture.

Although their roots were formed in an intellectual movement, the groups found their largest following to be mostly poor and uneducated urban youth cut off from their rural roots yet with no strong attachment to traditional urban culture (Schuyler 1993). These groups affected Moroccan musical culture in two major ways: first, they refocused the country's attention onto its diverse cultural heritage; second, by speaking to the concerns of a young generation experiencing geographic and social displacement due to urban migration, they set the stage for creating a national following that transcended local and the regional affiliations.

Tunisia enjoyed no such popularization of its black musical traditions and no such high-profile celebration of its cultural diversity. The cultural projects involving *sṭambēlī* have been much smaller in scope, and much more circumscribed in impact. But recently, the success of the Moroccan *gnāwa*, both in its international presence and acceptance as part of the Moroccan national fabric, has become increasingly influential in shaping the aspirations of *sṭambēlī* musicians and their interlocutors. Riadh Zaouch, the *ʿarīfa* who leads the Sīdī ʿAlī el-Asmar troupe, looks to the thriving *gnāwa* scene in Morocco for inspiration for his efforts to make *sṭambēlī* more visible and popular in Tunisia. His *sṭambēlī* troupe is public relations savvy, proactively seeking sponsorship from government and cultural institutions and publicity in newspapers and on television. It sends out flashy, bilingual (French and Arabic) invitations to journalists, government officials, and other members of the cultural elite and in 2001 secured the cosponsorship of the Tunisian Ministry of Culture, the Ministry of the Interior, the Tunis City Government, the Municipality of Tunis, and the newspaper *La Presse* for a *sṭambēlī* ceremony held at Sīdī ʿAlī el-Asmar for the *mūldiyya*, or celebration of the Prophet's birthday. Zaouch also looks to the *gnāwa* as a model for international success. He maintains a constantly updated file of clippings about *gnāwa* performances abroad from international newspapers; one folder I was shown had copies of articles about the *gnāwa* from German, Italian, Spanish, French, and Arabic newspapers. His image has become a standard accompaniment to press coverage of *sṭambēlī*, which recently suggested Zaouch might be heralding the era of the "*sṭambēlī* superstar."

Exhibit B: *Sṭambēlī* and the Global Marketplace (1998–2001)

Khemīsī's powerful, grainy voice, playing back on an old and weathered portable cassette deck, fills Bābā Majīd's small room at Dār Bārnū. Addressing Sīdī Manṣūr, he sings "mūl id-dīwān ʿajmī, bābā salem ʿalīh" (master of the non-Arab/sub-Saharan assembly, father, greetings to him), overpowering the track's *gumbrī* melody and *shqāshiq* rhythms, making it immediately clear that this recording was not meant to reproduce *sṭambēlī*'s ritual aesthetics (which do not foreground the solo voice). "Yā bābā salem ʿalīh, mūl id-dīwān" (O father, greetings to him, master of the assembly) answer the *ṣunnāʿ*, whose vocals are also lower in the sound mix than Khemīsī's. I am thinking to myself that the *gumbrī* strikes on the drumhead seem to be getting louder when Bābā Majīd points out, "That's the djembe." Indeed, a djembe drum's low tones are coinciding with the *gumbrī* strikes (which both correspond to the two syllables "bā-bā" in the response), while the drum's higher-pitched tones fill in the space between them. Soon I realize that I am lost. The djembe's emphasis on those two notes has resulted in a "gestalt flip" (Locke 1998) in which the first tone, which I had spent weeks working on finally hearing "correctly" as the "offbeat," was now "on" the beat;

put together, these two articulations now felt like the first two beats of a longer 6/4 pattern. The *gumbrī* melody, which was already low in the mix, now sounded entirely unfamiliar, as the relationship between the notes had been altered radically in my mind, a shift that was only reinforced as the cycle repeated over and over. Yet another surprise awaited me. About two minutes into the *nūba*, once I had become somewhat accustomed to the unfamiliar reversal of volume levels that foregrounded the lead voice and relegated the *shqāshiq* and vocal response to the background, the lead vocals dropped out as a saxophone entered the mix with hesitant, fleeting one- and two-note phrases that seemed to float over the distant *gumbrī* and *shqāshiq*. The saxophone improvisation did not adhere to the conventions of *sṭambēlī* improvisation, which involve repetitition, variation, and substitution, and it strayed far from the minor pentatonic mode proffered by the *gumbrī*'s melodic cycles. As the saxophone's phrasing became more elaborate and its insistence on free jazz aesthetics took root, it was not difficult to imagine the *gumbrī* being interpreted by a jazz musician as a bass ostinato and the *shqāshiq* as virtual hi-hats. Although the idea that Tunisian *sṭambēlī* and Moroccan *gnāwa* constitute the "African roots" of jazz, and are therefore naturally compatible with it, is a common sentiment shared by some African American musicians and members of the North African intelligentsia (and is discussed further below), this recording of Sīdī Manṣūr is the product of wider set of intersecting discourses, practices, and ideas.

This version of Sīdī Manṣūr was recorded for the 1999 film *Pomegranate Siestas* (Arabic *Qwayl ir-Rummān*; French *Les siestes grenadines*) by Tunisian director Mahmoud ben Mahmoud. More evocative in its original Tunisian Arabic, the title refers to the seasonal phenomenon we call "Indian summer," a time of ripening and temporarily suspended resolution. A film about displacement, belonging, and prejudice, it revolves around the character Soufiya, a teenager who grew up in Senegal with her authoritarian Tunisian father, who took her there as a child to avoid giving her up to her mother, the French wife he was divorcing. Soufiya, already out of place in Senegal, is drawn to local dance traditions to cope with her predicament but has experienced a level of acceptance and freedom that will be lacking when she is taken by her father back to Tunisia, where she encounters debilitating prejudice and corruption. But in Tunisia she also discovers *sṭambēlī*, which provides for her a space to escape, to become empowered by the very African-ness that disadvantages her socially. When she dances to the *nūba* of Bū Saʿdiyya, she merges her displacement and desperate search for identity and resolution into his, collapsing time and space in the act of embodiment. Her story shares some general themes with *sṭambēlī*: being under another's control, forcible trans-Saharan movements, prejudice, and the therapeutic potential of ritual trance music. Soufiya's experience of her Euro-African heritage is an uncomfortable one; she is an Arabic speaker in Dakar and then a Senegalese in Tunisia, while the specter of her mother, trying to track her down, is always close.

Although it was probably not the intent of the filmmaker, I sense a corresponding uncomfortable simultaneity and resultant ambiguity in the three intersecting domains of sound in this version of the *nūba*: *sṭambēlī*, djembe, and jazz, the latter two signifying locality precisely through their global circulation. Djembe drumming and jazz improvisation have a global presence, but also signify geoculturally, whether Senegal and the United States specifically, or sub-Saharan African drumming and Euro-American jazz more generally. Yet there is also the assumption that all three, as musics of the African diaspora, are closely related enough to be compatible in performance. Once again, Sīdī Manṣūr travels beyond the borders of the city of Sfax and the Tunisian nation-state (see chap. 7), drawing together into a shared space disparate traditions. Like the film, the *nūba* raises the issues of identity and border crossing without necessarily resolving them. Many readings are possible, and I do not presume to offer a definitive exegesis, but rather to simply highlight some of the forces at play.

In a similar vein, I consider below two sites of musical cosmopolitanism in which *sṭambēlī* was presented publicly, paying attention to some of the guiding motivations and implications of each project. Each example is characterized by slightly different relations between the centrifugal forces of "world music" and the centripetal forces of "exotica" (Bohlman 2002). In the first example, *sṭambēlī* as "world music" privileges centrifugal forces; that is, away from Tunisia and into the "global" imagination. In the second example, *sṭambēlī* as "exotica" privileges centripetal forces in France that draw the "authentic" other inward. What interests me here is that the listenership's cosmopolitanism involves the consumption of another, "diasporic" cosmopolitanism of *sṭambēlī*, whose musical relations themselves extend "indigenous ideologies of contact, exchange, and movement" (Stokes 2007: 9). Rather than merely providing new "world music" stages for the cosmopolitan gaze, they must be understood from within *sṭambēlī*'s history of performing for others. These examples, I believe, also complicate any homogeneous idea of the "global," for each demonstrates an engagement with different types of global forces, as well as different narratives of place, belonging, and authenticity.

"TRANSE-MISSION"

In the spring of 1998, the Centre des musiques arabes et méditerranéennes (CMAM), formerly the palace of the baron d'Erlanger,[7] in Sidi Bou Said,

Tunisia, held a concert event entitled "Stambali: Transe-Mission." The concept was initially proposed by Kays Rostom, an expatriate Tunisian living in Belgium, who designed and choreographed the performance. Rostom, a percussionist who has performed in Europe in numerous Afro-Cuban and jazz fusion groups, joined representatives of CMAM in scouting the major *sṭambēlī* groups in Tunis and chose to invite the musicians of Dār Bārnū to be the core musicians of the group.

A performance on stage was new to most members of the group. Khemīsī, the lead singer, for one, was uncomfortable singing into a microphone, since the call-and-response vocals of *sṭambēlī* are traditionally performed without amplification. As opposed to traditional rituals, where the unfolding of the event is malleable and based on direct interactions among musician, dancer, and spirit (including adhering to the conventions of spirit hierarchy), the dancing at the concert was all choreographed. This meant that there was a prescribed order to the succession of *nūba*s—represented in the printed program—and the musicians had to memorize when and where to enter and exit the music to accommodate the choreographic plans and musical arrangements, which featured two Senegalese percussionists as well as Rostom on the djembe (and for one performance, the saxophone and violin), which are not a part of the *sṭambēlī* ritual context.

This concert brought a vast repertoire of songs and dances out of the private sphere and into the public gaze. It is crucial to note, however, that this concert was not meant to be a representation of an "authentic" *sṭambēlī* ritual session; rather, it was self-consciously innovative, nontraditional, and secular. In his program notes, Rostom wrote, "This spectacle is not an experiment in cultural admixture, nor the result of a thesis on magico-religious ritual, and less still a therapeutic or socio-musicological session. It is a concert of music." The program consisted of thirty-two *nūba*s that in some ways followed the general logic of the *silsila*, grouping most *nūba*s together in appropriate succession, but with some noteworthy exceptions. The program began, in typical Dār Bārnū fashion, with the three opening *nūba*s of Ṣlāt in-Nabī, Jerma, and Bū Ḥijba. Immediately thereafter, however, came the *nūba*s for Miryamu and Nana ʿAysha, the two *nūba*s that appear together at the very end of traditional Dār Bārnū ceremonies. The saints, including Sīdī ʿAbd el-Qādir, Sīdī Saʿd, Sīdī Frej, and Sīdī ʿAbd es-Salēm, among others, were invoked next, followed by ʿArabiyya and Bambara (a rarely performed *nūba* about the Bambara people of Dār Bambara). *Silsila*s for the Baḥriyya and Banū Kūrī were played before ending with Gindīma, Bū Ḥijba (the only repeated *nūba*), Sīdī Marzūg, and Bū Saʿdiyya, which was intended as a finale featuring the impressive masked costume as well as the "reintroduction" of the *dūndūfa* drum, performed by Kays Rostom on what, according to the center's director, was possibly the last surviving specimen of the instrument in Tunisia.

What were the guiding motivations for this performance? For its director, it was a means of paying homage to the cultural treasures produced by the "increasingly rare, precious, and vulnerable" *sṭambēlī* musicians. "I quickly realized," however, writes Rostom, "that work on sonic and musical arrangements was obviously necessary to make it accessible to a public not initiated in the ritual ceremonies, where stambali is not only a music for the ears and mind but also a demonstration of the unity between music, body, and mind. . . . It seemed very natural then to invite Africa, original source of so many musical riches of the world, to give once again its substance, its energy, and its magic to stambali, one of its vast number of children, like its brothers, from Brazil to Haita, from Jamaica to Cuba, from jazz to SALSA" (Rostom 1998: n.p., capitals in original).

There is a certain irony to the perceived need to make *sṭambēlī*—already stigmatized as too "African"—more palatable to Tunisian listeners by incorporating other "African" musical elements into it. Moreover, Rostom suggests that such aesthetic changes might enable *sṭambēlī* to join other musical expressions of the African musical diaspora, namely, jazz and salsa, that have become global in scope. Tunisian newspaper reviews reinforced these fantasies and credited the organizers with "rescuscitating this traditional musical heritage" without "mummifying" or "museumizing" it (Ammar 1997; Zouaoui 1998). Underlying these sentiments is the issue of ownership. During the "era of the beys," the *sṭambēlī* community organized itself, presented itself to the court, and was understood on its own terms. The "Transe-Mission" concert, on the other hand, relied on outsiders to conceive and organize the show and depended on the world music phenomenon (including its assumptions about the "natural" compatibility of "African" diasporic musics) in order to generate interest and become comprehensible to the audience. Since *sṭambēlī* is simultaneously defined as Tunisian national heritage and as an inclusive African diasporic space for musical interaction, an initiative by a creative, energetic expatriate (Rostom) and a national cultural authority (CMAM) to salvage the *sṭambēlī* tradition went uninterrogated, at least in the press.

How did the Dār Bārnū musicians perceive these dynamics? They, too, understood the members of their Tunisians audience to be outsiders unfamiliar with the tradition. But unlike Europeans, Americans, and Japanese, whom they described as *maghrūm* (fond) of *sṭambēlī*, Tunisians were believed to have either misconceptions about, or strong prejudices against, *sṭambēlī*. Tunisians who attended the concert, according to Bābā Majīd, lost their bias only after witnessing firsthand that this was not a "simple" practice, but rather involved expert musical technique and an extensive repertoire. He told me that before the concert started, those in the audience "stared at me like predators, but I counter-attacked with the *gumbrī*. . . . [Then] they saw there was good playing here, there is rhythm, there is melody. . . . [After the concert, they said,] 'Kiss me here, and here [on the cheeks]; God bless you.'" For Bābā Majīd, it was not the addition of Senegalese musical elements that changed their outlook, but rather the opportunity to witness and experience the central, defining musical elements of *sṭambēlī*, namely, the *gumbrī*, the *shqāshiq*, and the vocals. But these sounds, exotic to even most of this Tunisian audience, became just that: musical sounds, like any other, that could be combined with others, like paints on a palette, to create a new aesthetic musical object. Of course, these sounds still signified; they enabled, indeed implored, the audience to imagine the ritual setting of *sṭambēlī*, not to mention an imagined "Africa." But they were recontextualized so that music, as object, could be mobilized and manipulated in new ways in order to render it comprehensible to its others. This corresponds to one of Stuart Hall's (1991) forms of globalization, that of the "global postmodern," which is characterized by "trying to live with, and at the same moment, overcome, sublate, get hold of, and incorporate difference." By privileging hybridity, mixing, and border crossing, "world music" aesthetics and discourses seek to make connections, to diminish the space between self and other. Exotica, and its centripetal forces, on the other hand, as we shall see, is grounded in forces that attempt to keep self and other at a greater distance.

POSTCOLONIAL (RE)PRESENTATIONS

The Transe-Mission concert series served as a catalyst generating opportunities for performing *sṭambēlī* in new contexts. One of these came in the form of an invitation to perform at the fifth *Festival de l'imaginaire* in Paris in 2001. This performance carried with it very different expectations, revealing a different set of tensions between the local and global. The festival was produced by the Maison des Cultures du Monde, a component of the French Ministry of Culture, and took place at the Théâtre Équestre Zingaro in Paris. *Sṭambēlī* was presented as part of the "cycle extase et possession," alongside spirit possession practices from Uzbekistan, South India, and Korea. As opposed to the organizers of the "Transe-Mission" concert, the organizers of the festival demanded an "authentic" ritual performance. It was "exotic" and needed to remain so; innovation was undesirable. However, in this case, the organizers demanded fundamental change to the Dār Bārnū troupe to fit their image of authentic *sṭambēlī*. According to Bābā Majīd, when the organizers conveyed to him their desire to have his troupe perform at the festival, they stipulated that because three of his accompanying musicians were "not black enough" to represent authentically a practice they defined in the program notes as *négro-africaine*, *afro-tunisien*, and performed exclusively by descendants of black slaves, Bābā Majīd would need to find appropriately pigmented replacements for the Arab Tunisians in his troupe. Bābā Majīd was reluctant to put together an all-black group, because, by chance, only the younger, inexperienced musicians looked "black enough," which meant replacing seasoned performers with younger, less disciplined musicians. However, seeing this as an opportunity not to be missed, Bābā Majīd bought the younger musicians their passports, visas, and even new clothing for the performances in Paris. Once in Paris, however—and before finishing the series of concerts—these three musicians decided to flee (*yaḥraq* in Tunisian slang; lit. "burn," referring to the burning of identification papers to avoid deportation) to become illegal immigrants in France. One, who had left behind a wife and child in Tunisia, was caught when he injured himself trying to climb a fence to cross the Italian border. Another returned after nearly a year in France.

From within, this performance was embraced as an opportunity to gain recognition from an international audience already conditioned to be interested in, and respectful of, traditions like *sṭambēlī*. Furthermore, Bābā Majīd mentioned that there were many Africans attending the concert who were visibly physically moved by the music. He felt they understood it, and that it reminded them of home. That they were staging a ritual-like performance did not seem to bother any of the musicians, who felt it put less pressure on them, since they were merely performing as they would in their regular ritual work. Bābā Majīd was willing to put aside this curious demand for "blacker" musicians for practical reasons: getting paid and having the opportunity to perform in Europe. Commodifying their racial identity went hand in hand with commodifying their spirituality, while the French culture brokers capitalized on the demand for racialized and spiritualized commodities (Kapchan 2007: 156). This nonritual performance was a reproduction of a ritual performance and was shaped to adhere to the imagined ideal in the minds of the organizers and audience. As opposed to the "Transe-Mission" concert, which relied on a musical compatibility, exotica ascribes and emphasizes difference and distance. At the same time, it participates in the construction of a supposedly universal category of "trance" ritual, adhering to its own tautology by presenting *sṭambēlī* alongside otherwise unrelated ritual traditions from South India, Uzbekistan, and Korea (see Kapchan 2007, but also Bohlman 1997 and Shannon 2007 on the construction of "sacred," especially Sufi, music in the world music market).

ARGUING AUTHENTICITY

The recent and modest renewed interest in *sṭambēlī* has produced an increasingly competitive market of musicians. The examples cited above prompted debates within the *sṭambēlī* community, despite the fact that the transfer of money is an integral part of the ritual process in *sṭambēlī*. While aesthetics and ritual knowledge provide important criteria for evaluation and acceptance of other musicians in the world of *sṭambēlī*, the narrative strategies for arguing authenticity are most often ethical in nature. Within the Dār Bārnū community, the term *fenniste* is used to praise respected *sṭambēlī* musicians. Derived from the Arabic *fann* (art), which is then entered into a French construction, the term could be translated as "artist." *Fenniste*, however, implies much more than a talented musician who can succeed, for example, on the concert stage. It assumes that the musician has a great deal of ritual efficacy, for good musical aesthetics are requisite for a successful healing ceremony. The spirits and saints will not descend, nor will they be placated, by inferior performances. Furthermore, the *nūba*s must be distributed effectively throughout the ceremony, with certain ones repeated at different times for particular spirits. Being able to control the pace and structure of the ceremony requires the *fenniste* to be an effective improviser; he must be able to adapt quickly to the emergent needs of dancers and spirits alike. This kind of awareness of the needs of the community, along with a commitment to and respect for the *sṭambēlī* tradition, marks the *fenniste* above all as characterized by a strong sense of ethics.

The *khubziste* is the ethical opposite of the *fenniste*. Derived from the Arabic *khubz* (bread), *khubziste* refers to one who is interested only in making money ("bread" in Tunisian slang). Making money, or performing in more commercialized or mass-mediated settings of *sṭambēlī*, however, is not enough to warrant the label *khubziste*. This term is reserved for those who make money at the expense of betraying others and compromising the *sṭambēlī* tradition.

The *khubziste-fenniste* dualism grows louder as new performance contexts emerge. The centripetal forces of the Paris performance, for instance, also gave rise to centrifugal forces that resonated back in Tunis. An *ʿarīfa* at Dār Bārnū spoke with the mother of one of the musicians who emigrated illegally to Europe and convinced her that if she held a *sṭambēlī* ceremony, her son would return. The *ʿarīfa* went to Dār Bārnū, proudly announcing that she had secured more work for the group. I was told that Bābā Majīd, upon hearing how this *ʿarīfa* misled a potential client, responded, "What? I'll pick up my *gumbrī* and play, and all of a sudden an airplane carrying the boy will appear? This is absurd. Leave, and don't come back." He sighed, shaking his head, and said, "khubziste . . ." The increasing escalation of the perceived *khubziste* mentality is a result of many factors, including the poor economic state of members of the community during (and since) the 1990s.

Global and Cosmopolitan

Sṭambēlī's movements and placements within the discourses of the world music market and the transnational imaginary have generated new challenges along with new opportunities for its performers. While the "modern" and the "global" generated new performance contexts, made available new technologies, and imposed new vocabularies and geocultural referents on *sṭambēlī*, it would be misleading to propose an analysis that assumed a radical clash of *sṭambēlī* with the ideologies of modernization and globalization, or, for that matter, that this is a one-way street of appropriation by cultural authorities, whose projects are always incomplete and unstable. Rather than seeing practices such as *sṭambēlī* as premodern or nonmodern, we could position them as "beyond modernity," as predating the modern, remaining relevant throughout it and beyond, and anticipating this era of the global.

Marc Augé (1999), who argues convincingly that "cults born of contact" such as *sṭambēlī*, which are generally understood as being peripheral to, or at least lagging or late in encountering, globalization, were perhaps the first to experience such senses as the acceleration of history, the shrinking of space, and the individualizing of identities that define the experience of globalization. The moments of "world music" and "exotica" discussed in this chapter suggest that they are congruent with *sṭambēlī*'s history of ritually adapting to new circumstances, and, moreover, that *sṭambēlī* has always been musically cosmopolitan—creating spaces for engagement and interaction with other traveling musical traditions—just as it has always been "global"—defined by, and ritually negotiating, previously unimagined levels of far-reaching social encounter.

CHAPTER NINE

Conclusion

MUSIC, TRANCE, AND ALTERITY

The *sṭambēlī* of Dār Bārnū charts a vast historical and geocultural terrain. At the same time, it is primarily concerned with the immediacy of making localized interventions to alleviate suffering and manage relationships between selves and others. I have attempted to show how the music of *sṭambēlī* ritual guides participants along journeys of the body and the imagination, conjoining and making inseparable these domains of the imaginal and the therapeutic. I have avoided seeking universals, such as an "explanation" of trance, as well as the "egological reflexivity" of a sustained phenomenological project (Bourdieu 2003), both of which tend to be concerned, either explicitly or obliquely, with the mechanisms or causes of trance and questions of consciousness. Mobilizing the concept of ritual dynamics has enabled me to avoid these two extremes while pursuing a path of inquiry that may be of some relevance beyond the context of *sṭambēlī* and maintaining my conviction that aesthetic sensations constitute vital, if analytically elusive, ways of knowing (Stoller 1997; Kapferer and Hobart 2005; Sklar 2001; see also Taussig 1993). Musical sensibilities and techniques, bodily gestures and movements, as well as visual displays and olfactory and gustatory absorptions, activate these embodied epistemologies, which contain not only the therapeutic knowledge necessary for healing, but also the capacity to ritually reconcile sub-Saharan Africanness and Tunisian Islamic praxis by aesthetically joining the two to produce a singular and unified system of musico-therapeutic knowledge.

"Simultaneously centers of new belonging and products of a prior realm," write Ronald Radano and Philip Bohlman, "musical migrations express a paradoxical concentration of sameness and difference . . . [and] destabilize fixities of place" (2000: 31). Situating Dār Bārnū at the center of my inquiry has enabled me to work from within, so to speak, to examine the senses of place cultivated and negotiated by *sṭambēlī*, as well as to recognize the ways in which its interaction with circulating forces, actions, and discourses both complicates and reinforces those senses. The historical, geocultural, and musical concerns expressed by members of Dār Bārnū emphasize movements and encounters, trajectories and intersections. The migrations and movements of sounds, sights, tastes, smells, things, ideas, people, and spirits converge in music and ritual, where they are recollected and reconfigured. I have situated these movements historically and socially, tracing the paths of humans, spirits, and musical materials and sensibilities across the Sahara, paying particular attention to modes of emplacement that involved processes of synthesis and profound changes in meanings as sub-Saharans, their spirits, and aesthetics became minorities, became alter, in their new environment.

I have also paid a great deal of attention to the musical routes followed by *sṭambēlī* musicians. These routes underscore the scope of ritual knowledge cultivated by musicians and highlight their responsibility to humans and the various and numerous members of the pantheon. I have tried to show that ritual is more than a symbolic reflection of realities or ideas external to it. Rather, it is a methodology for producing meaning for those involved; ritual is "its own exegesis" (Kapferer 1991: 241). It is here, in this recursive space of ritual, that musical aesthetics call attention to *sṭambēlī*'s own ontological premises, which recognize the spiritual authority of black bodies as well as the musical instruments they master. *Sūdānī* and *ʿajmī* become positive descriptors celebrating aesthetic ideals as they simultaneously distinguish *sṭambēlī* from the discourse of musical aesthetics dominant in the Tunisian context, which applies these terms in negative ways. *Sṭambēlī* thus challenges listeners to reconcile these worlds, worlds that have been constructed in the Tunisian imagination as oppositional and even mutually exclusive. But reconciling them does not mean erasing difference; rather, it expands what Vincent Crapanzano refers to as one's "imaginative horizons," a crucial component of which is the notion of a hinterland, a place that lies "elsewhere, *ailleurs*, beyond where one is and yet intimately related to it. It is in an owing relation, a reciprocal one, with the here-and-now from which it is declared a hinterland" (Crapanzano 2004: 15). That hinterland, he emphasizes, is blurry and fuzzy; it is what lies behind the horizon. But in the very act of being imagined it creates possibilities. In many ways, it is this relation to the beyond, cultivated by *sṭambēlī* musicians situated in the between, that reinforces people's commitment to the *sṭambēlī* tradition. John Blacking has argued powerfully that ritual aesthetics and their generation of transcendent experiences reinforce people's motivation and commitment to people and institutions. In her thoughtful reconsideration of John Blacking's theorization of the "other self," Rebecca Sager (2006) draws attention to the social implications of musically transcendent experiences by position-

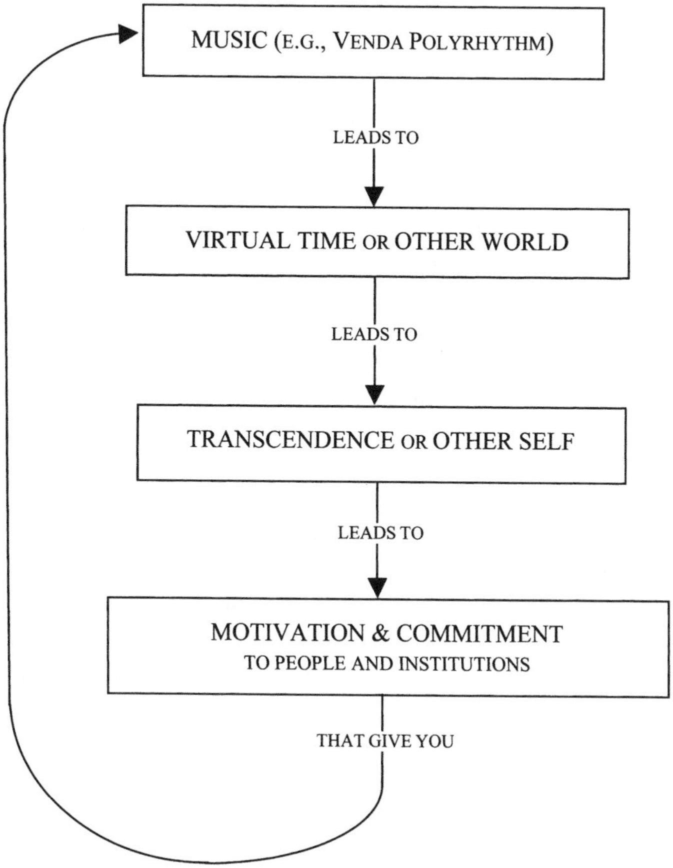

FIGURE. 13. John Blacking's theory of musical-institutional motivation. From Sager (2006: 149)

ing music within a conceptual feedback loop that connects to the virtual time or other world it constructs in ritual, the experience of transcendence and encountering other selves, and commitments to others and the social institutions that produce the music (see fig.13).

When I was first welcomed into the world of Dār Bārnū, it was at a profound historical moment marking the end of the slow demise of the *dār* system, an end literally embodied in the death of Khemīsī. During this transition to a post-*dār sṭambēlī*, relations to the idea of "Africa" have also been changing. For a while, Bābā Majīd's son and his counterparts prized, and wore in ritual, the kind of "African" outfits that Bābā Majīd refused to wear on television in the 1960s, and they now take part in *gnāwa* festivals in Morocco. Yet they are active within a sociohistorical context in which local knowledge about "Africa" is increasingly scarce, and the interaction with large communities of Africans from multiple sub-Saharan origins is entirely absent. But while the "African" presence in Tunis has unquestionably diminished over the twentieth century, making the *dār* system obsolete, the twenty-first century brings new modalities of connectivity to Africa through easier travel and communications. Along with the new figurations of distance and familiarity these may produce, however, come new racialisms that may reinscribe difference; at the turn of the twenty-first century, "all evidence indicates that music is playing an even more powerful role in the construction of racial imaginaries" (Radano and Bohlman 2000: 33). But for musicians as well as their multiple and overlapping publics, fractures in prior coherences may give way to new imaginaries of belonging and identity (Radano and Bohlman 2000: 33). *Sṭambēlī* as Bābā Majīd knew it may be gone, but as the historical and social contexts of *sṭambēlī* change, so have some practices and meanings. Yet traditional trance healing practices have proven to be remarkably resilient and adaptive to change. In fact, I would agree with Fritz Kramer that this resilience, adaptivity, and refusal to be contained by categories imposed from without constitute some of their most significant defining characteristics. Kramer explains that such practices "in which Africans portrayed the 'other' to their own respective cultures, did not fulfil a homogenous task; they served to heal and divert, to criticize divergencies and to legitimate them; to fuse to a festive oneness and to differentiate the individual from his corporate group. . . . They fixated alien phenomena, raising them to the status of types and making them part of their own tradition. . . . It is not possible to explain them from the perspective of some institution in our own society based on division of labour, for they are always both more and less than therapy, art, entertainment, social criticism, profession, fashion, or ethnography" (Kramer 1993: 240).

Alterity, as Michael Taussig (1993) notes, is not a thing, but rather a relationship, and relationships are both historically contingent and vulnerable to the vicissitudes of new opportunities and demands. I am often asked what the future of *sṭambēlī* holds, or even if it has a future. I am not one to prognosticate, though I am not pessimistic. As long as we continue to consider the organization of musical sound as "total social facts, saturated with messages about time, place, feeling, style, belonging, and identity" (Feld and Fox 1994: 38), then it is likely that *sṭambēlī* will continue to signify, negotiate, and accommodate relations between self and other, albeit among different publics with different needs and expectations, and in ways we may not be able to predict.

EPILOGUE

(WITH NOTES ON AUDIO EXAMPLES)

The Dār Bārnū household was devastated by the death of Bābā Majīd in 2008. He passed away during the month of Ramadan, at the age of eighty-six. I returned to Dār Bārnū in the spring of 2009 to pay my respects and to spend time with the house's *sṭambēlī* troupe, now led by the forty-year-old Ṣālaḥ Wārglī, who years ago had been Bābā Majīd's apprentice. Belḥassen is the troupe's lead *shqāshiq* player, accompanied by Nūr ed-Dīn Sūdānī. Although they sometimes perform as a trio, for most ceremonies they add one or two other *shqāshiq* players. During my visit, another elder, Nūr ed-Dīn's father, Ṣādiq Sūdānī—the last of his generation to regularly enter possession trance by the *silsila* of Brāwnā spirits—also passed away. In addition to the great personal loss felt by the Dār Bārnū household and the wider *sṭambēlī* community, these two deaths have brought definitive closure to the era of a *sṭambēlī dār* system animated by individuals with firsthand knowledge and memories of multiple and diverse communal houses, with their different languages, traditions, and shared, experience-near memories of slavery and servitude.

Despite these losses, *sṭambēlī* remains in demand, as clients old and new must placate their afflicting spirits, and pilgrimages must be made to assuage saints such as Sīdī Frej. Moreover, as *sṭambēlī*'s public presence increased in the early years of the new century, so did opportunities for festival performances and new musical collaborations. During my two-month stay in Tunisia in 2009, the Dār Bārnū troupe's activities included several private healing ceremonies, two out-of-town festival performances, and three days and nights of ceremonies at the annual pilgrimage to the shrine of Sīdī ʿAlī Ḥaṭāb, which brings *sṭambēlī* into the same sacred performance space as Sufi groups such as the ʿĪsāwiyya, Sulāmiyya, and Ḥaṭābiyya. While this pilgrimage, like any social event that brings together hundreds of people in Tunisia, was cloaked as a "festival" by the government (and thus suffers from the requisite opening speeches and parading of participating groups around a horse ring for officials to view), it nevertheless maintained its function as a space for several traditions of saint (and spirit) veneration to operate on their terms. There was no shortage of new trancers, including some Sufi adepts as well as individuals who participate in other trance traditions such as the Tijaniyya (a women's Sufi trance group). There was also no shortage of new audience members, mostly teenagers and young adults, many of whom recorded clips on their cell phones, reacting with words and gestures exhibiting a range of attitudes, from astonishment and curiosity to dismissal and scorn.

These attitudes continue to be shaped in part by the twin concerns of religion and modernity that conditioned public attitudes toward *sṭambēlī* throughout the twentieth century. But technological changes have perhaps intensified things a bit. Connectivity via cell phones, the Internet, and satellite television keeps Tunisian youth in continual contact with friends and family at home and abroad and keeps them attuned to the latest European and American music and fashion trends. Computers and mp3 players are filled with Western rap, rock, and pop music alongside the latest Arabic pop songs. Social and ritual lives are far more likely to revolve around texting, shopping, and attending parties than visits to shrines or healing ceremonies. Decades of French-style schooling and nationalist politics have also entrenched ideologies of empiricism and cultural uniformity in the psyche of the younger generations. During this trip I heard *sṭambēlī* dismissed as "superstition" because "spirits are not real," and several attendees described it as *mūsh normale* (lit. "not normal"), a popular phrase among Tunisian youth to express amazement at the bizarre (in some contexts, though not this one, it can be applied positively, e.g., if something is so beautiful it is beyond "normal").

Technology has also intensified religious-based criticism of *sṭambēlī*. Many Tunisians blame satellite television broadcasts from the Middle East for inspiring a new religious conservatism in the country, including a resurgence in women wearing the Islamic headscarf (*ḥijāb*), that has sparked heated debate over religion and Tunisian identity. I noticed more outright religious-based criticism of *sṭambēlī* (often based on the inaccurate assumption that *sṭambēlī* involves exorcizing the *jinn*) during this trip than I had in previous years. In fact, at least one such incident occurred at each of the ceremonies I attended in 2009.

The situation, however, is not bleak, as *sṭambēlī* has always been a niche tradition that does not rely on widespread appeal for its survival. Moreover, there is no consensus in attitude among the tech-savvy youth or the religious minded: some members of the younger generations are beginning to invite *sṭambēlī* musicians to perform at their house parties, and some *sṭambēlī* clients and occasional trancers are devout wearers of the *ḥijāb*. I have even heard that a Tunisian airline holds a *sṭambēlī* ceremony inside each new airplane it purchases before it is put into service. *Sṭambēlī* has proven to be a highly adaptive cultural practice, capable of producing multiple meanings for its participants and audiences. Its past resilience bodes well for its future.

* * *

The accompanying compact disc tries to capture this moment of transition in the Dār Bārnū tradition by juxtaposing Bābā Majīd's musical narratives of *sṭambēlī* history with *nūba*s performed by the Dār Bārnū troupe in 2009, led by his successor, Ṣālaḥ Wārglī. The first recording is Bābā's performance of the *nūba* of Bū Saʿdiyya, described in detail in chapter 2 for its evocative portrayal of *sṭambēlī*'s early history. The other recording of Bābā Majīd (track 6) is a medley of three *nūba*s he played for me to highlight the cultural diversity of the black population of the communal houses. The track begins with "ʿAysha Līla," described by Bābā Majīd as a Tuareg (*ṭargiyya*) song. He follows this with "Wīta Tatanī," a Barnāwī song. He told me that "*tatanī*" is Kanuri for "my child," and near the beginning of this *nūba* you can hear him explain that "wīta tatanī" is about a mother calling her child as she prepares a meal. The third song is the *nūba* Bambara, whose lyrics call attention to the numerous places migrant or displaced Bambara have settled in. Most of this *nūba* consists of inserting the name of a different country or region after singing the phrase "Bambara, *awlēd* . . ." (which means "Bambara, people of . . ." [lit. "sons of . . ."]). Thus, "Bambara, *awlēd* Togo," or "Bambara, people of Togo." After singing "Bambara, *awlēd* Congo" and "Bambara, *awlēd* Senegal," Bābā Majīd added "Bambara, *awlēd* Ghana" in recognition of my Ghanaian friend and colleague Ismael Musah Montana (who was present for this recording), and then, with a wink and a laugh, "Bambara, *awlēd* Chicago!" to acknowledge my home at the time.

Tracks 2–5 document the Dār Bārnū troupe, under the leadership of Ṣālaḥ Wārglī, performing in ritual. Tracks 2, 3, and 4 are examined in detail in chapter 5. Track 5 is a portion of the Banū Kūrī *silsila*, chosen in part because it includes some lesser-known *nūba*s such as Dundurūsū, Ḥaddād, and Garūjī, in addition to the Banū Kūrī mainstays.

Track Listing

1. Bū Saʿdiyya (6:27). *Gambara* and vocals: Bābā Majīd Barnāwī. Recorded at Dār Bārnū, August 15, 2001.
2. Ṣlāt in-Nabī, Jerma, and Bū Ḥijba (7:17). *Gumbrī* and lead vocals: Ṣālaḥ

Wārglī; *shqāshiq* and vocals: Belḥassen Barnāwī [Mihoub], Noureddine Soudani, and Lotfi. Recorded at Dār Bārnū, May 23, 2009.

3. Sīdī Marzūg (6:57). *Gumbrī* and lead vocals: Ṣālaḥ Wārglī; *shqāshiq* and vocals: Belḥassen Barnāwī [Mihoub], Noureddine Soudani, and Noureddine Jouini. Recorded in Bizerte, Tunisia, May 1, 2009.
4. Sīdī Bū Ra's el-ʿAjmī (4:23). *Gumbrī* and lead vocals: Ṣālaḥ Wārglī; *shqāshiq* and vocals: Belḥassen Barnāwī [Mihoub], Noureddine Soudani, and Lotfi. Recorded at Dār Bārnū, May 23, 2009.
5. *Silsila* of Banū Kūrī spirits (18:57). Includes Istifṭāḥ il-Kḥūl, Sārkin Kūfa, Dundurūsū (in two parts), Ḥaddād, Garūjī, Kūrī, Migzū, Jamarkay, Bābā Magojay, and Danīlya. *Gumbrī* and lead vocals: Ṣālaḥ Wārglī; *shqāshiq* and vocals: Belḥassen Barnāwī [Mihoub], Noureddine Soudani, and Lotfi. Recorded at Dār Bārnū, May 23, 2009.
6. "ʿAysha Līla" (Tuareg song), "Wīta Tatanī" (Barnāwī song), and Bambara (5:33). *Gambara* and vocals: Bābā Majīd Barnāwī. Recorded at Dār Bārnū, July 16, 2001.

Additional audio, video, and other materials are posted on this book's companion Web site, www.stambeli.com.

NOTES

Introduction

1. The only recognizable influence of sub-Saharan aesthetics in other musical contexts is the rarely performed pentatonic *maqām* called *rast ʿabīdī*, literally, "slave's *rast*."

2. Learning these healings and histories—whether learning to heal or be healed, or to perform or absorb the histories—is likewise a bodily process (Stoller 1997).

3. For particularly insightful accounts of ethnographic apprenticeship, see Stoller and Olkes (1987) and Chernoff (1979).

Chapter 1

1. The difficulty in assigning an accurate term to the segment of the black population that has practiced *sṭambēlī* in Tunis is evident in the multitude of descriptors employed by different scholars. Categorizations such as the misleadingly specific "Hausas of Tunis" (Tremearne 1914) and the more general and geographically dubious *afro-maghrébine* (Gouja 1996; Rahal 2000) have been used in the English and local French-language scholarship. A Muslim cleric from Timbuktu used the compound *sūdān-tūnis*, which combines the Arabic term for "black Africa" (*sūdān*) with "Tunisia," in his description of *sṭambēlī* practitioners in the early 1800s (Montana 2004a).

2. Further complicating race relations is the fact that sub-Saharans often made up entire military regiments and served as guards for the French during their colonial endeavors in the Maghrib. See Ennaji (1999) and Meyers (1983).

3. Tremearne notes that this was also a prevalent belief in Europe, where the word "necromancy" was corrupted into "negromancy," or black magic (1914: 453 n1).

4. On contemporary colactation practices in the Maghrib, see Ensel (2002).

5. Dutch scholar Snouck Hurgronje described the *ṭumbura* rituals and weekly dance "festivals" of black slaves in Mecca in the 1880s. Although such rituals have since been banned, there is anecdotal evidence that they continued to be performed undergro
in Saudi Arabia in the late twentieth century (Makris 2000: 369 n53).

6. There are reports from the early nineteenth century that slaves in
their musical ceremonies *sambānī* (Montana 2004a: 189), which is w
dition—as well as the slaves who practiced it—is called in Liby
Sambānī is also the name of the iron clappers, similar to the
regions of West Africa.

7. In Arabic, a root form language, adding a *t* (an

way typically creates a variant of the original word with a related meaning. For example, *ijtamaʿ*, "to assemble or meet," is related to *ijmaʿ*, "to collect or acquire."

8. Interestingly, similar uncertainty exists over the etymological origins of related traditions such as *gnāwa* in Morocco and *zār* in Egypt and the Sudan. The word *gnāwa* has been described as a corruption of Guinea (Dermenghem 1954: 285), Djinawa (Chlyeh 1998: 17), and the Berber word meaning "black" (Hunwick 2004: 165). Competing theories on the origins of *zār* are discussed in Morsy (1991) and Boddy (1989).

9. At times I sensed that these interactions were partially based on the assumption that I, as an educated Westerner, would need a "rational" explanation, or that they believed that a foreigner might develop a negative view of Tunisian Islam or culture by attending a *sṭambēlī* ceremony.

10. The desire for the modern is virtually inescapable in contemporary Tunis, where, for example, one bank's recent advertising campaign promoted debit card accounts not because they are more convenient or efficient, but simply because, as their simple, two-word slogan asserted, "C'est moderne!"

11. See, for instance, the newspaper articles that began to appear just before the "Stambali: Transe-mission" concert at the Center for Mediterranean and Arab Musics. These articles all had to explain and define *sṭambēlī* and often did so by comparing it to Moroccan *gnāwa*, which was presumably more well known to the readership (Alya 2001; Ben Ammar 1997, 1998; Zouaoui 1998).

12. There is a great deal of slippage between the concepts of "trance" and "possession" in the literature, and no consensus on the definition of either term. For the purposes of the present discussion, "trance" refers to a ritualized altered state of consciousness, while "possession" is the act of a spirit entering the body to cause trance. In other words, trance is a *behavior*, and possession is a *cultural theory for explaining that behavior*. See Lambek (1989: 37).

13. It is, I believe, no coincidence that the "Moroccan experiments" (Dwyer 1982; Crapanzano 1980; Rabinow 1977) in reflexive anthropology all involved the anthropologist's encounter with seemingly incommensurable practices involving the agency of spirits and saints.

14. David Locke (2006) has recently argued that a more appropriate analogy may be that of cubist art, which allows for a multitude (rather than only two) of perspectives on the work's many interpenetrating planes.

15. While this conclusion has been construed as coming "very close to musical reductionism" (Janzen 2000: 62), Friedson did clarify in a subsequent article that he was not suggesting a causal relationship between music and trance (Friedson 2005: 124).

16. This connection between music and emotion, especially in the context of repetitive musical stimuli and brain wave activity, has been furthered by recent studies providing intriguing arguments for incorporating drum-based rhythmic entrainment into the practice of Western music therapy (e.g., Bittman et al. 2001; Maurer et al. 1997; Mastnak 1993; see also Clayton, Sager, and Will 2004: 18).

17. See Stoller (2009) on the power of the between. He points out that while the between poses the danger of "indecision, fusion, and lethargy," if we "draw strength from both sides of the between and breathe in the creative air of indeterminacy, we can find ourselves in a space of enormous growth, a space of power and creativity" (4). See also Crapanzano (2004), Pandolfo (1997), and Chittick (1989) on Sufi conceptions of the between.

18. Examining the importance of spirit possession in everyday practice, of course,

can involve more than situating possession within the quotidian. Drawing on thinkers such as John Dewey and Ludwig Wittgenstein, Robert Desjarlais (1992) suggests that it is in the realm of aesthetics (and embodiment) that personhood, illness, and the quotidian experience interface. While the present study follows the spirit of Desjarlais's convictions, especially for the descendants of slaves in Tunisia, it also diverges from it by considering how otherness and dimensions of the nonordinary factor in to the nonblack experience of *sṭambēlī*.

19. The term "Berber" is highly problematic and often understood as a pejorative. Its etymology is unclear: it may be a native Arabic term or may be derived from the Latin *barbari* (barbarian; the Greeks used the term "Libyan" for North Africa's native population, after the region's Libu tribe). Since Berbers are not ethnically homogenous and share cultural and religious practices with their neighbors, the primary criterion for referring to them as a collective is essentially linguistic (Battenburg 1999: 149; Abun-Nasr 1987: 2). In other parts of North Africa, where there are many more Berber speakers and Berber identity is much more public and politicized, members of this group often designate themselves *Imazighen* (freeborn or noble), or a related term, instead of Berber.

20. On the importance of music to Berber identity and contemporary politics in Algeria, see Goodman (2005). There is a rich ethnographic literature on Berber music in Morocco, including Rovsing Olsen (1997), Lortat-Jacob (1980, 1981), Hoffman (2002), and Schuyler (1978, 1984). Due to the reported near extinction of Berber culture in Tunisia, as well as the official discouragement of ethnographic research on the subject, there are, to my knowledge, no published studies of Tunisian Berber music or culture.

21. For postindependence changes in attitude toward the medina of Tunis, see Micaud (1978).

22. Richard Lobban's (1997) otherwise useful overview of Tunis's informal economy neglects the activities of musicians and healers.

23. Tremearne (1914: 431) echoes this etymology but allows for the possibility that it derives from *baḥar nūḥ*, or Noah's Sea, that is, Lake Chad (29). Noah, like Jesus, is an acknowledged prophet in Islam. H. R. Palmer (1928) reports that the term "Bornu" is also the Zaghāwī plural for "man" (*bar*), which is why the Bornu people have also been called "Barri-barri" or "Beriberi."

24. See Stoller (1997: 32–36) on personal implication and ethnography.

Chapter 2

1. Masked costumes are rare in Tunisia, and masked dances virtually unknown, as such practices are usually considered idolatrous in the context of Islam. This aversion may be a reason why Bū Saʿdiyya's masked dance in the context of a possession ceremony is considered "entertainment" (*jāw*, lit. "ambience") and no trance or possession occurs to his *nūba*.

2. The sale of white Christian slaves had already been successfully abolished in 1816. Tunisia was not unique in enslaving white Europeans, often captured through pirate raids on the Mediterranean Sea. These slaves, however, served a much different purpose and did not experience the same racial prejudice and social marginalization as sub-Saharans.

3. Entire slave regiments were not rare in North Africa; they had already existed in Tunisia as early as the Aghlabid era (800–909) (Hunwick 1978: 30). For an illuminating account of Morocco's black slave corps, see Ennaji (1999).

4. It is unclear whether Tremearne's use of the term *gidan* reflected actual usage in Tunis or whether he instead used the Hausa term the term as a translation of the Arabic *dār*. Tremearne, who spoke Hausa fluently and became a *bori* medicine man during his seven years in Nigeria, bemoaned the Arabization of Hausa language and practice among displaced Hausa in North Africa.

5. Multiples of seven are highly symbolic in Tunisian Islam.

6. It is also common among Hausa and Songhay-Zarma populations in other diasporas to couch nonbiogenetic alliances in terms of familial relations that transcend or recalibrate ethnic identities. See Stoller (2002) and Amselle (1971).

7. *Shwāshnā* also referred to more ancient generations of slaves but should not to be confused with the concentration of black groups in southern Tunisia called *shwāshin*, who lived in local polities (*ʿurūsh*) and had as their patron saint Sīdī Marzūg (Montana 2004b: 94).

8. The *takai* is also a popular dance with sticks among the Dagbamba, an Islamicized people in northern Ghana. There it is performed with *gun-gon* (a barrel drum almost identical to the *sṭambēlī ṭabla*) and *lunga* (talking drum) (see Chernoff 1979; Locke and Lunna 1990). The dance movements are also similar to those described by Bābā Majīd. Tremearne (1914: 191) notes that the *takai* had become a war dance in Nigeria.

9. The change in status from slave to indentured servant was also the norm in rural areas in the Tunisian south, where a freed slave would become a *khammās* (one-fifth sharecropper) with little discernible difference in workload or reward (Pâques 1964).

10. While some saints were particular to Jewish communities in Tunisia, many were venerated by Jews, Arab Muslims, and sub-Saharans alike. Sīdī Maḥrez, the "patron saint" of Tunis, was central to the Jewish community's mythological narratives of establishing the *hara*, or Jewish quarter, of the Tunis medina. Jews, like sub-Saharans, were prohibited from owning homes beginning during the reign of Ḥammūda Pāshā (Larguèche 1999: 358). According to legend, Sīdī Maḥrez saw the suffering of the Jews and initiated the establishment of a quarter of the medina for them. Sīdī Maḥrez was also important to the black community, and it was at his shrine where slaves received their official documents awarding them freedom after the abolition of slavery.

11. In his largely autobiographical 1955 novel, *The Pillar of Salt*, Albert Memmi describes a *sṭambēlī* performance held at his home. As a Jewish teenager living in an Arab-Islamic country but educated in the schools of the French colonizers, his extreme but conflicting reactions, and ultimately unresolved attitude toward his mother's participation in *sṭambēlī*, evoke vividly the simultaneous sense of difference and interdependence between two Tunisian minorities. It also provides a compelling account of some of the ambiguities of interpretation of *sṭambēlī* for a Tunisian subjugated to colonization by the French but also indoctrinated in the French educational system. Hoping to miss the ceremony he despised so much, Memmi's character returned home late, only to find it was still in full swing: "The whole band was in a frenzy, in response to the clashing cymbals that never ceased sounding. . . . They must have all become quite deaf, if not insane, from this awful music. . . . I forced my way through the throng of women, all of them familiar faces, aunts, cousins, neighbors, but each one of them now a stranger under the spell that had overcome her" (158).

The problem for Memmi's character was his own mother's excitement over, and participation in, this ceremony that was arranged to "exorcize" his aunt's demons: "Nor was the woman dancing a simulator. That the musicians should be possessed in this manner was far from surprising: they were from some tribe of the deep South, a strange offshoot of Negro Africa sent out toward the Mediterranean. But the woman was a sensible housewife, with children who went to school; did she deserve my anger or my contempt for allowing herself to become hysterical, limp as a rag, a jointless doll tossed back and forth, without any conscience, in this manner?" (160).

12. For smaller, private ceremonies for Jewish clients, the Dār Bārnū troupe would usually play only the *ṭabla* and *shqāshiq*. They would play only certain *nūbas* for these ceremonies, including Kūrī (whom the Jews called Shwarā'). The Jewish connection left a strong imprint on the historical memory at Dār Bārnū. Bābā Majīd waxed nostalgic about his experience playing for Jewish clients such as Bū ʿAtga and Khaylū. "They loved the music, and they loved to dance. They would drink *ʿaraq* and dance." He smiled as he recalled that the Jewish community referred to the *sṭambēlī* troupe as "the sirs" (*al-asiyyāt*). Not only did they pay well, but "they respected us," he said. "Not like it is today." Attesting to the importance of this connection is the fact that fifty years later, Bābā Majīd still remembers some of the *sṭambēlī* vocabulary specific to the Jewish community. Rather than "we're holding a *sṭambēlī*," his Jewish clients would say "ʿandinā nāwb," and if they wanted the *gumbrī* instead of the *ṭabla*, they would ask them to bring the *gnāybra*. An especially popular *nūba* was Bū Saʿdiyya, whom they called Shasharaya. Although the Jewish community hired *sṭambēlī* troupes for specific and unique ceremonies, some Jews also played important roles within the *sṭambēlī* community. Bābā Majīd remembers two male Jewish *ʿarīfas* (a role they called *sarraʿ*), named Nahūm and Gagū, with whom he worked occasionally.

13. Tunisian Jewish immigrants in Israel continue to hold *sṭambēlī* ceremonies but use the *mizwid* instead of the *gumbrī*, along with the *shqāshiq*, and sing in Tunisian Arabic (Somer and Saadon 2000). Although blacks are not the musicians in this new context, *sṭambēlī* is serving therapeutic needs of a minority, in this case Maghribi Jewish immigrants facing societal and institutional prejudice in Israel.

Chapter 3

1. In referring to tunes associated with specific spirits, I find Rouget's (1986) use of the phrase "musical motto" somewhat problematic, as "motto" suggests that the tune is merely identifying or describing the spirit. Closer to the *sṭambēlī* experience, perhaps, would be a variation on Mircea Eliade's "hierophany," a term he uses to designate the dual, even paradoxical, nature of the sacred object: it is simultaneously an object (stone, tree, or, I should add, sound, etc.) as well as a manifestation of the sacred (Eliade 1959). In earlier drafts, I considered subtly transforming Eliade's "hierophany" into "hierophony," another neologism, evoking the musical or sonic manifestation of the sacred. I prefer, however, to use the indigenous term, *nūba*, which is at once more ambiguous, more nuanced, and more specifically evocative of the inseparability of sound and spirit.

2. This is not to be confused with the *nūba* (pl. *nūbēt*) of *ma'lūf*, the Arab-Andalusian art music designated as Tunisia's official national music. In *ma'lūf*, *nūba* refers to an entire cycle of songs in the same *maqām*, or, less frequently now, *ṭbaʿ* (lit. "stamp" or "character"), or melodic mode. In both *sṭambēlī* and *ma'lūf*, then, the term "*nūba*" designates successive musical entities. For the *nūba* of *ma'lūf*, see Davis (2004).

3. For a musical mapping of social relations in the context of Sufi *qawwali* in India and Pakistan, see Qureshi (1995).

4. In *tumbura*, they are known as Nuba, Banda, and Gumuz, three pagan tribes that are always invoked first in the ceremony (Makris 2000).

5. These spirits came "from the west," which in this context referred specifically to the Zarma-Songhay people, who ruled the Nigerien government that was seen by many Hausa as favoring the western regions of the country and complicit in allowing the famine to continue by not taking action against it. The famine years also witnessed the arrival of new "cricket" spirits who also hailed "from the west" (Echard 1989). Among the Mawri of Niger, Zarma spirits are believed to have generated numerous fatal incidents in the 1960s involving lightning and constitute the most feared, and therefore most honored, spirits in *bori* rituals there (Masquelier 2001).

6. The Black-White dichotomy may also have moral implications, but again this binarism is often blurred. Fremont Besmer notes that since black spirits are generally associated with evil in the context of Nigerian *bori*, a white spirit may be described as black if its modes of afflicting someone are especially malicious, or even if the spirit's attire is dark in color. Moreover, a spirit who is perceived as black by others may be considered white by an individual who venerates, and is thus protected by, that spirit (Besmer 1983: 63).

7. It is often transliterated as Djerma or Zarma.

8. See Montana (2004a) for a critique of Tunisian scholar Ahmed Rahal's (2000) insistence on labeling *sṭambēlī* a "cult of Bilāl."

9. My decision to translate *walī* as "saint" is a compromise. The term "saint" carries with it the historical and religious connotations of the word's meaning in Christianity, which includes elements (e.g., the process of beatification, the institution of the monastery, and the relationship of saint to church) that are not present in the Islamic context. Some scholars suggest translating *walī* as "pious one" instead, but this is perhaps even more misleading, since many Muslim saints in the Maghrib were not particularly pious during their lives, but rather demonstrated their blessing from God through miraculous acts. I feel that the term "saint" is acceptable for our purposes, since it conveys the general idea of a deceased historical figure with a special closeness to God, to whom offerings and prayers are made in hopes of the saint's intervening on behalf of the supplicant.

10. Rahal (2000: 61) reports the use of the verb "stung" (*daggu*) in such cases, but I have not heard an attack by a saint described as such.

11. A slight exception to both of these characterizations is Sīdī ʿAbd es-Salēm. While he may induce a more or less standard trance in an uninitiated dancer, he will select only initiates to perform his preferred trance patterns, which involve dancing with fire and reciting the *fātiḥa*.

12. One reason for this debate is that while ʿAbd el-Qādir el-Jīlānī was awarded the Sufi robe (*khirqa*) by his Sufi teacher al-Mukharrimī, he continued to wear the clothing associated with religious scholars (Braune 1960; Trimingham 1971). At the heart of the issue is the definition of "a Sufi," a contested topic throughout the centuries within the world of Sufism as well as without.

13. While some *sṭambēlī* saints and spirits may be able to protect their hosts from attacks by malevolent *jinn*, possession by the *jinn* is not treatable by *sṭambēlī*. Exorcism of *jinn* may be sought from traditional healers such as *ʿazzāma* (magicians or sorcerers), religious healers who use the words of the Qur'ān to chase away *jinn*, and healers associated with certain saints (Abdmouleh 1993).

14. Most North Africans use *ṣāliḥ/ṣālḥīn* interchangeably with *walī/awliyāʾ* to refer to a Muslim saint. Indeed, the two terms are often combined into the phrase *walī ṣāliḥ*, or "holy saint." The distinction between the two (as well as their mutual compatibility), however, is crucial in the *sṭambēlī* context.

15. According to Trimingham, Lake Chad, the great lake of Bornu, was also known

as "Kūrī" (Trimingham 1962). Tremearne (1914) notes that Kūrī was chief of the pagan spirits.

16. The parenthetical references to Hausa translations and aliases of Banū Kūrī spirits in this section are drawn from Tremearne (1914).

17. The successive or simultaneous appearance of Kūrī, Jamarkay, and Dakākī in Tunisia was also noted by Tremearne (1914: 287).

18. Cf. Rahal (2000), who lists the Arnawēt as a distinct spirit family including Arnī, Bābā Kūrī, Ummī Yenna, Dan Droso, May Ska, Kasare Ye, May Kiri, May Lima, and Yakūba. My question to Bābā Majīd was a result of my reading of Rahal's study.

19. In Tunisia, the *mattanza* sacrifice at the shrine of Sīdī Dāwd (or Daoud), introduced by Italian tuna fishermen, continues to be performed annually at the beginning of the tuna fishing season (Ammaïria 1996). Like the trans-Saharan movement described in this book, this trans-Mediterranean movement demonstrates the compatibility of certain rituals and beliefs, though between southern Europe and North Africa in this case.

Chapter 4

1. In other troupes, he may be known by the apparently related term *inagambara* (Gouja 1996).

2. The terms *ṣunnāʿ* and *mʿallim* are also defining concepts of the master-apprentice hierarchy associated more broadly with traditional North African trade guilds and Sufi orders, where *mʿallim* is the "master" while *ṣunnāʿ* are "companion-grade craftsmen" (Trimingham 1998: 25, 310).

3. While failure on the part of other *sṭambēlī* musicians to address the *yinna* in such a deferential manner may be perceived as inconsiderate, failure to do so by members of the Dār Bārnū troupe is perceived as downright rude and shows a lack of appreciation for the knowledge and economic opportunities that the *yinna* has provided. During my stay in the summer of 2002, members of Dār Bārnū conveyed to me several times how disturbed they were that one of Bābā Majīd's apprentices—one who, along with his mother, had lived for years at Dār Bārnū and had recently started his own troupe—entered the house a few weeks earlier and asked for Bābā Majīd by demanding "Where is he?" (wīnūh?) rather than "Where is Bābā?" (wīnūh bābā?).

4. A small wooden box may also be used to hold this money, especially at larger ceremonies such as the annual pilgrimage, so that the *ṣunnāʿ* can make change for attendees wishing to make an offering.

5. Bābā Majīd bemoaned the use of the term "donkey" (*bhīm*) sometimes used to refer to the bridge, finding the imagery disrespectful to the *gumbrī*.

6. These include, but are by no means limited to, what Eric Charry (1996) calls "griot lutes" such as the Maninka and Xasonke *koni*, Bambara *ngoni*, Mandinka *kontingo*, Wolof *xalam*, Soninke *gambare*, Fulbe *hoddu*, and the Moorish *tidinit*, as well as "non-griot lutes" such as those used by the Hausa of Nigeria. Semispiked lutes, whose necks only partially penetrate the body of the instrument, are more common in West Africa and Morocco.

7. Henry George Farmer's assertion that the ancestry of the *gumbrī* was "clearly traceable" to ancient Egyptian lutes (1928: 6) has been challenged by Eric Charry (1996).

8. Such a system of naming strings, based on associations with animate beings and the human voice, is not uncommon in sub-Saharan Africa. Ames and King (1971: 40–41) report that among the Hausa, the lower-pitched string is called either "huge camel" (*amale*) or "little elephant" (*giwa*) while the highest-pitched is called "ululator" (*magudiya*). Further afield, Paul Berliner reports that the lower-register keys of the Shona

mbira are called "old men's voices," while the middle and higher registers are called "young men's voices" and "women's voices," respectively (1993: 56).

9. For video examples of these timbres and techniques, see the solo footage of Bābā Majīd online at this book's accompanying Web site, www.stambeli.com.

10. Besmer (1983) reports a similar centrality of instrumental melody for attracting the spirits in the context of Nigerian *bori*.

11. Command of a vast repertoire of *nūba*s is at the heart of the *sṭambēlī* system of knowledge, and access to that knowledge is granted only through an arduous apprenticeship process. There is a great deal of anxiety over guarding one's repertoire from being "stolen" by aspiring *yinna*s attending the performance. Bābā Majīd once told me the story of one such aspiring *yinna* who was unwilling to devote the necessary time and energy to learning the repertoire at the pace dictated by Bābā Majīd. The apprentice asked if he could record the next ceremony to help him learn. Bābā Majīd agreed, but used the situation as an opportunity to teach his student a lesson by placing the microphone in front of the troupe, knowing that the *gumbrī* lines would be inaudible due to the overpowering volume of the closer *shqāshiq*.

12. For a distributional study of the monochord fiddle in West Africa, see DjeDje (1980).

Chapter 5

1. In embarking on an exploration of the relationships between music and time, I should point out that I am not in search of any kind of homology between musical form and cosmology, as has been advocated by some scholars for cyclical musical forms in Indonesia. Michael Tenzer (2006) provides a critique of the anthropological and ethnomusicological tendency to distinguish between "linear" (i.e., Western) and "cyclical" (non-Western) forms. I sympathize with Martin Clayton (2000), who finds such generalized correlations between cultural norms or ideologies and musical structure intriguing but highly problematic.

2. See Lortat-Jacob's (1980) study of the *aḥwash* in the North African High Atlas Mountains for a discussion of a rhythmic cell that gradually compresses such that its eight pulses become seven. Lortat-Jacob argues that previous scholars have misunderstood fundamental tenets of *aḥwash* music and dance by making aural assumptions based on the rules of Western art music.

3. For accounts of microrhythmic nuances that blur the binary-ternary distinction in American jazz and Brazilian samba, see Benadon (2006) and Gerischer (2006), respectively. It is worth noting that, in contrast to *sṭambēlī*, these genres involve a commonly accepted and theorized framework of regular, subdivisible pulses.

4. Microrhythmic measurements were made using sonograms generated by Peak Pro 5.2 software. Using the application's "marker" feature, I marked the beginning of each major event of the rhythmic cell, calculated the time difference between them, and divided the resulting numbers by the length of the entire cell. The goal of making the measurements, I should emphasize, was to illuminate the relative spacing between articulations and how it transforms as the *nūba* progresses.

5. It is worth reiterating that the point I am making is not one about the practicalities or ethics of representing non-Western musics in Western notation (or audio software, or even the written word in a foreign language, for that matter). I am not suggesting that *sṭambēlī* or any other music "should" fit into the framework of Western notation, nor am I trying to demonstrate that Western notation is an inappropriate mode of representa-

tion. Rather, I am using the tools of Western notation to help us gain access to a rhythmic system that is organized in ways that Western notation does not adequately approximate. The logic underlying the system of Western notation—namely, the assumption that rhythmically regular music can be fitted into a framework of regular underlying pulses—is also fundamental to Arabic music theory and therefore highlights further the otherness of the *sṭambēlī* rhythmic system in the context of Arab Tunisia.

6. This particular kind of metrical ambiguity is far more representative of musico-cultural alterity in the context of Tunisia than in, say, Morocco, where it can be found in a diversity of musical practices such as the Berber *aḥwash* and the urban Arab *daqqa* (which also utilizes iron clappers). Although acceleration is a common feature of many Tunisian musics, it is rare to encounter normative changes in the relative spacing between articulations. Nevertheless, it does seem that the metrical ambiguity found in *sṭambēlī*, however rare (as in Tunisia) or common (as in Morocco), is in fact more characteristic of the Maghrib than of sub-Saharan Africa.

7. *Saʿdāwī* is also the name of a 12/8 rhythm commonly heard in Tunisian folk music such as *mizwid*.

8. The elongation of temporal space preceding regularly accented tones has been discussed by Christiane Gerischer (2006) in the context of Brazilian samba.

9. Simha Arom (1989: 91) refers usefully to such a reordering of accentual organization in quotidian activities, such as "when one listens for some time to the binary cycle of the 'tick-tock' of a clock: the stress feature, which is first attributed to the 'tick' (TICK-tock), suddenly shifts onto the 'tock' (TOCK-tick)."

10. The "*accelerando crescendo*," according to Rouget, is perhaps the only nearly universal feature of possession musics (1986: 91).

11. The performance on the accompanying compact disc adheres to these tendencies: Ṣlāt in-Nabī has a starting tempo of 94 cells per minute and ends at 124 (a 31.9 percent increase); Jerma's *nūba* ends at 130 (a 4.8 percent increase), and Bū Ḥijba's *nūba* ends at 145 (an 11.5 percent increase).

12. The flattened second usually takes the form of a "blue" note, situated between a fully natural and fully flatted interval. I found that in contexts in which a greater number of less experienced *shqāshiq* players participate (such as the annual pilgrimage) there is a tendency in the choral response to sing the note closer to a major second.

13. Jean Rouch's films *Porto Novo* and *Horendi*, undertaken in collaboration with Gilbert Rouget, draw attention to the dynamic and shifting relationships between musicians and possession dancers in Benin and Niger, respectively (Stoller 1992: 192).

14. In her otherwise illuminating and convincing account of *bori* in Niger, Adeline Masquelier concludes that despite her Mawri friends' insistence that *bori* "has not changed," the development over time of new spirits reveals that it in fact has changed (2001: 291). Could it be, however, that they are not referring to such empirical manifestations of change, but, rather, to the ritual dynamics of *bori*—its musical triangulation between musician, spirit, and host, as well as its capacity for adaptation, among others—which have not changed fundamentally over time?

Chapter 6

1. The commodity value of the sacrifice is demonstrated in the transactions of Maghribi clairvoyants (*shuwāffa*) in France, where afflicting spirits may demand a "sacrifice" (given to the clairvoyant) of a television, refrigerator, or portable telephone.

2. Equivalent to about four U.S. dollars at the time.

3. Among the female participants at an Aissawa ceremony in Morocco, Tony Langlois notes the ubiquity of the *zaghrāt* (in Moroccan Arabic sometimes called *yu-yu*) across North Africa and notes that this semianonymous, communal, and high-volume outburst is common in North African life rituals or "wherever the structures of everyday life [are] being publically reconfigured" (Langlois 1999).

Chapter 7

1. Here Bābā Majīd is simply using a conventional Tunisian term for saint, *rājil ṣāliḥ* (lit. "holy man"), which is equivalent to *walī*. This is not to be confused with the *ṣāliḥ/ṣālḥīn* of the *sṭambēlī* pantheon, who are unequivocally spirits and not saints. By using the term *rājil* (man) in the phrase *rājil ṣāliḥ*, Bābā Majīd is also drawing attention to the fact that Sīdī Frej was a human, which also excludes him from the *sṭambēlī* category of *ṣāliḥ/ṣālḥīn*.

2. Recorded examples and transcriptions from the 2005 *ziyāra* are available at www.stambeli.com.

3. The repertoire of the *gnāwa* of Morocco features more explicit narratives of displacement and the experience of slavery (Fuson 2003).

Chapter 8

1. Curiously, although the term *sūrī* means "Syrian" in standard Arabic, in Tunisian dialectical Arabic it means "French." (It is quite common, for instance, to hear someone say "yaḥkī b-sūrī," or "He speaks French.") Depending on the context, *sūrī* may also refer more generally to something imported or foreign. While none of the numerous Tunisian I asked, including a professor of linguistics, was able to account for the possible origins of this peculiar Tunisian usage of the term, most agreed it had nothing to do with Syria. Some speculated that it may be derived from the Tunisian Arabic term for "shirt" (*sūriyya*), as Tunisians during colonial times may have referred to the French as the ones wearing Western clothing, symbolized by the button-up shirt (as opposed to the traditional Tunisian *jallabiyya*, a flowing robe).

2. In this passage, Bābā Majīd used the terms *mutadīnīyīn* (a general term for Islamic fundamentalists) and *khumaynīyīn* (radical Islamists inspired by the success of the Iranian revolution). As the era under discussion was pre-1979 (the year of the Iranian Revolution), Bābā Majīd's reference to the *khumaynīyīn* was either anachronistic or part of a more general reference to Bourguiba's problems with Islamists, which continued to the end of his presidency in 1987.

3. More broadly, both Ottoman and French colonial ruling strategies in North Africa (and elsewhere) involved the selective employment of local minorities or foreigners, especially to intercede with indigenous populations.

4. A *gumbrī* player, not affiliated with Dār Bārnū, is reported to have penned a "*sṭambēlī* for Bourguiba" (Lapassade and Ventura 1966: 3).

5. Of course, song and album titles alone do not necessarily constitute African influences or associative intentions. Consider, for example, Dizzy Gillespie's "Night in Tunisia," which he wrote in 1942 under the title "Interlude," long before he had the opportunity to visit the country. The new name was only adopted after Earl Hines suggested that Tunisia, which had been appearing in American news stories at the time, provided a sufficiently "exotic" image to match the foreign—but, of course, Afro-Cuban!—rhythms of the piece.

6. Such claims were not limited to exponents of popular culture. Abdellah Hammoudi (1993) provides a trenchant critique of colonial-era anthropologists who made similar arguments about the supposed European origins of North African religious traditions.

7. D'Erlanger was an expatriate French artistocrat who dedicated himself to notating and theorizing *ma'lūf.* His activities, influence, and legacy are described in Davis (2004).

GLOSSARY

ʿabīd	slaves (sing. *ʿabd*)
ʿajmī	non-Arab or non-Arabic
ʿarīfa	*sṭambēlī* healer or diviner (lit. "she who knows"; pl. *ʿarāyif*)
ʿatīg	freed slaves (sing. *ʿatg*; *ʿatīq* and *ʿatq* in classical Arabic)
Baḥriyya	Water spirits (lit. "those of the water")
Banū Kūrī	a family of spirits (lit. "Kūrī's Tribe" or "Those of Kūrī")
baraka	blessing from God bestowed on Muslim saints
bash agha	black slave eunuch of the Husaynid era, responsible for overseeing the court's harem and carrying out administrative duties
bendīr	frame drum with snare (pl. *bnādir*)
bey	head of the Tunisian state under the Husaynids
Bēyēt	Royalty spirits (lit. "the Beys")
bkhūr	incense
bori	ritual spirit possession tradition of the Hausa people
Brāwnā	a category of spirits from Bornu
Bū Saʿdiyya	mythico-historic first musician of *sṭambēlī*
dār	house, but also evokes a genealogy (pl. *diyār*)
dār jamāʿa	"communal house"; a house that gathered displaced sub-Saharans in Tunis (pl. *diyār jamāʿa*)
debdabū	percussion ensemble featured in the annual *ziyāra*
dindrī	drink composed of soured milk, sorghum, water, and sugar
dūkh	the act of fainting or passing out, especially at the end of a trance
fātiḥa	opening verse of the Qur'ān
gaʿīd	overseer of, and spokesman for, the black community in Tunis during the Husaynid era
gambara	three-stringed lute with rectangular body
gaṣʿa	drum resembling an overturned bowl
gūgāy	one- or two-stringed fiddle
gumbrī	three-stringed lute with cylindrical body
jinn	a certain class of often malevolent spirits in the Islamic world (also, *jnūn*; m. sing. *jinnī*, f. sing. *jinniya*)
kashabiyya	hooded cloak worn by dancers possessed by certain spirits
kharja	street procession of the *ziyāra* (lit. "departure")

kūlū	highest-pitched string of the *gumbrī*
kurkutū	small kettledrum (pl. *kurkutūwāt*)
mīdān	ritual dance space surrounded by musicians
muthallith	a four-note rhythmic pattern
nūba	a tune for a *sṭambēlī* spirit or saint (lit. "[one's] turn"; pl. *nuwab*)
sa'dāwī	a four-note rhythmic pattern
ṣālḥīn	the *sṭambēlī* spirits (lit. "holy ones")
Sghār	youth spirits (lit. "Children")
shayb	lowest-pitched string of the *gumbrī*
shēb	middle-pitched string of the *gumbrī*
shaqshaqa	resonating plate attached to the strings of the *gumbrī*
shqāshiq	handheld iron clappers
shūshān	child of slaves (pl. *shwāshin*)
silsila	succession of *nūbas* associated with a specific group of saints or spirits (lit. "chain"; pl. *silsilēt*)
sṭambēlī	ritual trance music tradition developed by Tunisian slaves
sūdānī	sub-Saharan; also the name of a three-note rhythmic pattern
sūga	musical pattern of increased intensity and repetition
sunjuq	banner whose color and pattern represent a specific saint or spirit (pl. *snājaq*)
ṣunnā'	praise singers and *shqāshiq* players of the *sṭambēlī* troupe (lit. "workers" or "craftsmen"; sing. *ṣāni'*)
ṭabla	double-headed barrel drum (pl. *ṭabālī*)
ṭarīqa	Sufi order (lit. "path" or "way"; pl. *ṭuruq*)
walī	a Muslim saint (lit. "close [to God]"; pl. *awliyā'*)
waṣfān	most common term for blacks in Tunisian Arabic (lit. "servants")
yashṭaḥ	to dance (lit. "to roam")
yinna	master *gumbrī* player and leader of *sṭambēlī* troupe
zār	ritual spirit possession tradition in East Africa and the Middle East
zāwiya	shrine of a Muslim saint (pl. *zwāya*)
ziyāra	annual pilgrimage to a saint's shrine (lit. "visit")

BIBLIOGRAPHY

Abdmouleh, Ridha. 1993. Les catégories de guérisseurs opérant aujourd'hui en Tunisie. *Revue de l'Institut des belles lettres arabes (IBLA)* 56 (172): 247–259.

Abu-Lughod, Lila. 1991. Writing against Culture. In *Recapturing Anthropology: Working in the Present*, edited by R. G. Fox. Santa Fe, NM: School of American Research Press.

Abun-Nasr, Jamil M. 1987. *A History of the Maghrib in the Islamic Period.* Cambridge: Cambridge University Press.

Alexander, Christopher. 1997. Authoritarianism and Civil Society in Tunisia. *Middle East Report* 27 (4): 34–38.

Alpers, Edward A. 2000. Recollecting Africa: Diasporic Memory in the Indian Ocean World. *African Studies Review* 43 (1): 83–99.

Alya. 2001. Le retour du *stambali. La Presse* (Tunis), 7 June.

Ames, David W., and Anthony V. King. 1971. *Glossary of Hausa Music and Its Social Contexts.* Evanston, IL: Northwestern University Press.

Ammaïria, Hafnaoui. 1996. La Mattanza: Fête et sacrifice. *Cahiers des Arts et Traditions Populaires* 11:101–108.

Amselle, Jean-Loup. 1971. Parenté et commerce chez les Kookoro. In *Development of Indigenous Trade and Markets in West Africa*, edited by C. Meillassoux. London: Oxford University Press.

Anderson, Lisa. 1986. *The State and Social Transformation in Tunisia and Libya, 1830–1980.* Princeton Series on the Near East. Princeton, NJ: Princeton University Press.

———. 1996. North Africa: Changes and Challenges. *Dissent* 43 (3): 113–116.

Andrews, J. B. 1903. *Les Fontaines des Génies (Seba' Aioun): Croyances soudanaises à Alger.* Alger: Adolphe Jourdan.

Apter, Andrew H. 1992. *Black Critics and Kings: The Hermeneutics of Power in Yoruba Society.* Chicago: University of Chicago Press.

———. 2002. On African Origins: Creolization and *Connaissance* in Haitian *Vodou. American Ethnologist* 29 (2): 233–260.

Arafat, W. 1960. Bilāl bin Rabaḥ. In *Encyclopedia of Islam*, edited by H. A. R. Gibb. Leiden: Brill.

Arom, Simha. 1989. Time Structure in the Music of Central Africa: Periodicity, Meter, Rhythm and Polyrhythmics. *Leonardo Music Journal* 22 (1): 91–99.

Augé, Marc. 1999. *An Anthropology for Contemporaneous Worlds.* Translated by Amy Jacobs. Stanford, CA: Stanford University Press.

Austen, Ralph A. 1979. The Trans-Saharan Slave Trade: A Tentative Census. In *The Uncommon Market: Essays in the Economic History of the Atlantic Slave Trade*, edited by H. A. Gemery and J. S. Hogendon. New York: Academic Press.

Ayoub, Abderrahman. 2000. The Arab Folklorist in a Postcolonial Period. In *Beyond Colonialism and Nationalism in the Maghrib: History, Culture, and Politics*, edited by A. A. Ahmida. New York: Palgrave MacMillan.

Baily, John. 1977. Movement Patterns in Playing the Herati *Dutar*. In *The Anthropology of the Body*, edited by J. Blacking. London: Academic Press.

———. 1992. Music Performance, Motor Structure, and Cognitive Models. In *European Studies in Ethnomusicology: Historical Developments and Recent Trends*, edited by M. P. Baumann, A. Simon, and U. Wegner. Wilhelmshaven: Florian Noetzel Verlag.

Bargery, G. P. 1934. *A Hausa-English Dictionary and English-Hausa Vocabulary*. London: Oxford University Press/Humphrey Milford.

Barz, Gregory F., and Timothy J. Cooley, eds. 1997. *Shadows in the Field: New Perspectives for Fieldwork in Ethnomusicology*. New York: Oxford University Press.

Battenburg, John. 1999. The Gradual Death of the Berber Language in Tunisia. *International Journal of the Sociology of Language* 137:147–161.

Bauman, Gerd. 1995. Music and Dance: The Royal Road to Affective Culture? *World of Music* 37 (2): 31–42.

Becker, Judith. 2004. *Deep Listeners: Music, Emotion, and Trancing*. Bloomington: University of Indiana Press.

Ben Abdallah, Chadly. 1988. *Fêtes religieuses et rythmes de Tunisie*. Tunis: JPS Editions.

Benadon, Fernando. 2006. Slicing the Beat: Jazz Eighth-Notes as Expressive Microrhythm. *Ethnomusicology* 50 (1): 73–98.

Ben Ammar, Mustapha. 1997. L'interrogation de la mémoire culturelle: *Stambali*, Transe-mission, *Le Renouveau* (Tunis), 28 December.

———. 1998. Synthèse de la culture africaine: *Derdeba* au maroc—*stambali* en Tunisie. *Le Renouveau* (Tunis), 28 January.

Berliner, Paul. 1993. *The Soul of Mbira: Music and Traditions of the Shona People of Zimbabwe*. Chicago: University of Chicago Press.

Berlioux, Étienne Félix. 1872. *The Slave Trade in Africa in 1872, Principally Carried on for the Supply of Turkey, Egypt, Persia, and Zanzibar*. London: E. Marsh.

Besmer, Fremont. 1983. *Horses, Musicians, and Gods: The Hausa Cult of Possession-Trance*. South Hadley, MA: Bergin and Garvey.

Bhabha, Homi, ed. 1990. *Nation and Narration*. London: Routledge.

Bittman, Barry B., Lee S. Berk, David L. Felten, James Westengard, O. Carl Simonton, James Pappas, and Melissa Ninehouser. 2001. Composite Effects of Group Drumming Music Therapy on Modulation of Neuroendocrine-Immune Parameters in Normal Subjects. *Alternative Therapies in Health and Medicine* 7 (1): 38–47.

Blacking, John. 1985. The Context of Venda Possession Music: Reflections on the Effectiveness of Symbols. *Yearbook for Traditional Music* 17:64–87.

———. 1995. Expressing Human Experience through Music. In *Music, Culture, and Experience: Selected Papers of John Blacking*, edited by R. Byron. Chicago: University of Chicago Press.

Blench, Roger. 1984. The Morphology and Distribution of Sub-Saharan Musical Instruments of North-African, Middle Eastern, and Asian Origin. *Musica Asiatica* 4:155–191.

Boahen, A. A. 1962. The Caravan Trade in the Nineteenth Century. *Journal of African History* 3 (2): 349–359.

Boddy, Janice. 1989. *Wombs and Alien Spirits: Women, Men, and the Zār Cult in Northern Sudan*. Madison: University of Wisconsin Press.

———. 1994. Spirit Possession Revisited: Beyond Instrumentality. *Annual Review of Anthropology* 23:407–434.

Bohlman, Philip V. 1996. The Final Borderpost. *Journal of Musicology* 14 (4): 427–452.

———. 1997. World Musics and World Religions: *Whose World?* In *Enchanting Powers: Music in the World's Religions*, edited by L. E. Sullivan. Cambridge, MA: Harvard University Press.

———. 2002. World Music at the "End of History." *Ethnomusicology* 46 (1): 1–32.

Boissevain-Souid, Katia. 2000. Saïda Manoubiya, son culte aujourd'hui, quelles spécificités? *Revue de l'Institut des Belles Lettres Arabes* 63 (186): 137–164.

Bourdieu, Pierre. 2003. Participant Objectivation. *Journal of the Royal Anthropological Institute* 9:281–294.

Brandel, Rose. 1959. The African Hemiola Style. *Ethnomusicology* 3 (3): 106–117.

Braune, W. 1960. ʿAbd al-Qādir al-Jilānī. In *Encyclopaedia of Islam*, edited by H. A. R. Gibb. Leiden: Brill.

Brett, Michael. 1969. *Ifriqiya* as a Market for Saharan Trade from the Tenth to the Twelfth Century A.D. *Journal of African History* 10 (3): 347–364.

Brown, L. Carl. 1964. The Islamic Reformist Movement in North Africa. *Journal of Modern African Studies* 2 (1): 55–63.

———. 1974. *The Tunisia of Ahmad Bey, 1837–1855*. Princeton, NJ: Princeton University Press.

Brunel, René. 1926. *Essai sur la confrérie religieuse des ʿAîssâoua au Maroc*. Paris: Paul Geuthner.

Casey, Edward. 1996. How to Get from Space to Place in a Fairly Short Stretch of Time: Phenomenological Prolegomena. In *Senses of Place*, edited by S. Feld and K. H. Basso. Santa Fe: School of American Research Press.

Charry, Eric. 1996. Plucked Lutes in West Africa: An Overview. *Galpin Society Journal* 49:3–37.

Chernoff, John Miller. 1979. *African Rhythm and African Sensibility: Aesthetics and Social Action in African Musical Idioms*. Chicago: University of Chicago Press.

Chittick, W. C. 1989. *The Sufi Path of Knowledge: Ibn al-ʿArabi's Metaphysics of the Imagination*. Albany: State University of New York Press.

Chlyeh, Abdelhafid. 1998. *Les Gnaoua du Maroc: Itineraires, initiatiques, transe et possession*. Casablanca: La Pensée Sauvage.

Clancy-Smith, Julia A. 1990. Between Cairo and the Algerian Kabylia: The Rahmaniyya Tariqa, 1715–1800. In *Muslim Travellers: Pilgrimage, Migration, and the Religious Imagination*, edited by D. F. Eickelman and J. P. Piscatori. Berkeley: University of California Press.

———. 1994. *Rebel and Saint: Muslim Notables, Populist Protest, Colonial Encounters (Algeria and Tunisia, 1800–1904)*. Berkeley: University of California Press.

Clayton, Martin. 2000. *Time in Indian Music: Rhythm, Metre, and Form in North Indian Rāg Performance*. Oxford: Oxford University Press.

Clayton, Martin, Rebecca Sager, and Udo Will. 2004. In Time with the Music: The Concept of Entrainment and Its Significance for Ethnomusicology. *ESEM Counterpoint* 1:1–81.

Clifford, James, and George E. Marcus, eds. 1986. *Writing Culture: The Poetics and Politics of Ethnography*. Berkeley: University of California Press.
Crapanzano, Vincent. 1973. *The Ḥamadsha: A Study in Moroccan Ethnopsychiatry*. Berkeley: University of California Press.
———. 1980. *Tuhami: Portrait of a Moroccan*. Chicago: University of Chicago Press.
———. 2004. *Imaginative Horizons: An Essay in Literary-Philosophical Anthropology*. Chicago: University of Chicago Press.
Csikszentmihályi, Mihály. 1990. *Flow: The Psychology of Optimal Experience*. New York: Harper and Row.
Csordas, Thomas J. 2002. *Body/Meaning/Healing*. New York: Palgrave.
Dakhlia, Jocelyne. 1993. Collective Memory and the Story of History: Lineage and Nation in a North African Oasis. *History and Theory* 32 (4): 57–79.
Danforth, Loring M. 1989. *Firewalking and Religious Healing: The Anastenaria of Greece and the American Firewalking Movement*. Princeton, NJ: Princeton University Press.
Danfulani, Umar Habila Dadem. 1999. Factors Contributing to the Survival of the Bori Cult in Northern Nigeria. *Numen* 46 (4): 412–447.
Danielson, Virginia. 1997. *The Voice of Egypt: Umm Kulthum, Arabic Song, and Egyptian Society in the Twentieth Century*. Chicago: University of Chicago Press.
Davis, Ruth. 1997. Cultural Policy and the Tunisian Ma'luf: Redefining a Tradition. *Ethnomusicology* 41 (1): 1–21.
———. 2004. *Ma'luf: Reflections on the Arab-Andalusian Music of Tunisia*. Lanham, MD: Scarecrow Press.
Dekhil, Ezeddine. 1993. Le phénomène de transe corps possèdes. *Revue de l'Institut des Belles Lettres Arabes* 56 (172): 261–275.
Dermenghem, Émile. 1954. *Le culte des saints dans l'islam maghrébin*. Paris: Gamillard.
Desjarlais, Robert. 1992. *Body and Emotion: The Aesthetics of Illness and Healing in the Nepal Himalayas*. Philadelphia: University of Pennsylvania Press.
DjeDje, Jacqueline Cogdell. 1980. *Distribution of the One-String Fiddle in West Africa*. Los Angeles: University of California Press.
Dubouloz-Laffin, Marie-Louise. 1941. Le bouri à Sfax. *En Terre d'Islam* 13:50–60.
During, Jean. 1997. African Winds and Muslim Djinns: Trance, Healing, and Devotion in Baluchistan. *Yearbook for Traditional Music* 29:39–56.
Dwyer, Kevin. 1982. *Moroccan Dialogues: Anthropology in Question*. Baltimore: Johns Hopkins University Press.
Echard, Nicole. 1989. *Bori: Aspects d'un culte de possession hausa dans l'Ader et le Kurfey (Niger)*. Paris: École des Hautes Études en Sciences Sociales.
Eickelman, Dale F. 1976. *Moroccan Islam: Tradition and Society in a Pilgrimage Center*. Austin: University of Texas Press.
———. 1998. *The Middle East and Central Asia: An Anthropological Approach*. 3rd ed. Upper Saddle River, NJ: Prentice-Hall.
Eliade, Mircea. 1959. *The Sacred and the Profane: The Nature of Religion*. Translated by W. R. Trask. New York: Harcourt.
Emoff, Ron. 2003. *Recollecting from the Past: Musical Practice and Spirit Possession on the East Coast of Madagascar*. Middletown, CT: Wesleyan University Press.
Ennaji, Mohammed. 1999. *Serving the Master: Slavery and Society in Nineteenth-Century Morocco*. Translated by S. Graebner. New York: St. Martin's Press.
Ensel, Remco. 2002. Colactation and Fictive Kinship as Rites of Incorporation and Reversal in Morocco. *Journal of North African Studies* 7 (4): 83–96.

Erlmann, Veit. 1982. Trance and Music in the Hausa Bòorii Spirit Possession Cult in Niger. *Ethnomusicology* 26 (1): 49–58.

———. 1986. *Music and the Islamic Reform in the Early Sokoto Empire: Sources, Ideology, Effects.* Stuttgart: Steiner-Verlag-Wiesbaden-GmbH.

Erlmann, Veit, and Habou Magagi. 1989. *Girkaa: Une cérémonie d'initiation au culte de possession boorii des Hausa de la région de Maradi (Niger).* Berlin: Dietrich Reimer Verlag.

Fabian, Johannes. 1983. *Time and the Other: How Anthropology Makes Its Object.* New York: Columbia University Press.

———. 1990. *Power and Performance: Ethnographic Explorations through Proverbial Wisdom and Theater in Shaba, Zaire.* Madison: University of Wisconsin Press.

Fales, Cornelia, and Stephen McAdams. 1994. The Fusion and Layering of Noise and Tone: Implications for Timbre in African Instruments. *Leonardo Music Journal* 4:69–77.

Farmer, Henry George. 1928. A North African Folk Instrument. *Journal of the Royal Asiatic Society* 1:24–34.

Feld, Steven. 1988. Aesthetics as Iconicity of Style, or "Lift-Up-Over Sounding": Getting into the Kaluli Groove. *Yearbook for Traditional Music* 20:74–113.

———. 1994. From Schizophonia to Schismogenesis: On the Discourses and Practices of World Music and World Beat. In *Music Grooves,* edited by C. Keil and S. Feld. Chicago: University of Chicago Press.

———. 2000. The Poetics and Politics of Pygmy Pop. In *Western Music and Its Others: Difference Representation, and Appropriation in Music,* edited by G. Born and D. Hesmondhalgh. Berkeley: University of California Press.

Feld, Steven, and Keith H. Basso. 1996. Introduction. In *Senses of Place,* edited by S. Feld and K. H. Basso. Santa Fe: School of American Research Press.

Feld, Steven, and Aaron Fox. 1994. Music and Language. *Annual Review of Anthropology* 23:25–53.

Ferchiou, Sophie. 1972. Survivances mystiques et culte de possession dans le maraboutisme tunisien. *L'Homme* 12 (3): 47–69.

———. 1991. La Possession: Forme de Marginalité Féminine. *Annuaire de l'Afrique du Nord* 30:191–200.

Friedson, Steven M. 1996. *Dancing Prophets: Musical Experience in Tumbuka Healing.* Chicago: University of Chicago Press.

———. 2005. Where Divine Horsemen Ride: Trance Dancing in West Africa. In *Aesthetics in Performance: Formations of Symbolic Construction and Experience,* edited by Angela Hobart and Bruce Kapferer, 109–128. New York: Berghahn.

Fuson, Tim Abdellah. 1996. Renewed Pandemonium: The Continuing Legend of the Master Musicians of Jajouka. *Journal of the International Institute* 3 (2): 26–28.

———. 2003. Slavery's Past in the Musical Present: Ritual and Memory in the Moroccan *Gnāwa Līla.* Paper presented at the Society for Ethnomusicology annual conference, Miami, 5 October.

Geertz, Hildred. 1979. The Meanings of Family Ties. In *Meaning and Order in Moroccan Society: Three Essays in Cultural Analysis,* edited by C. Geertz, H. Geertz, and L. Rosen. Cambridge: Cambridge University Press.

Gerischer, Christiane. 2006. *O Suingue Baiano*: Rhythmic Feeling and Microrhythmic Phenomena in Brazilian Percussion. *Ethnomusicology* 50 (1): 99–119.

Gibb, Camilla C. T. 1999. *Baraka* without Borders: Integrating Communities in the City of Saints. *Journal of Religion in Africa* 29 (1): 88–108.

Gilsenan, Michael. 1973. *Saint and Sufi in Modern Egypt: An Essay in the Sociology of Religion*. Oxford: Clarendon Press.

Goodman, Jane E. 2005. *Berber Culture on the World Stage: From Village to Video.* Bloomington: Indiana University Press.

Gouja, Zouhir. 1996. Une tradition musical de transe afro-maghrébine: Stambali. *Cahiers des Arts et Traditions Populaires* 11:71–99.

Gouk, Penelope, ed. 2000. *Musical Healing in Cultural Contexts.* Aldershot: Ashgate.

Hagedorn, Katherine. 2001. *Divine Utterances: The Performance of Afro-Cuban Santería.* Washington, DC: Smithsonian Institution Press.

Hall, Stuart. 1991. The Local and the Global: Globalisation and Ethnicity. In *Culture, Globalisation, and the World-System: Contemporary Conditions for the Representation of Identity*, edited by A. V. King. London: MacMillan.

Hammoudi, Abdellah. 1993. *The Victim and Its Masks: An Essay on Sacrifice and Masquerade in the Maghreb.* Translated by P. Wissing. Chicago: University of Chicago Press.

Harris, Rachel, and Barley Norton. 2002. Introduction: Ritual Music and Communism. *British Journal of Ethnomusicology* 11 (1): 1–8.

Hell, Bertrand. 1999. *Possession et chamanisme: Les maîtres du désordre.* Paris: Flammarion.

Herzfeld, Michael. 1997. *Cultural Intimacy: Social Poetics in the Nation-State.* New York: Routledge.

———. 2001. *Anthropology: Theoretical Practice in Culture and Society.* Oxford: Blackwell.

Hesmondhalgh, David. 2000. International Times: Fusions, Exoticism, and Antiracism in Electronic Dance Music. In *Western Music and Its Others: Difference Representation, and Appropriation in Music*, edited by G. Born and D. Hesmondhalgh. Berkeley: University of California Press.

Hoffman, Katherine E. 2002. Generational Change in Berber Women's Song of the Anti-Atlas Mountains, Morocco. *Ethnomusicology* 46 (3): 510–540.

Hunwick, John. 1978. Black Africans in the Islamic World: An Understudied Dimension of the Black Diaspora. *Tarikh* 5 (4): 20–40.

———. 2004. The Religious Practices of Black Slaves in the Mediterranean Islamic World. In *Slavery on the Frontiers of Islam*, edited by P. E. Lovejoy. Princeton, NJ: Markus Wiener.

Imām, Rashād al-. 1980. *Siyāsat Ḥammūdah Bāshā fī Tūnis, 1782–1814.* Tunis: Manshūrāt al-Jāmiʿah al-Tūnisīyah.

——— [Limam, Rashed]. 1981. Some Documents Concerning Slavery in Tunisia at the End of the 18th Century. *Revue d'Histoire Maghrébine* 23–24:349–357.

Jackson, Anthony. 1968. Sound and Ritual. *Man* 3:293–299.

Jankowsky, Richard C. 2006. Black Spirits, White Saints: Music, Spirit Possession, and Sub-Saharans in Tunisia. *Ethnomusicology* 50 (3): 373–410.

———. 2007. Music, Spirit Possession and the In-Between: Ethnomusicological Inquiry and the Challenge of Trance. *Ethnomusicology Forum* 16 (2): 185–208.

Janzen, John M. 2000. Theories of Music in African *Ngoma* Healing. In *Musical Healing in Cultural Contexts*, edited by Penelope Gouk, 46–66. Aldershot: Ashgate.

Jones, Lura JaFran. 1977. The ʿĪsāwīya of Tunisia and Their Music. PhD dissertation, University of Washington, Seattle.

Kapchan, Deborah. 2002. Possessing Gnawa Culture: Displaying Sound, Creating History in an Unofficial Museum. *Music and Anthropology: Journal of Musical Anthropology of the Mediterranean*, vol. 7.

———. 2007. *Traveling Spirit Masters: Moroccan Gnawa Trance and Music in the Global Marketplace*. Middletown, CT: Wesleyan University Press.

Kapferer, Bruce. 1991. *A Celebration of Demons: Exorcism and the Aesthetics of Healing in Sri Lanka*. 2nd ed. Oxford: Berg; Washington, DC: Smithsonian Institution. (Original edition, 1983.)

———. 2005a. Ritual Dynamics and Virtual Practice: Beyond Representation and Meaning. In *Ritual in Its Own Right: Exploring the Dynamics of Transformation*, edited by D. Handelman and G. Lindquist. New York: Berghahn.

———. 2005b. Sorcery and the Beautiful: A Discourse on the Aesthetics of Ritual. In *Aesthetics in Performance: Formations of Symbolic Construction and Experience*, edited by A. Hobart and B. Kapferer. New York: Berghahn.

Kapferer, Bruce, and Angela Hobart. 2005. The Aesthetics of Symbolic Construction and Experience. In *Aesthetics in Performance: Formations of Symbolic Construction and Experience*, edited by A. Hobart and B. Kapferer. New York: Berghahn.

Kauffman, Robert. 1980. African Rhythm: A Reassessment. *Ethnomusicology* 24 (3): 393–415.

King, A. V. 1966. *A Bòoríi Liturgy from Katsina (Introduction and Kíráarì Texts)*. Collected Papers in Oriental and African Studies: African Language Studies 7. London: School of Oriental and African Studies, University of London.

Kleinman, Arthur. 1980. *Patients and Healers in the Context of Culture: An Exploration of the Borderland between Anthropology, Medicine, and Psychiatry*. Berkeley: University of California Press.

Kramer, Fritz. 1993. *The Red Fez: Art and Spirit Possession in Africa*. Translated by M. R. Green. London: Verso.

Lambek, Michael. 1981. *Human Spirits: A Cultural Account of Trance in Mayotte*. Cambridge: Cambridge University Press.

———. 1989. From Disease to Discourse: Remarks on the Conceptualization of Trance and Spirit Possession. In *Altered States of Consciousness and Mental Health: A Cross-cultural Perspective*, edited by C. A. Ward. London: Sage.

———. 1993. *Knowledge and Practice in Mayotte: Local Discourses of Islam, Sorcery, and Spirit Possession*. Toronto: University of Toronto Press.

———. 1998. The Sakalava Poiesis of History: Realizing the Past through Spirit Possession in Madagascar. *American Ethnologist* 29 (2): 106–127.

———. 2006. Provincializing God? Post-religious Cogitations, Post-secular Apprehensions of the Continuing Problems of an Anthropology of Religion. Paper presented at the SOAS Anthropology Seminar Series, School of Oriental and African Studies, London, England, February 8.

Lan, David. 1985. *Guns and Rain: Guerrillas and Spirit Mediums in Zimbabwe*. Berkeley: University of California Press.

Langlois, Tony. 1999. Heard but Not Seen: Music among the Aissawa Women of Oujda, Morocco. *Music and Anthropology: Journal of Musical Anthropology of the Mediterranean*, vol. 4.

Lapassade, Georges. 1998. Les Gnawa, thérapeutes de la différence (entretien avec Georges Lapassade). *Africultures* 13:15–21.

Lapassade, Georges, and Flavio Ventura. 1966. Les dieux africains ont rendez-vous aujourd'hui à Sidi Saad. *La Presse*, 18 February, 3.

Larguèche, Abdelhamid. 1995. L'abolition de l'esclavage en Tunisie (1841–1846). In *Les abolitions de l'esclavage: De L. F. Sonthonax à V. Schoelcher 1793—1794—1848*, edited by M. Dorigny. Vincennes: Éditions Presses Universitaires de Vincennes.

———. 1999. *Les ombres de la ville: Pauvres, marginaux et minoritaires à Tunis (XVIIème et XIXème siècles)*. Tunis: Centre de Publication Universitaire, Faculté des Lettres de Manouba.

———. 2003. The Abolition of Slavery in Tunisia: Towards a History of the Black Community. In *The Abolitions of Slavery: From L. F. Sonthonax to Victor Schoelcher—1793, 1794 , 1848*, edited by M. Dorigny. New York: Berghahn.

Larguèche, Dalenda, and Abdelhamid Larguèche. 1992. *Marginales en terre d'Islam.* Tunis: Cérès.

Limam, Rashed. *See* Imām, Rashād al-.

Lobban, Richard A. 1997. Responding to Middle Eastern Urban Poverty: The Informal Economy in Tunis. In *Population, Poverty, and Politics in Middle East Cities*, edited by Michael E. Bonine, 85–112. Gainesville: University Press of Florida.

Locke, David. 1998. *Drum Gahu: An Introduction to African Rhythm.* Crown Point, IN: White Cliffs Media.

———. 2006. Cubism in African Music Improvisation. Paper presented at the Society for Ethnomusicology annual conference, Honolulu, 17 November.

Locke, David, and Abubakari Lunna. 1990. *Drum Damba: Talking Drum Lessons.* Crown Point, IN: White Cliffs Media.

Lortat-Jacob, Bernard. 1980. *Musique et fêtes au Haut-Atlas.* Paris: EHESS.

———. 1981. Community Music as an Obstacle to Professionalism: A Berber Example. *Ethnomusicology* 25 (1): 87–98.

Lovejoy, Paul, ed. 2000. *Transformations in Slavery: A History of Slavery in Africa.* Cambridge: Cambridge University Press,

———. 2004. Slavery, the Bilād al-Sūdān, and the Frontiers of the African Diaspora. In *Slavery on the Frontiers of Islam*, edited by P. E. Lovejoy. Princeton, NJ: Markus Wiener.

Makris, G. P. 1996. Slavery, Possession, and History: The Construction of Self among Slave Descendants in the Sudan. *Journal of African History* 66 (2): 159–182.

———. 2000. *Changing Masters: Spirit Possession and Identity Construction among Slave Descendants and Other Subordinates in the Sudan.* Evanston, IL: Northwestern University Press.

Masquelier, Adeline Marie. 2001. *Prayer Has Spoiled Everything: Possession, Power, and Identity in an Islamic Town of Niger.* Durham, NC: Duke University Press.

Maurer, Ronald, V. K. Kumar, Lisa Woodside, and Ronald Pekala. 1997. Phenomenological Experience in Response to Monotonous Drumming and Hypnotizability. *American Journal of Clinical Hypnosis* 40 (2): 130–145.

Mastnak, Wolfgang. 1993. Non-Western Practices of Healing-Music and Applications for Modern Psychotherapy. *International Review of the Aesthetics and Sociology of Music* 24 (1): 77–84.

Meillassoux, Claude. 1991. *The Anthropology of Slavery: The Womb of Iron and Gold.* Translated by A. Dasnois. Chicago: University of Chicago.

Mernissi, Fatima. 1977. Women, Saints, and Sanctuaries. *Signs* 3 (1): 101–112.

Messaoud, J. I. R. 1984. La situation de la population noire d'Afrique du Nord. *Présence Africaine*, no. 155:185–197.

Meyers, Allen R. 1983. Slave Soldiers and State Politics in Early ʿAlawi Morocco, 1668–1727. *International Journal of African Historical Studies* 16 (1): 39–48.

Micaud, Ellen C. 1978. Urbanization, Urbanism, and the Medina of Tunis. *International Journal of Middle Eastern Studies* 9 (3): 431–447.

Monfouga-Nicolas, Jacqueline. 1972. Ambivalence et culte de possession: Contribution à l'étude de bori hausa. Paris: Anthropos.

Monson, Ingrid. 2007. *Freedom Sounds: Civil Rights Call Out to Jazz and Africa.* Oxford: Oxford University Press.

Montana, Ismael Musah. 2004a. Aḥmad ibn al-Qāḍī al-Timbuktāwī on the Bori Ceremonies of Tunis. In *Slavery on the Frontiers of Islam,* edited by P. E. Lovejoy. Princeton, NJ: Markus Wiener.

———. 2004b. Enslavable Infidels: Sūdān-Tūnis as a Classificatory Categorization for New Wave of Enslaved Africans in the Regency of Tunis. *Maghreb Review* 29 (1–4): 78–98.

Morsy, Soheir A. 1991. Spirit Possession in Egyptian Ethnomedicine: Origins, Comparison and Historical Specificity. In *Women's Medicine: The Zar-Bori Cult in Africa and Beyond,* edited by. I. M. Lewis, Ahmed Al-Safi, and Sayyid Hurreiz, 189–208. Edinburgh: Edinburgh University Press (for the International African Institute).

Nachtigal, Gustav. 1971 [1879]. *Sahara and Sudan.* Vol. 1, *Tripoli and Fezzan, Tibesti or Tu.* Translated by A. G. B. Fisher and H. J. Fisher. Berkeley: University of California.

Natvig, Richard. 1991. Some Notes on the History of the *Zar* Cult in Egypt. In *Women's Medicine: The Zar-Bori Cult in Africa and Beyond,* edited by I. M. Lewis, A. Al-Safi and S. Hurreiz. Edinburgh: Edinburgh University Press (for the International African Institute).

Needham, Rodney. 1967. Percussion and Transition. *Man* 2:606–614.

Neher, Andrew. 1961. Auditory Driving Observed with Scalp Electrodes in Normal Subjects. *Electroencephalography and Clinical Neurophysiology* 13:449–451.

———. 1962. A Physiological Explanation of Unusual Behaviour in Ceremonies Involving Drums. *Human Biology* 34:151–160.

Nketia, J. H. Kwabena. 1974. *The Music of Africa.* New York: Norton.

Palmer, H. K. 1928. The Origin of the Name Bornu. *African Affairs* 28 (109): 36–42

Pandolfo, Stefania. 1997. *Impasse of the Angels: Scenes from a Moroccan Space of Memory.* Chicago: University of Chicago Press.

Pâques, Viviana. 1964. *L'arbre cosmique dans la pensée populaire et dans la vie quotidienne du Nord-Ouest Africain.* Paris: Institut d'Ethnologie.

Perkins, Kenneth J. 1986. *Tunisia: Crossroads of the Islamic and European Worlds.* Boulder, CO: Westview Press.

———. 2004. *A History of Modern Tunisia.* Cambridge: Cambridge University Press.

Qureshi, Regula Burckhardt. 1995. *Sufi Music of India and Pakistan: Sound, Context, and Meaning in Qawwali.* 2nd ed. Chicago: University of Chicago. (Original edition, 1986.)

Rabinow, Paul. 1977. *Reflections on Fieldwork in Morocco.* Berkeley: University of California Press.

Radano, Ronald, and Philip V. Bohlman. 2000. Introduction: Music and Race, Their Past, Their Presence. In *Music and the Racial Imagination,* edited by R. Radano and P. V. Bohlman. Chicago: University of Chicago Press.

Rahal, Ahmed. 2000. *La Communauté Noire de Tunis: Thérapie initiatique et rite de possession.* Paris: L'Harmattan.

Reily, Suzel Ana. 2002. *Voices of the Magi: Enchanted Journeys in Southeast Brazil.* Chicago: University of Chicago Press.

Reporters without Borders. 2007. *Tunisia: Annual Report*. Available from http://www.rsf.org/article.php3?id_article=20780&Valider=OK (accessed 16 November 2008).

———. 2008. *Tunisia: Annual Report*. Available from http://www.rsf.org/article.php3?id_article=25442&Valider=OK (accessed 16 November 2008).

Richardson, James. 1853. *Narrative of a Mission to Central Africa, 1850–51*. London: Chapman and Hall.

Rizgī, Ṣādiq. 1989 [1968]. *Al-Aghānī al-Tūnisiyya*. Reprint, 2nd ed. Tunis: Dār al-Tūnisiyya lil-Nashr.

Roseman, Marina. 1991. *Healing Sounds from the Malaysian Rainforest: Temiar Music and Medicine*. Berkeley: University of California Press.

Rostom, Kays. 1998. Program Notes to Stambali: Transe-Mission Concert. Sidi Bou Said, Tunisia: Centre des Musiques Arabes et Méditerranéennes.

Rouget, Gilbert. 1986. *Music and Trance: A Theory of the Relations between Music and Possession*. Translated by B. Biebuyck. Chicago: University of Chicago Press.

Rovsing-Olsen, Miriam. 1997. *Chants et danses de l'Atlas*. Arles: Actes Sud.

Sager, Rebecca. 2006. Creating a Musical Space for Experiencing the Other-Self Within. In *The Musical Human: Rethinking John Blacking's Ethnomusicology in the Twenty-first Century*, edited by S. A. Reily. Aldershot: Ashgate.

Schutz, Alfred. 1964. *Collected Papers II: Studies in Social Theory*. The Hague: Martinus Nijhoff.

Schuyler, Philip D. 1978. The *Rwais* and *Ahwash*: Opposing Tendencies in Moroccan Music and Society. *World of Music* 21 (1): 65–80.

———. 1984. Berber Professional Musicians in Performance. In *Performance Practice: Ethnomusicological Perspectives*, edited by G. Béhague. New Haven, CT: Greenwood Press.

———. 1993. A Folk Revival in Morocco. In *Everyday Life in the Muslim Middle East*, edited by E. A. Early and D. L. Bowen. Bloomington: Indiana University Press.

———. 2000. Joujouka/Jajouka/Zahjoukah: Moroccan Music and Euro-American Imagination. In *Mass Mediations: New Approaches to Popular Culture in the Middle East and Beyond*, edited by W. Armbrust. Berkeley: University of California Press.

Sebag, Paul. 1998. *Tunis: Histoire d'une ville*. Paris: Harmattan.

Segal, Ronald. 2001. *Islam's Black Slaves: The Other Black Diaspora*. New York: Farrar, Straus and Giroux.

Shannon, Jonathan. 2003. Sultans of Spin: Syrian Sacred Music on the World Stage. *American Anthropologist* 105 (3): 266–277.

———. 2007. Suficized Musics of Syria at the Intersection of Heritage and the War on Terror. Paper presented at the Society for Ethnomusicology annual conference, Columbus, OH.

Signoles, Pierre, Amor Belhedi, Jean-Marie Miossec, and Habib Dlala. 1980. *Tunis: Evolution et fonctionnement de l'espace urbain*. Paris: CNRS; Poitiers: Centre inter-universitaire d'études méditerranéennes; Tours: Conseil scientifique de l'université de Tours.

Sklar, Deidre. 2001. *Dancing with the Virgin: Body and Faith in the Fiesta of Tortugas, New Mexico*. Berkeley: University of California Press.

Somer, Eli, and Meir Saadon. 2000. Stambali: Dissociative Possession and Trance in a Tunisian Healing Dance. *Transcultural Psychiatry* 37 (4): 580–600.

Stambouli, Fredj, and A. Zghal. 1976. Urban Life in Pre-colonial North Africa. *British Journal of Sociology* 27 (1): 1–20.

Stokes, Martin. 1994. Introduction. In *Ethnicity, Identity, and Music: The Musical Construction of Place*, edited by M. Stokes. Oxford: Berg.

———. 1997. Place, Exchange, and Meaning: Black Sea Musicians in the West Coast of Ireland. In *Ethnicity, Identity, and Music: The Musical Construction of Place*, edited by M. Stokes. Oxford: Berg.

———. 2004. Music and the Global Order. *Annual Review of Anthropology* 33:47–72.

———. 2007. On Musical Cosmopolitanism. Paper presented at the Institute for Global Citizenship, Macalester College. In *Macalester International Roundtable*, paper 3. Available at http://www.digitalcommons.macalester.edu/intlrdtable/3.

Stoller, Paul. 1989. *Fusion of the Worlds: An Ethnography of Possession among the Songhay of Niger*. Chicago: University of Chicago Press.

———. 1992. *The Cinematic Griot: The Ethnography of Jean Rouch*. Chicago: University of Chicago Press.

———. 1995. *Embodying Colonial Memories: Spirit Possession, Power, and the Hauka in West Africa*. New York: Routledge.

———. 1996. Sounds and Things: Pulsations of Power in Songhay. In *The Performance of Healing*, edited by C. Laderman and M. Roseman. New York: Routledge.

———. 1997. *Sensuous Scholarship*. Philadelphia: University of Pennsylvania.

———. 2002. *Money Has No Smell: The Africanization of New York City*. Chicago: University of Chicago Press.

———. 2009. *The Power of the Between: An Anthropological Odyssey*. Chicago: University of Chicago Press.

Stoller, Paul, and Cheryl Olkes. 1987. *In Sorcery's Shadow: A Memoir of Apprenticeship among the Songhay of Niger*. Chicago: University of Chicago Press.

Surugue, Bernard. 1972. *Contribution à l'étude de la musique sacrée Zarma Songhay (Republique du Niger)*. Niamey: Centre Nigérien de Recherches en Sciences Humaines.

Takaki, Keiko. 1997. Les Stambâlî: Leurs rites et leur culture sonore. In *Cultures sonores d'afrique*, edited by K. Janzo. Tokyo: L'Institute d'recherches sur les langues et cultures d'Asie et d'Afrique.

Tapper, Nancy, and Richard Tapper. 1987. The Birth of the Prophet: Ritual and Gender in Turkish Islam. *Man* 22:69–92.

Taussig, Michael. 1993. *Mimesis and Alterity: A Particular History of the Senses*. New York: Routledge.

Taylor, Timothy D. 1997. *Global Pop: World Music, World Markets*. New York: Routledge.

Tenzer, Michael. 2006. *Oleg Tumulilingan*: Layers of Time and Melody in Balinese Music. In *Analytical Studies in World Music*, edited by M. Tenzer. New York: Oxford University Press.

Tessler, Mark. 1978. The Identity of Religious Minorities in Non-secular States: Jews in Tunisia and Morocco and Arabs in Israel. *Comparative Studies in Society and History* 20:359–373.

Tolbert, Elizabeth. 2001. The Enigma of Music, the Voice of Reason: "Music," "Language," and Becoming Human. *New Literary History* 32 (3): 451–465.

Tremearne, Arthur John Newman. 1914. *The Ban of the Bori: Demons and Demon-Dancing in West and North Africa*. London: Heath, Cranton and Ouseley.

Trimingham, J. Spencer. 1962. *A History of Islam in West Africa*. Oxford: Oxford University Press.

———. 1971. *The Sufi Orders in Islam*. Oxford: Clarendon Press.

———. 1998. *The Sufi Orders in Islam.* New York: Oxford University Press.

Turino, Thomas. 2000. *Nationalists, Cosmopolitans, and Popular Music in Zimbabwe.* Chicago: University of Chicago Press.

Turner, Victor. 1969. *The Ritual Process: Structure and Anti-structure.* Chicago: Aldine.

———. 1973. The Center Out There: Pilgrim's Goal. *History of Religions* 12 (3): 191–230.

Valensi, Lucette. 1967. Esclaves chrétiens et esclaves noirs à Tunis au XVIIIe siècle. *Annales, Économies, Sociétés, Civilisations* 6:1267–1288.

Vischer, Hanns. 1910. *Across the Sahara from Tripoli to Bornu.* London: Edward Arnold.

Wafer, Jim. 1991. *The Taste of Blood: Spirit Possession in Brazilian Candomblé.* Philadelphia: University of Pennsylvania Press.

Walker, Sheila. 1972. *Ceremonial Spirit Possession in Africa and Afro-America.* Leiden: E. J. Brill.

Wehr, Hans. 1994. *The Hans Wehr Dictionary of Modern Written Arabic.* Edited by J. M. Cowan. 4th ed. Ithaca, NY: Spoken Language Services.

Weinstein, Norman C. 1993. *A Night in Tunisia: Imaginings of Africa in Jazz.* New York: Limelight.

Zawadowski, G. 1942. Le rôle des Nègres parmi la population tunisienne. *En Terre d'Islam* 19:146–152.

Zeghonda, Fethi. 1991. *al-Ṭarīqa al-Sulāmiyya fī Tūnis: Ashʿārha wal-ḥānha.* Carthage: Dār al-Ḥikma.

Zouaoui, Zeïneb. 1998. Transe-Mission: Stambali à Ennajma Ezzahra. *Le Renouveau,* 25 January.

INDEX